IMAGES
of America

AFRICAN AMERICANS OF WICHITA

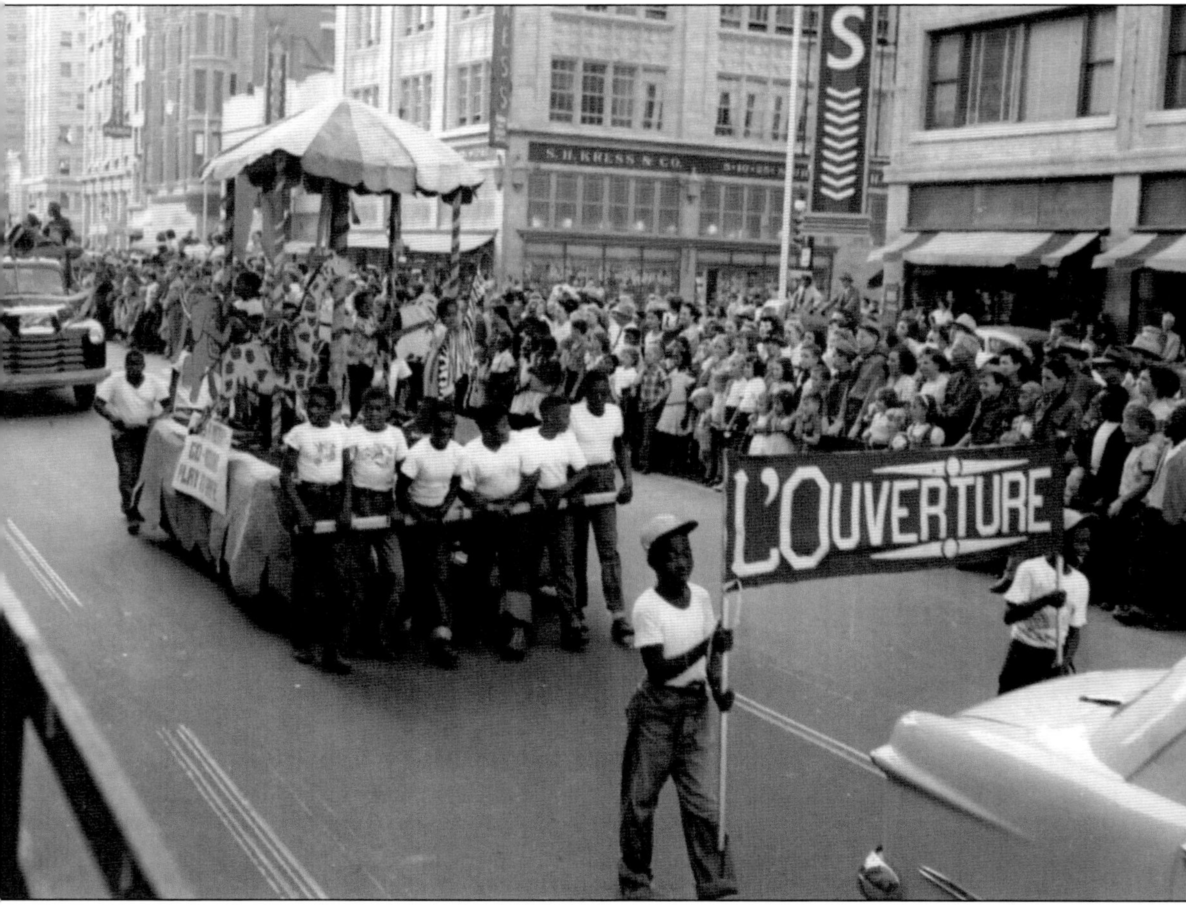

L'Ouverture Elementary students march in a downtown Wichita parade in 1958. This image shows the float on Douglas Avenue at Broadway. The photographer was in front of the Dockum Drug Store—the site of the sit-in that took place that summer. (Courtesy Kansas African American Museum.)

On the Cover: Members of Arkansas Valley Lodge No. 21 work on the construction of the Calvary Baptist Church. (Courtesy Kansas African American Museum.)

IMAGES
of America

AFRICAN AMERICANS OF WICHITA

The Kansas African American Museum

ARCADIA
PUBLISHING

ISBN 978-1-4671-1481-3

Published by Arcadia Publishing
Charleston, South Carolina

Printed in the United States of America

Library of Congress Control Number: 2015938033

For all general information, please contact Arcadia Publishing:
Telephone 843-853-2070
Fax 843-853-0044
E-mail sales@arcadiapublishing.com
For customer service and orders:
Toll-Free 1-888-313-2665

Visit us on the Internet at www.arcadiapublishing.com

To Doris Kerr Larkins and Samella Lewis, who made The Kansas African American Museum possible.

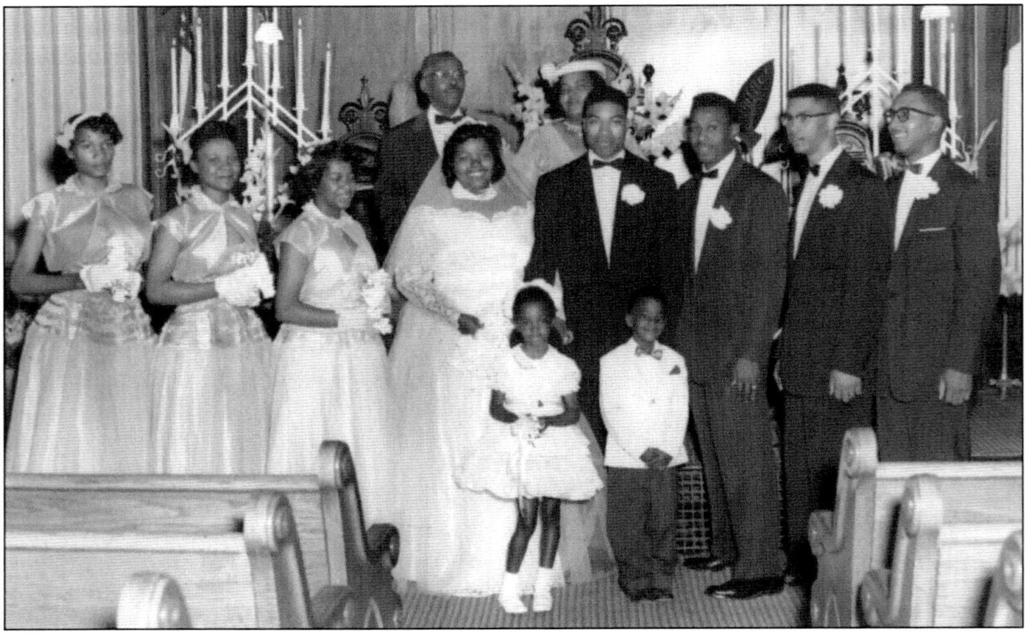

Doris Kerr Larkins is pictured here at center on her wedding day. (Courtesy Kansas African American Museum.)

Contents

ACKNOWLEDGMENTS

Book projects such as these draw on a wide range of sources. The team wants to thank *The Wichita Eagle*, *The Community Voice*, the Wichita–Sedgwick County Historical Museum, the Wichita Public Library, Wichita State University's Department of Special Collections, Old Cowtown Museum, the Butler County History Center, the Augusta Historical Museum, Fort Leavenworth, City of Wichita Planning Department, First Presbyterian Church, the Kansas Sports Hall of Fame, the Kansas State Historical Society, Spencer Library of the University of Kansas, St. Paul's AME, Holy Savior Catholic Church, Adorers of the Blood of Christ, Chisholm Trail Church of Christ, Greater Pentecostal Church of God in Christ, Hewitt's Antiques, Jackson Mortuary, *The Liberty Press*, NewsBank, the *Topeka Capital-Journal*, and the *Pittsburgh Courier*. The team appreciates the support of many people, including Robert Alford, Mrs. John E. Allen, Eric Anderson, Jean Pouncil-Burton, Brian Corn, Sherry Chisenhall, Mark Criner, Cynthia Elliott, Oletha Faust-Goudeau, Emmet M. Ford, U.L. "Rip" Gooch, Bonita Gooch, Bessie Halbrook, Yvette Harris, Anabelle Haupt, Karmina Hill, Grant Hewitt, Rosie Hughes, Barbara James, George T. Johnson, Dr. Donald Jackson, Charlie Jenkins, Mary Johnson, Jonathan Jones, Sheila Kinnard, Bly Jean Marcel Kouame, Florence Looney, Charles McAfee, Adrienne McAlpine, Melody McCray Miller, Gerald Norwood, Larry Muhammad, Chinyere Okafor, Carol Parks Hahn, Pat Patterson, Donna Rae Pearson, Carlota Ponds, Karen Porter, Katie Pott, Arlene Harris Ruffin, Eric and Kathy Sexton, Beccy Tanner, Pam Thompson, Galyn Vesey, Norman Williams, and Lavonta Williams. The team also appreciates the help of those in the community who assisted with photographs and other materials, including Jami Frazier Tracy, Deborah Dandridge, Michelle Enke, Barth Hague, Kevin Haskin, Gary Huffman, David Hughes, Charlie Jenkins, Jackie Lugrand, Rachelle Meinecke, Dr. Lorraine Madway, MyPictureman, Barb Myers, Mary Nelson, Sister Edwina Pope, Kathy Morgan, Kyle Palmer, Dr. Aaron Rife, Karen Porter, Janet Stewart, and Keith Wondra.

The project team regrets that not all of the images donated could be used. In addition, space precluded many persons and stories from being included. That significant persons, events, and institutions were not covered in as much detail as they deserve is, unfortunately, inevitable in projects of this type. The team hopes, however, that this book will inspire others to work to tell these and other stories as well as to donate and preserve the memories, records, and photographs that ensure that future generations know the African American Wichita story in its complexity and richness.

Unless otherwise noted, all images appear courtesy of the Kansas African American Museum and/or the project team members.

Project team members include Carole Branda, Gretchen Eick, Abril Marshall, Mark E. McCormick, Jay M. Price, Mark Strohminger, and Robert Weems.

Introduction

Even before Wichita's incorporation in 1870, African Americans represented a significant presence in what would become Kansas's largest city. They migrated to Kansas seeking opportunities in its towns and homesteads once it became a "free state." Many of them were veterans of the Civil War. In those early frontier years, black citizens were not officially segregated in Wichita, though the Jim Crow segregation laws that emerged in the Post-Reconstruction South would eventually make their way to the Great Plains.

In the late 19th and early 20th centuries, a small but influential community emerged in Wichita, concentrated especially along Water Street just west of the courthouse. Here, entrepreneurs founded businesses, people of faith erected churches, and civic leaders founded newspapers such as *The National Baptist World* and the *Kansas Reflector*. Others established clubs, fraternal organizations, and social groups. By the outbreak of World War I, black Wichitans numbered just under 2,500 and had family ties to black towns in Kansas and Oklahoma.

By the 1910s, Kansas's promise of freedom was under threat, despite the efforts of groups and individuals to resist growing racial restrictions. The creation of African American schools was perhaps the most visible sign of this growing segregation. That one school was named after abolitionist leader Frederick Douglass and the other for Haitian revolutionary Toussaint L'Ouverture is indicative of the sense of independence and pride that helped the community withstand growing white hostility. Wichita did not experience the traumatic white-against-black race riots that devastated 23 cities in 1919, and Tulsa in 1921, though some Tulsans migrated to Wichita as a result. The local Ku Klux Klan, job and housing discrimination, and public accommodations refusing admittance to African Americans severely challenged families who had come to the city with the expectation that the US Constitution's guarantees would be enforced.

In the 1920s, 1930s, and 1940s, the core of black Wichita shifted to the northeast and what came to be known as the McAdams neighborhood. There, the community faced social and economic changes, as well as literal division when Interstate 135 sliced through the community. The relaxation of residential segregation did not come until the last decades of the 20th century, when black citizens could finally reside throughout Wichita.

Besides geographic movement, the 20th century Wichita African American experience featured historic protests against racial discrimination. In 1942, an African American cafeteria worker in Wichita, James G. Thompson, gave *The Pittsburgh Courier* the idea for its famous World War II "Double V" campaign. Later, in 1958, a group of local high school youths, under the direction of the Wichita NAACP, conducted the nation's first successful student-led lunch counter sit-in, which eventually desegregated Rexall drugstores nationwide. Wichita was also the first city in the Midwest to be investigated by the federal government for school segregation, and Kansas black porters won an $8.5 million settlement from the Santa Fe Railroad for its employment discrimination thanks to Wichita lawyer Chester I. Lewis Jr.

The 1960s and 1970s saw new challenges and opportunities. This was a time of social unrest, as African Americans stood up to racism, prejudice, and discrimination even as the larger white society remained fearful of school integration, and white flight changed the complexion of neighborhoods. Federal anti-poverty programs opened jobs, and the city and state slowly abandoned discriminatory hiring practices. African Americans achieved leadership positions in the school system and, through the Wichita Alliance of Black School Educators, strategized how best to educate black children in the 1980s and 1990s. A Black Caucus was established in the state legislature, and a network of neighborhood organizations focused on providing residents with better opportunities. Where outsiders saw poverty, insiders in Northeast Wichita—especially zip code 67214—saw a vibrant community in which they felt pride. Black institutions—clubs, sororities and fraternities, churches, the Urban League, and the NAACP—focused on the possibilities and celebrated the richness of African American culture.

In contemporary Wichita, African Americans have achieved impressive visibility in the city's life, so much so that a number of African Americans have been elected to political office in both local and state government. A new generation of community leaders has stepped forward in the 21st century, often coming from McConnell Air Force Base or Wichita State University. The area also boasts a sizeable African immigrant population. Together, these citizens continue to redefine the African American community, even as issues of economic development, poverty, incarceration, and police/community tensions remain.

This book celebrates the African Americans of Wichita who built a strong foundation of self-reliance and community advocacy. The current generation stands on their shoulders with gratitude, empowered by their commitment and work.

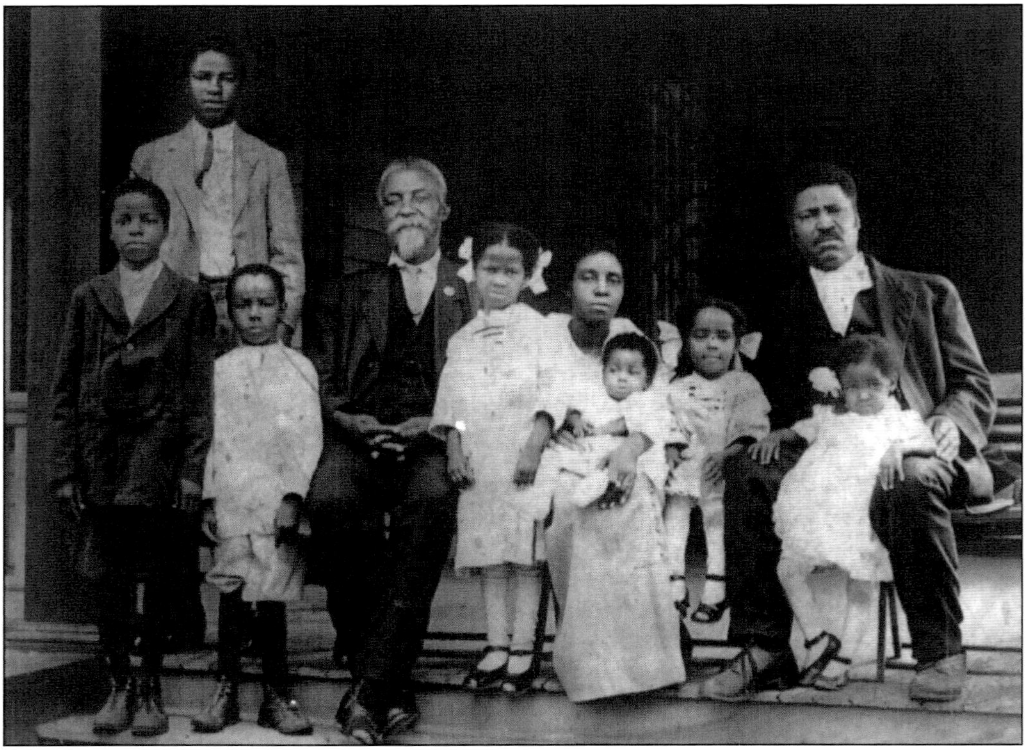

The Rev. John Henry Van Leu (seated at right) migrated to Wichita from South Carolina and married Julia Patton (holding toddler), whose family came from Tennessee. They raised 13 children. By 1897, Van Leu had become one of Sedgwick County's largest land owners. He was also a realtor, a pastor and missionary for the Kansas Baptist Convention, and founder of the Central Baptist Theological Seminary in Kansas City, Kansas. Julia's brother, Charlie Patton, ran a tailor shop.

One

Kansas: The Promised Land?

Africans first came to Kansas with Spanish conquistadors in the 1540s, most notably Estevanico, who came with Coronado. The main African American story in Kansas, however, begins with those individuals crossing into Kansas from Missouri to escape slavery. Congress had opened Kansas to Euro-American settlement in 1854, setting off violent clashes between pro-slavery forces and Free Staters, symbolized by figures such as John Brown. In 1861, Kansas entered the Union as a free state and some African Americans even joined the Kansas militia, protecting the new President Lincoln. In 1868, the state constitution guaranteed African Americans the right to vote, followed by the US Constitution two years later. This created the image of Kansas as a place of hope. Some 30,000 African Americans arrived between 1860 and 1890 in search of new opportunities. Whole African American towns developed, such as Nicodemus in northwestern Kansas, Hoggs Town near Lawrence, Juniper Town in Shawnee County, Quindaro along the Missouri River, Dunlap near Council Grove, Rattlebone Hollow west of Kansas City, Tennessee Town in Topeka, and the Daniel Votaw Colony near Coffeyville. Smaller black settlements also arose around family farms, such as in Wabaunsee and Hodgeman Counties. In south central Kansas, African Americans were fewer in number but predated the founding of Wichita itself.

In the 1870s, families such as the Robinsons, Hodges, and McAfees established themselves in business, real estate, and other ventures in Wichita. Others, such as Thomas Glover, rose to prominence in local politics. In 1874, Kansas law prohibited racial discrimination, reinforcing the image of Kansas as a place of hope. By the 1880s and 1890s, African Americans had founded businesses, churches, and newspapers that stretched along Water Street. By 1890, a thriving black community of over 1,200 included everyone from firemen, policemen, clergy, and business owners to laborers, porters, and servants. A major depression in the 1890s, however, brought economic distress across the United States and was followed by segregation laws. As the 20th century dawned, the promise that Kansas had held seemed to have evaporated. African Americans focused on separate development, building strong black institutions. Encouraged by W.E.B. DuBois, families educated their children for excellence in the new all-black schools. And encouraged by Booker T. Washington, churches and businesses erected proud new edifices and offered a positive racial identity amidst the resurgent racism.

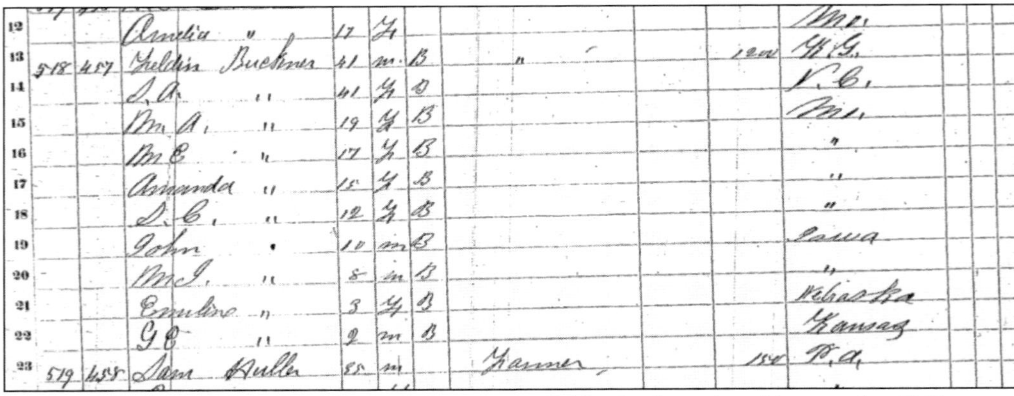

			Name		Age	Sex	Color	Occupation	Value	Birthplace
12			Amelia	"	17	F				Mo.
13	518	457	Feldin Buckner		41	M	B	"	1200	N.C.
14			S.A.	"	41	F	B			N.C.
15			Wm A.	"	19	F	B			Mo.
16			M.E.	"	17	F	B			"
17			Amanda	"	15	F	B			"
18			S.C.	"	12	F	B			"
19			John	"	10	M	B			Iowa
20			M.J.	"	8	M	B			"
21			Emeline	"	3	F	B			Nebraska
22			G.E.	"	2	M	B			Kansas
23	519	458	Sam Fuller		25	M		Farmer	150	N.Y.

One of the earliest residents of the Wichita area was Feldin Buckner, listed here in the 1860 census. Even before Kansas was a state, Buckner was a prominent landowner in the vicinity of what later became Towanda. In 1863, the Buckner family assisted the newly arrived James R. Mead. In this census chart, the letter "B" in the sixth column indicates black. Other early African Americans were designated with an "M" for mulatto.

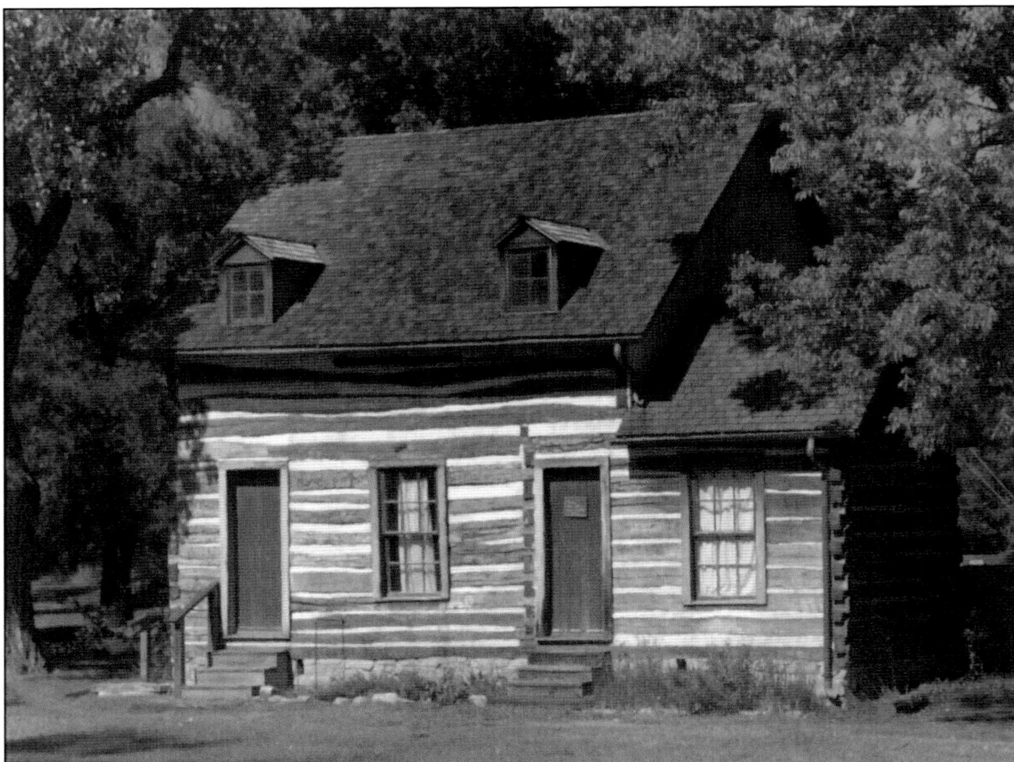

Another of Wichita's early black settlers was John Akles, a servant in the household of Darius Munger, who arrived in the area in 1868 as a representative of the Wichita Land and Town Company. By 1869, Munger had completed this house at what is now Waco Avenue and Ninth Street. The building also served as a post office, hotel, and meeting place. This structure was later moved to the site of what is now the Old Cowtown Museum. (Courtesy Old Cowtown Museum.)

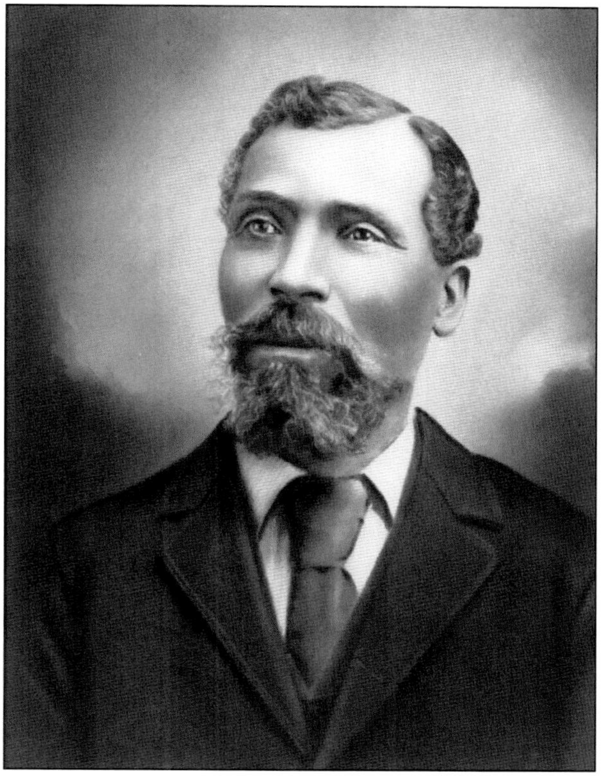

In early 1864, Jacob McAfee mustered into the 27th Regiment United States Colored Troops in Columbus, Ohio, and was wounded at Petersburg. When the Civil War ended the following year, McAfee, now a corporal at age 26, received his discharge and moved west—arriving in Wichita in the 1870s. By the 1880s, his son, Abraham, established a 50-acre farm in Garden Plain in Sedgwick County, where he raised corn, hogs, and potatoes. (Courtesy Charles McAfee.)

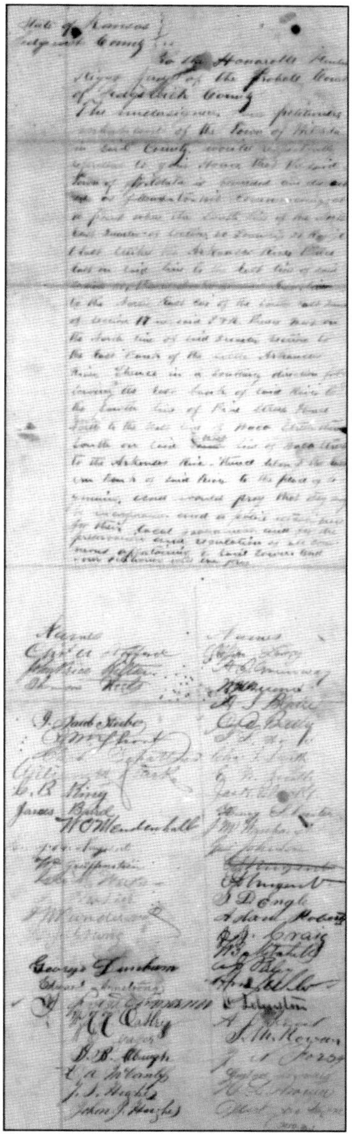

An African American, Richard Robinson, was among the 124 individuals who petitioned the Sedgwick County probate court to incorporate the city of Wichita on July 21, 1870. Originally from Virginia, Robinson came to Kansas from Pennsylvania and lived on the farm of James Gordy in 1870. One of several workers on the property, he lived with his wife, Sarah, and two young boys. (Courtesy Wichita–Sedgwick County Historical Museum.)

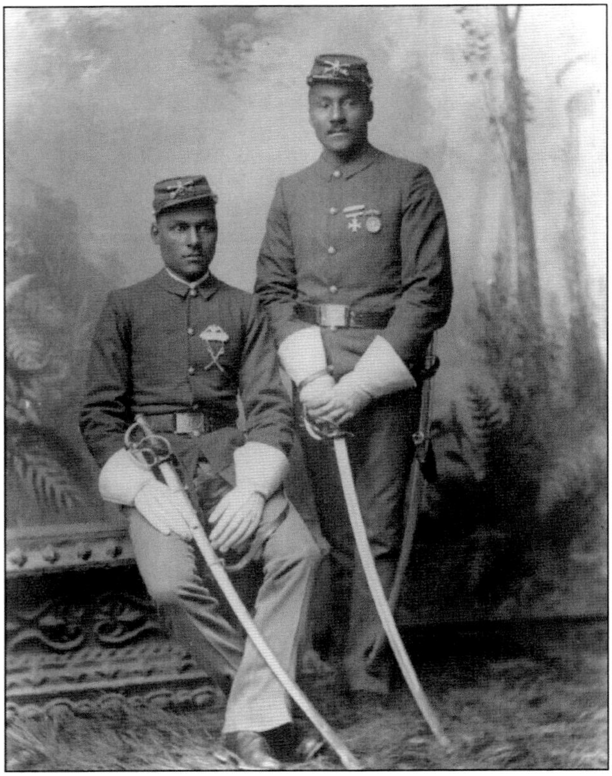

In the 1860s and 1870s, black soldiers and veterans—veterans of the First and Second Kansas Colored Regiments among them—were important in the settlement of Kansas. Others served in units such as the 9th and 10th Cavalry Regiments, which organized in 1866 to control Native American activities in the face of American settlement. Tradition says that African Americans' curly hair reminded native peoples of bison hides, giving rise to the term "Buffalo Soldier." (Courtesy Fort Leavenworth.)

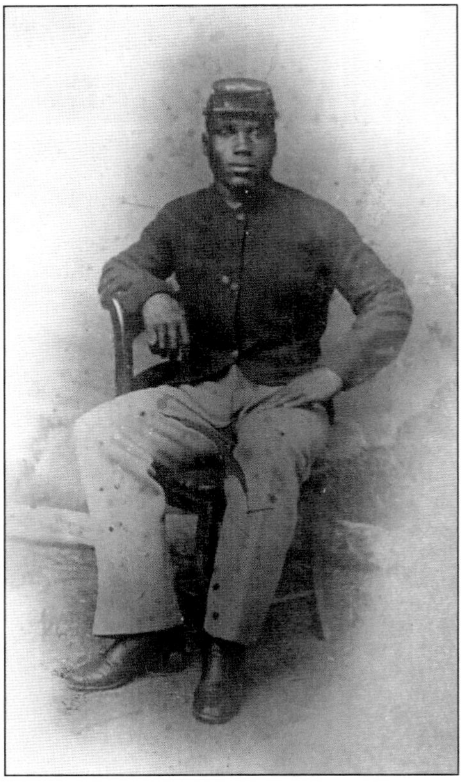

As slave to a Confederate general, Ruben Waller saw Civil War battles and witnessed the surrender of Gen. Robert E. Lee. After the war, he joined the Buffalo Soldiers, where he served 10 years and participated in the rescue of Major Forsyth's men at Beecher Island. After the Indian wars, Waller homesteaded in El Dorado, where he lived until his death in 1945 at age 105. (Courtesy Kansas State Historical Society.)

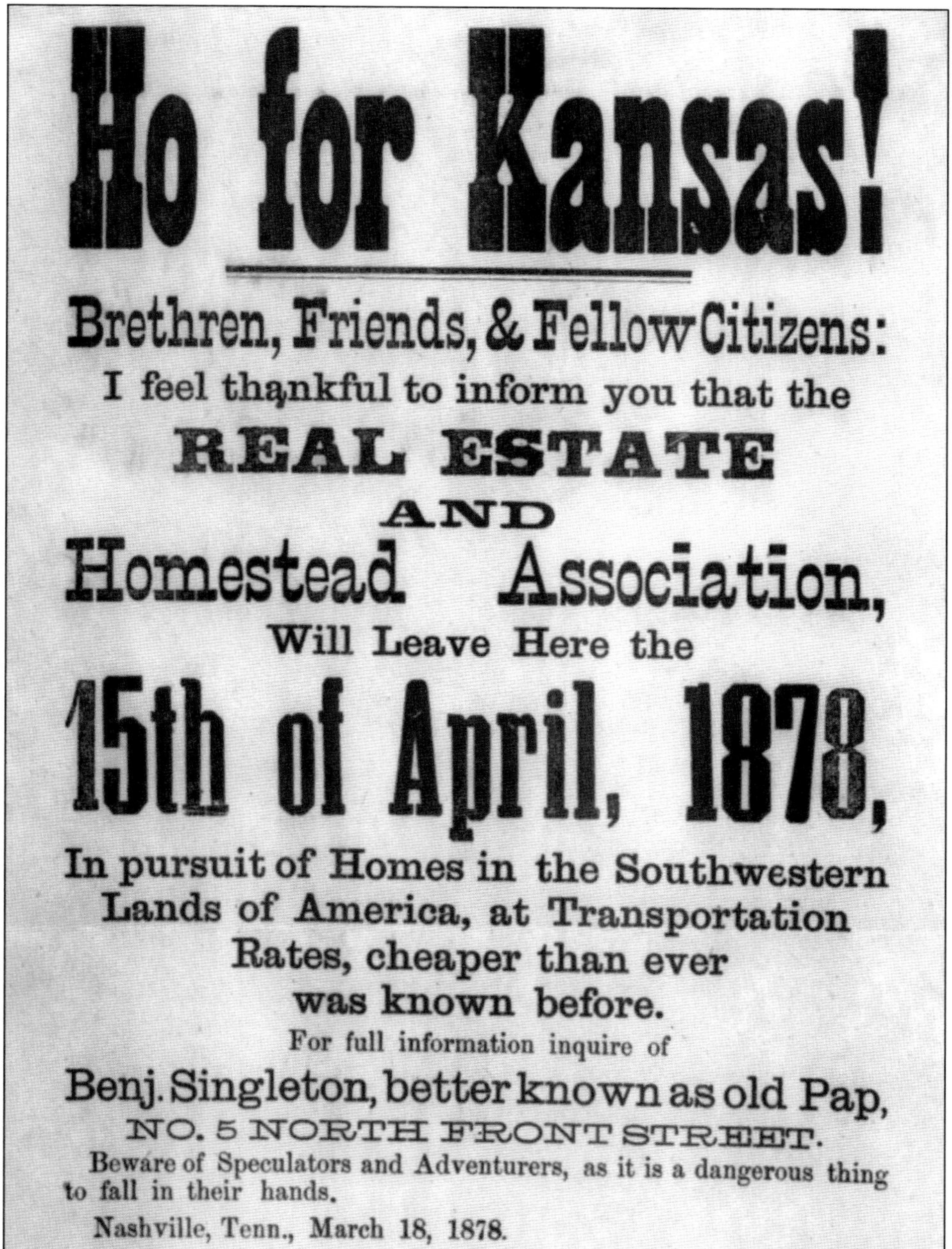
Ho for Kansas!

Brethren, Friends, & Fellow Citizens:
I feel thankful to inform you that the
REAL ESTATE
AND
Homestead Association,
Will Leave Here the
15th of April, 1878,
In pursuit of Homes in the Southwestern
Lands of America, at Transportation
Rates, cheaper than ever
was known before.
For full information inquire of
Benj. Singleton, better known as old Pap,
NO. 5 NORTH FRONT STREET.
Beware of Speculators and Adventurers, as it is a dangerous thing to fall in their hands.
Nashville, Tenn., March 18, 1878.

Thousands of black southerners fled the terrorism that punished any assertion of their constitutional rights, and many came to Kansas, which had an anti-discrimination law as early as 1874. By 1877, the Republican Party, in order to win the presidency, made a backroom deal to no longer enforce the 14th and 15th Amendments in the South—letting white supremacist Democrats, who had returned to power in southern states, police themselves as they saw fit. Terror tactics were used against newly freed people in the South, which made constitutional guarantees of equal treatment and due process meaningless—persuading tens of thousands to flee west. (Courtesy Kansas State Historical Society.)

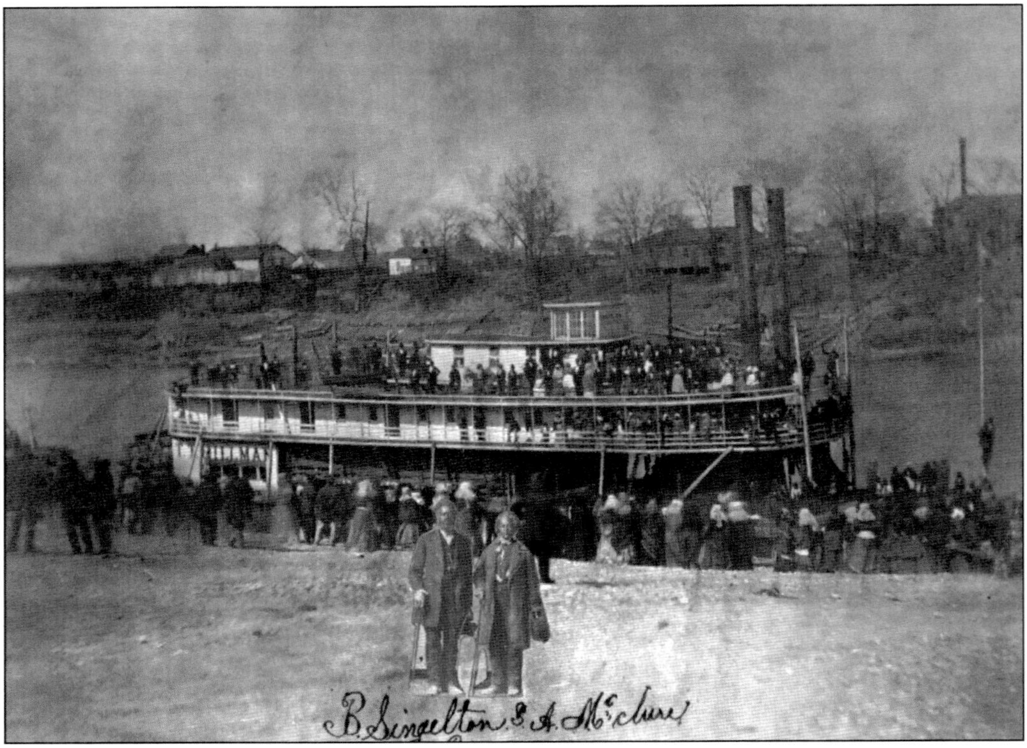

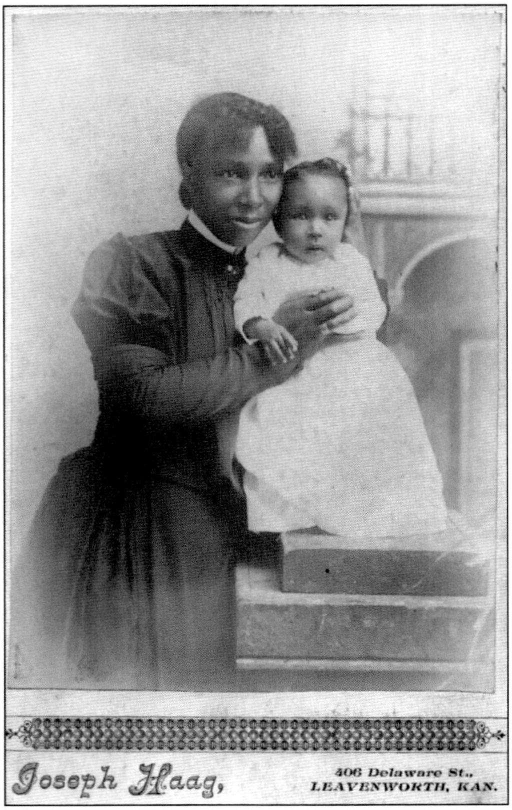

Many "Exodusters" arrived on steamboats such as the one pictured above, with an image of Benjamin "Pap" Singleton and S.A. McClure superimposed on the scene. Black communities such as Tennessee Town in Topeka, Quindaro near Kansas City, Nicodemus in northwest Kansas, and Dunlap near Council Grove emerged. Some went to western Kansas and into Oklahoma, where they farmed, ran businesses, were cowboys, and laid track for the railroads. Locals were not always welcoming to the new arrivals, however. *Wichita Eagle* editor and publisher Marshall Murdock charged Topeka with exporting black people "contaminated" with yellow fever to Wichita and got the city council to quarantine Exodusters. Among them, 14 were sent back to Topeka despite the absence of any evidence supporting his claim. (Above, courtesy Kansas State Historical Society.)

Wichita's early leaders hoped to tap into the drives of longhorns that traveled north out of Texas to the railheads in Kansas. From 1872 through 1876, cattle came into town to be loaded on trains that went back to Chicago. The drovers who moved the great herds were one of the most diverse populations in the American West, with some estimates suggesting that one in four cowboys was black. Below, Duane Nelson, a participant in the civil rights sit-ins of the 1960s, reenacts the black cowboy experience at the Old Cowtown Museum. (Right, courtesy Kansas State Historical Society; below, courtesy Old Cowtown Museum.)

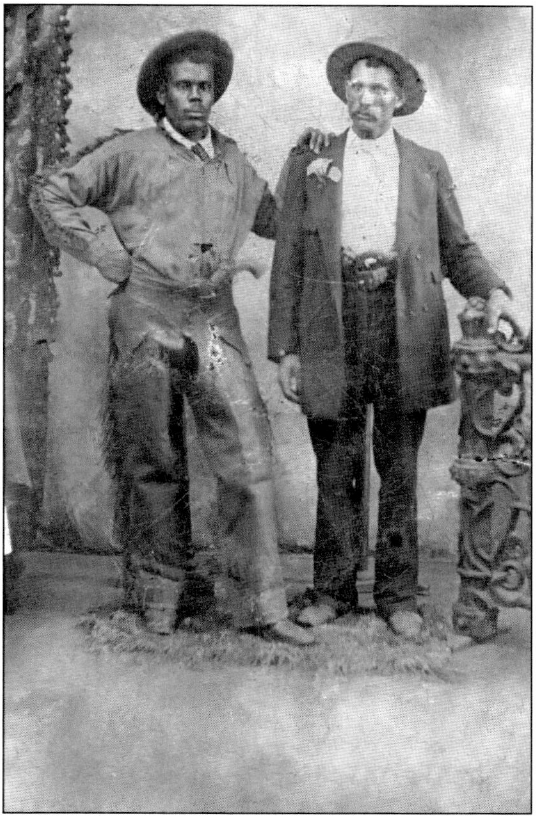

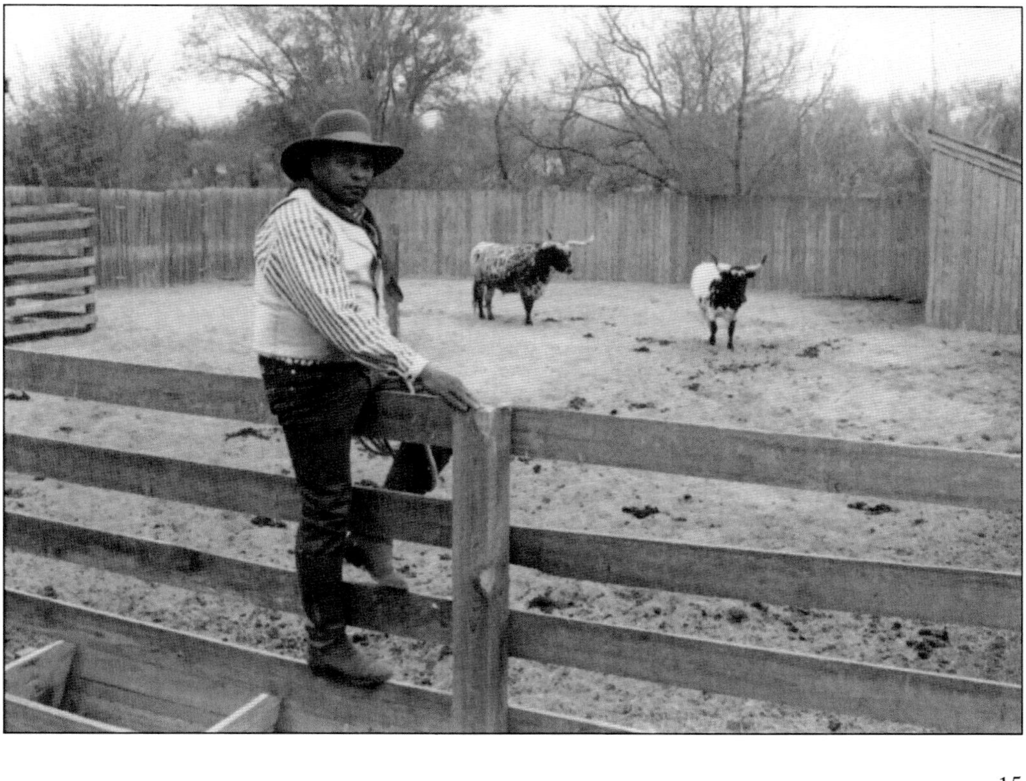

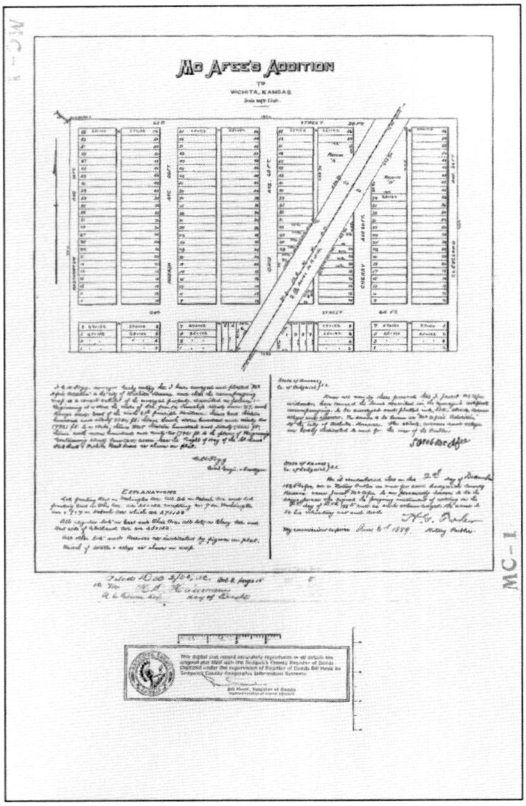

Several African Americans were involved in the city's 1870s and 1880s real estate boom. Among them was Jacob McAfee, whose acquisitions included a parcel north of Eighteenth Street. In 1885, he also platted the "McAfee Addition," which was north of Twenty-fourth Street next to land that eventually became the site of the city's stockyards and meat packing plants. (Courtesy Sedgwick County.)

The Perry family moved from Higginsville, Missouri, to Wichita around the turn of the 20th century. Thomas, standing second from left, established the first small animal hospital in Wichita, at 1325 North Cleveland Avenue. Eugene, standing second from right, graduated from the University of Kansas School of Music and taught music in several Midwestern states. Homer, standing at far right, found steady work as a postal carrier in Wichita.

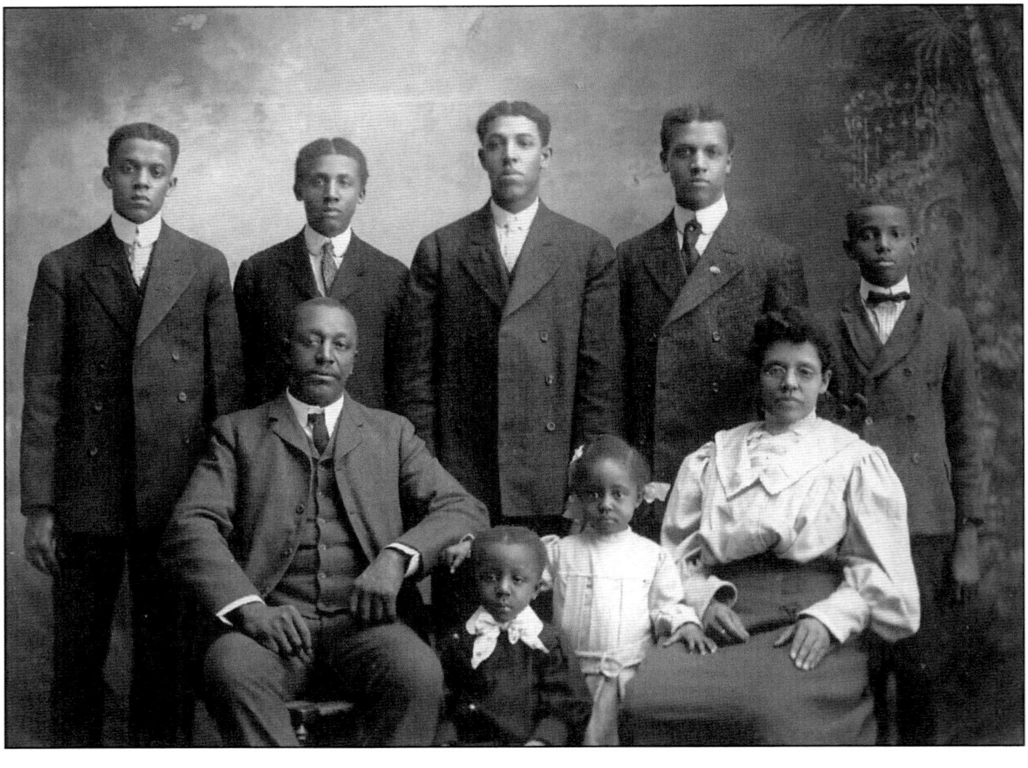

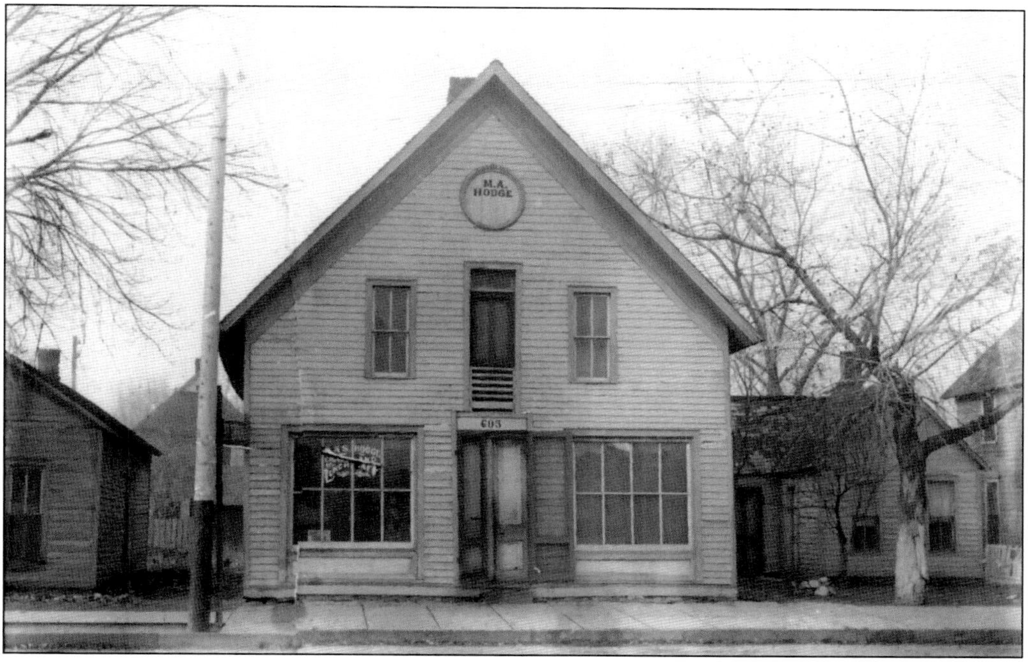

Wesley and Millie Hodge arrived in Wichita in 1876, constructing this home on North Main Street soon after. Wesley was a blacksmith and Millie was a charter member of Second Baptist Church (later Calvary Baptist), which was organized in the spring of 1878. In 1885, the family acquired the frame church that housed the city's first Presbyterian—and later, Catholic—congregation, moving it to 605 North Main Street to be converted into a hotel adjacent to their home. Both structures were later relocated to the Old Cowtown Museum (below) where the Hodge home was, until recently, misidentified as the church's parsonage. (Above, courtesy First Presbyterian Church Archives; below, courtesy Keith Wondra.)

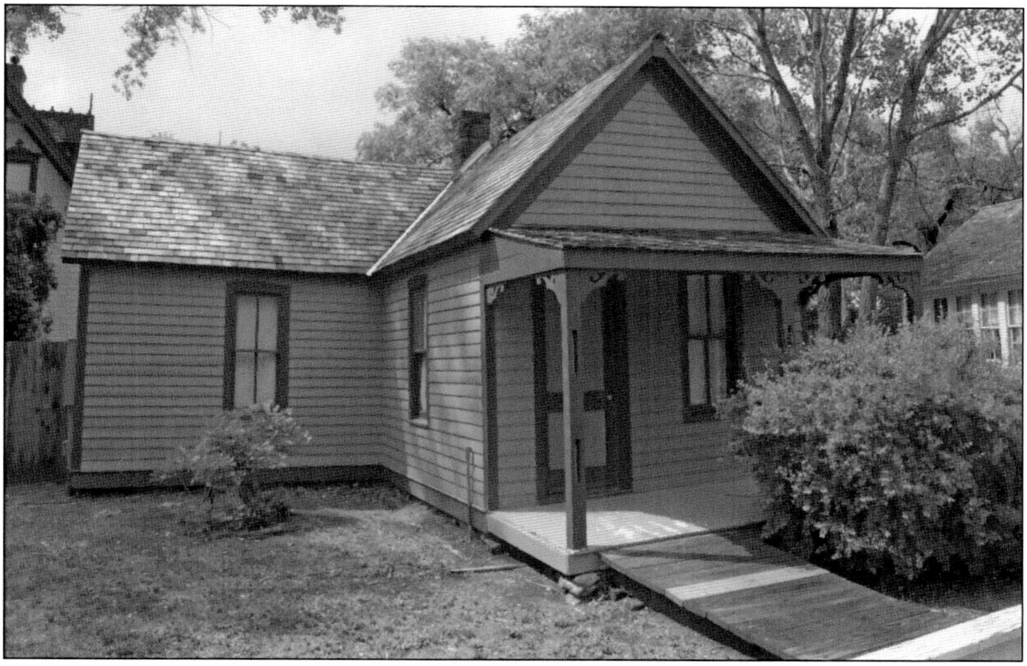

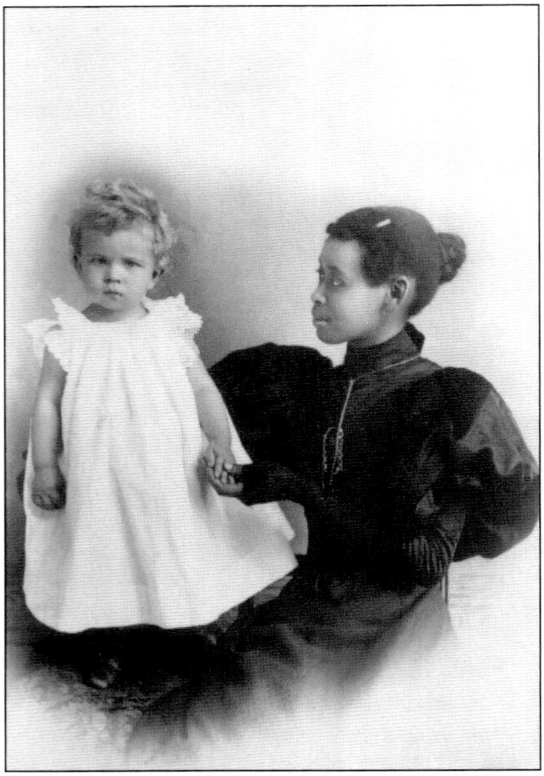

Several prominent white families had both white and black household servants. At left, George Fabrique Nolley, grandson of well-known early physician Dr. Andrew Fabrique, poses with an unidentified African American nurse. The photographic record contains many images of black residents whose names have been lost to local memory, such as the children below. (Left, courtesy Wichita–Sedgwick County Historical Museum.)

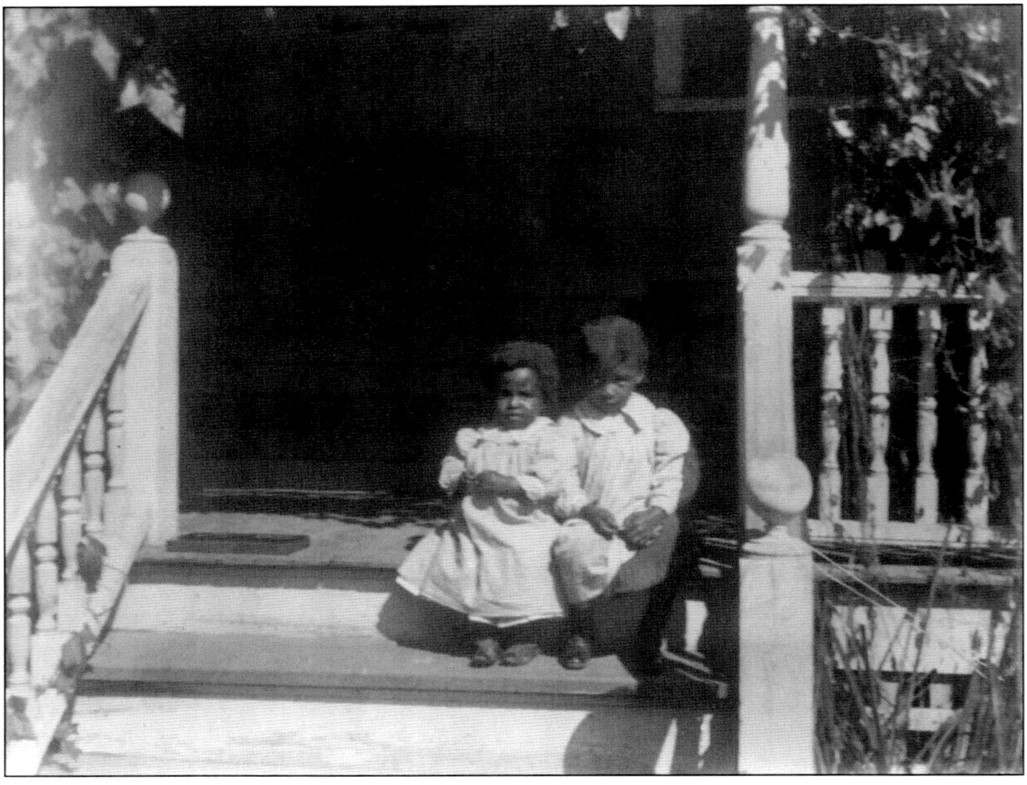

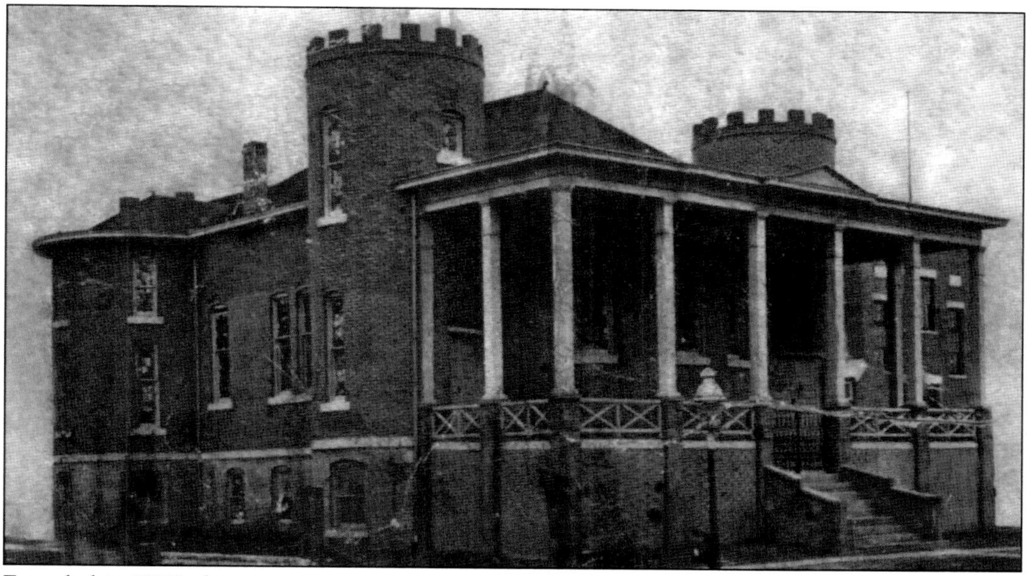

Founded in 1878, the congregation of Second Baptist (later Calvary Baptist) laid the cornerstone of its church at Elm and Water Streets on June 27, 1909. Under Pastor George W. Smith, this large brick building was erected on the site. They commissioned African American architect Josiah Joshua Walker to design the building. Second Baptist, St. Paul AME (founded in 1875), and Tabernacle Baptist (founded in 1883) were among Wichita's first African American churches.

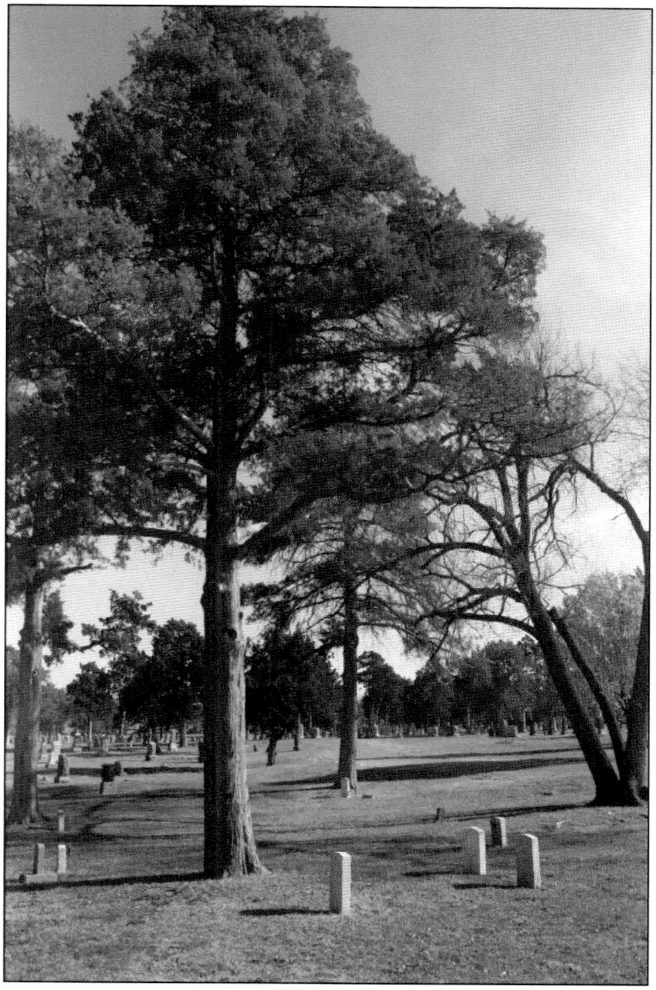

At first, cemeteries, like the rest of local life, were relatively integrated. Over time, policy, custom, family tradition, and finance often resulted in African Americans being buried separate from white people in local cemeteries. In some cases, black organizations purchased their own burial plots, such as this plot of African American Grand Army of the Republic veterans in Maple Grove Cemetery.

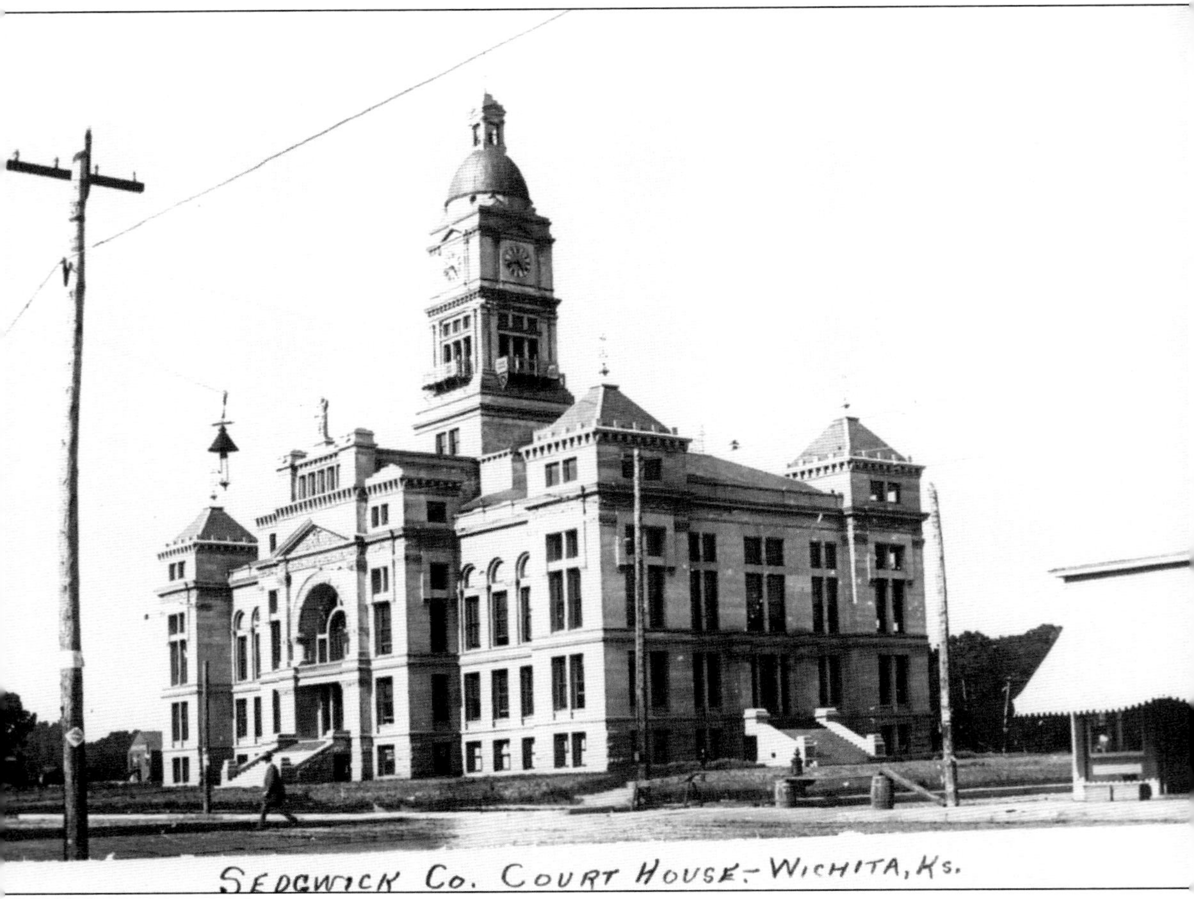

By the late 19th century, African Americans created a business district downtown, from Waco to Main Streets and just west of the city's courthouse—seen here. In the years that followed, the courthouse was a source of jobs and the backdrop for formal and informal pictures. Wichita's first African American businesses included an ox-yoke factory, blacksmith, and barber shop. Community members ranged from police and firemen to railroad porters, clergy, and people whose businesses served the community, including undertakers, barbers, and seamstresses. (Courtesy Wichita–Sedgwick County Historical Museum.)

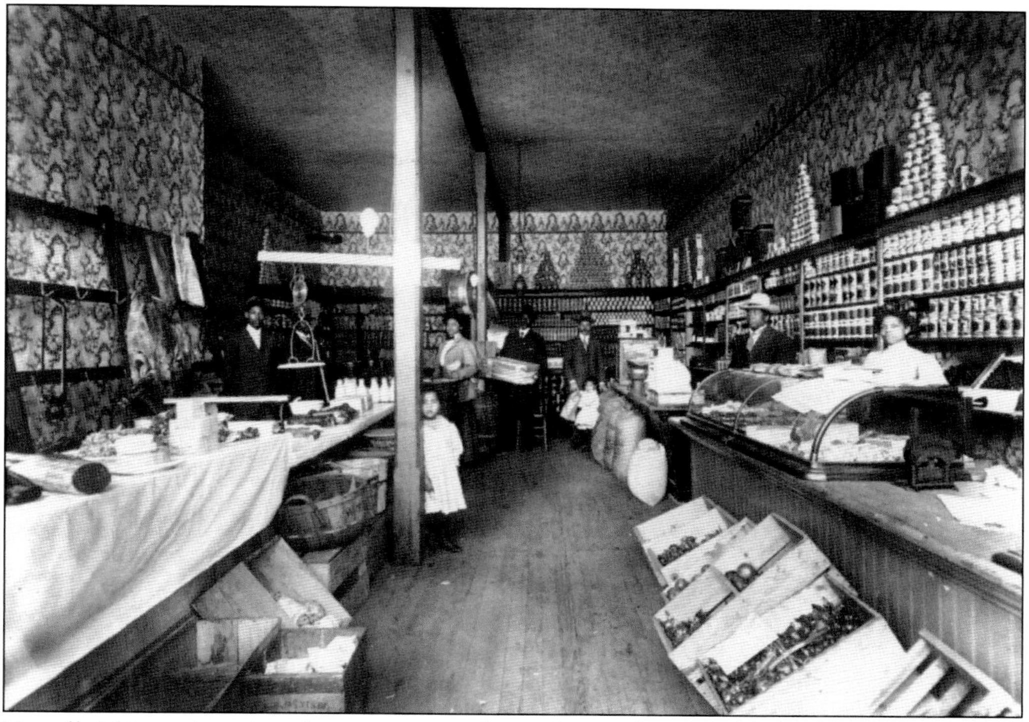

Not all African American businesses were located near downtown. The LeGrand Store, for example, was on North Mosley Street. (Courtesy Wichita Public Library.)

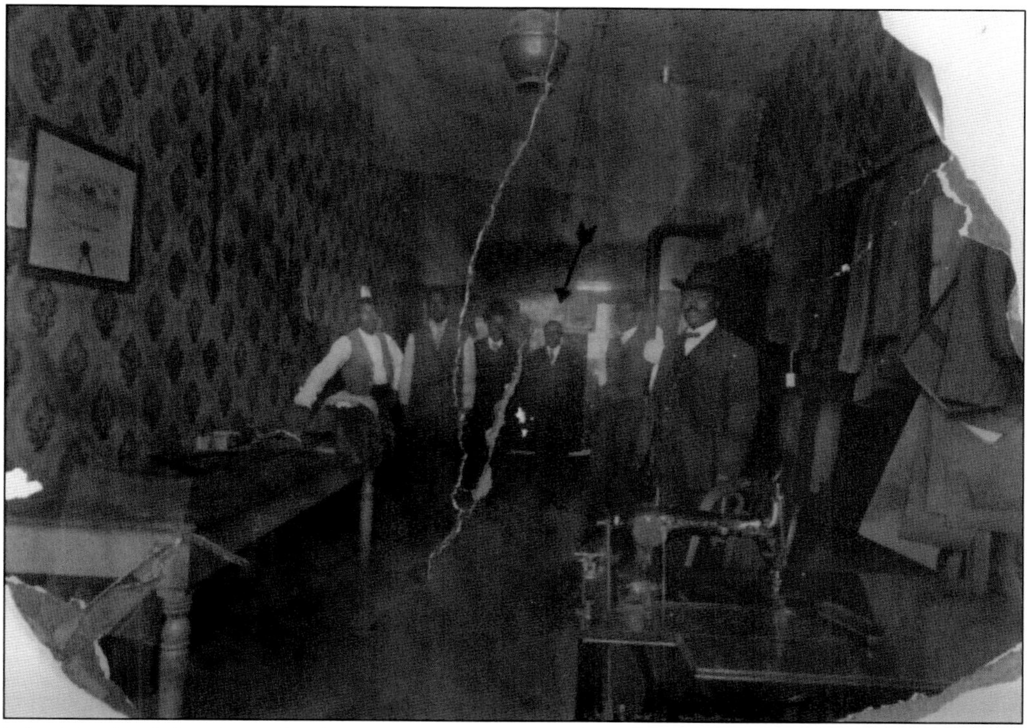

Julia Van Leu's brother, Charlie Patton, ran a tailor shop at 639 North Main Street. Patton is shown at center.

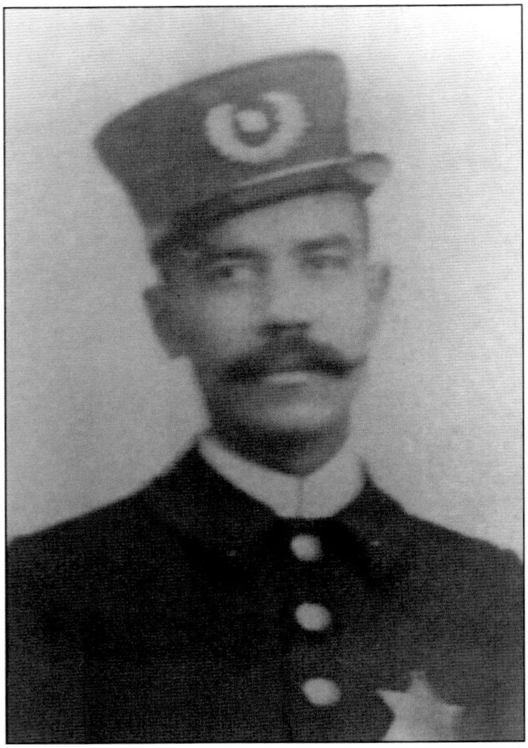

Sam Jones came to Wichita with his parents in 1874 and attended the old Fourth Ward School. Before he became a plumber, he held a variety of jobs that included police officer and fireman. He was also a musician with a traveling minstrel show and the editor of a local newspaper, *The National Baptist World*. In 1893, he became the first African American elected to county office—serving two terms as constable.

George Walter Robinson, top center, joined Wichita's fire department on November 17, 1896, and served for 43 years. A member of one of Wichita's oldest African American families, Robinson was the son of Richard and Sarah Robinson and was two years old when Wichita was incorporated. George was one of the first African Americans to work for the Wichita Fire Department and became a fire captain.

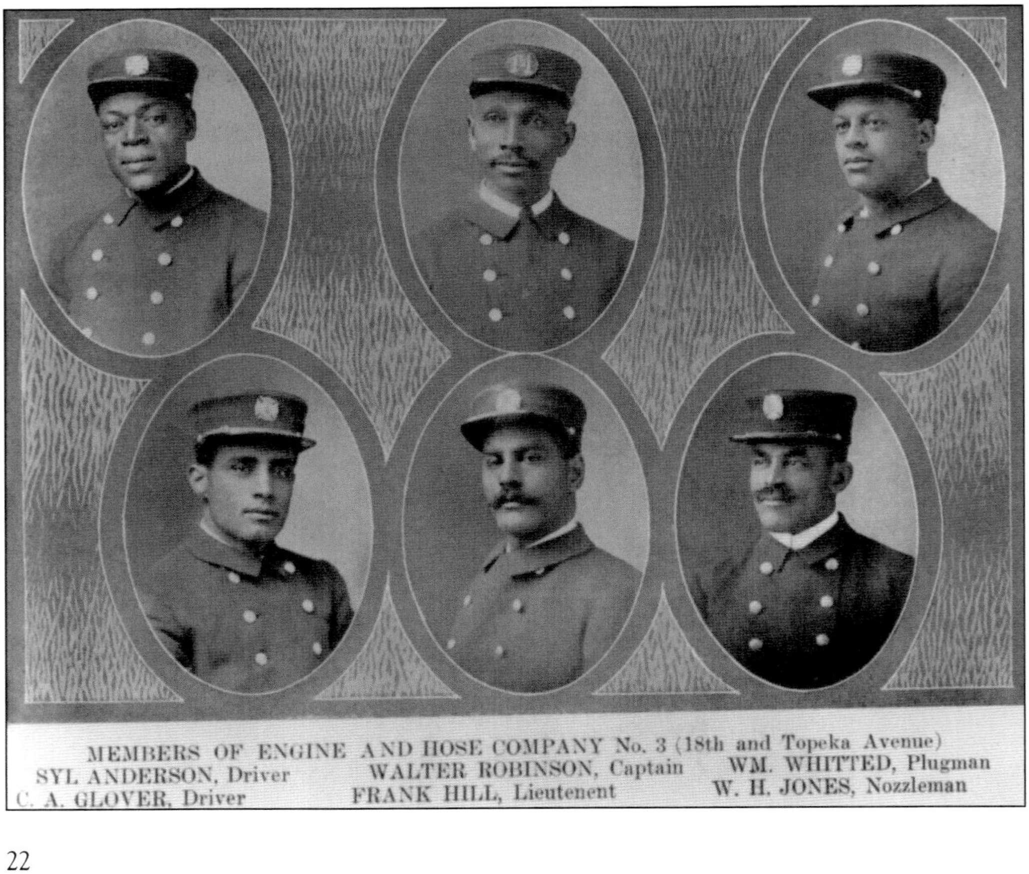

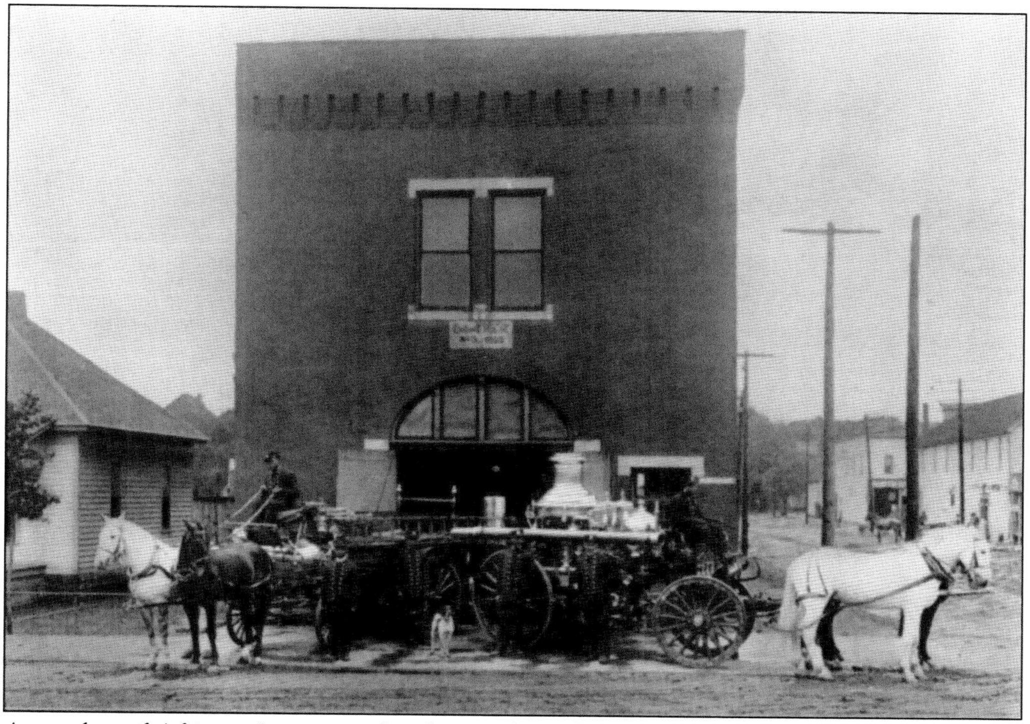

A number of African Americans lived near the railroad tracks on what was then the city's northern edge. Above, Syl Anderson, Frank Hill, C.A. Glover, George Walter Robinson, W.H. Jones, and William Whitted pose in front of Engine House No. 3, located at Eighteenth Street and North Topeka Avenue. The image below shows that, a few years later, the station had replaced its horses with a fire truck.

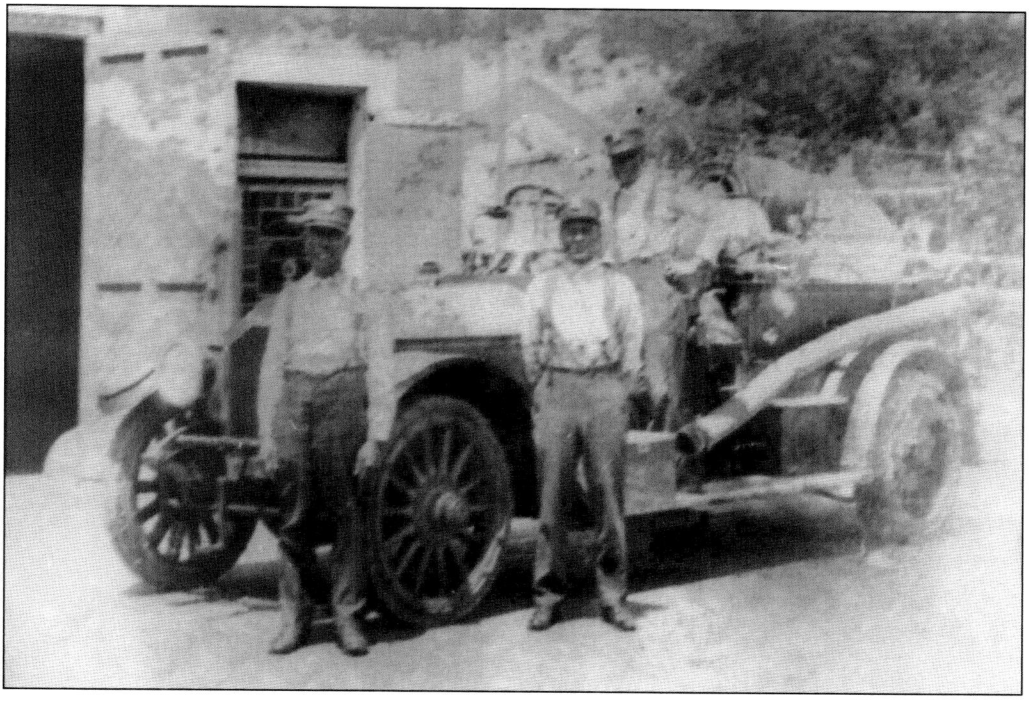

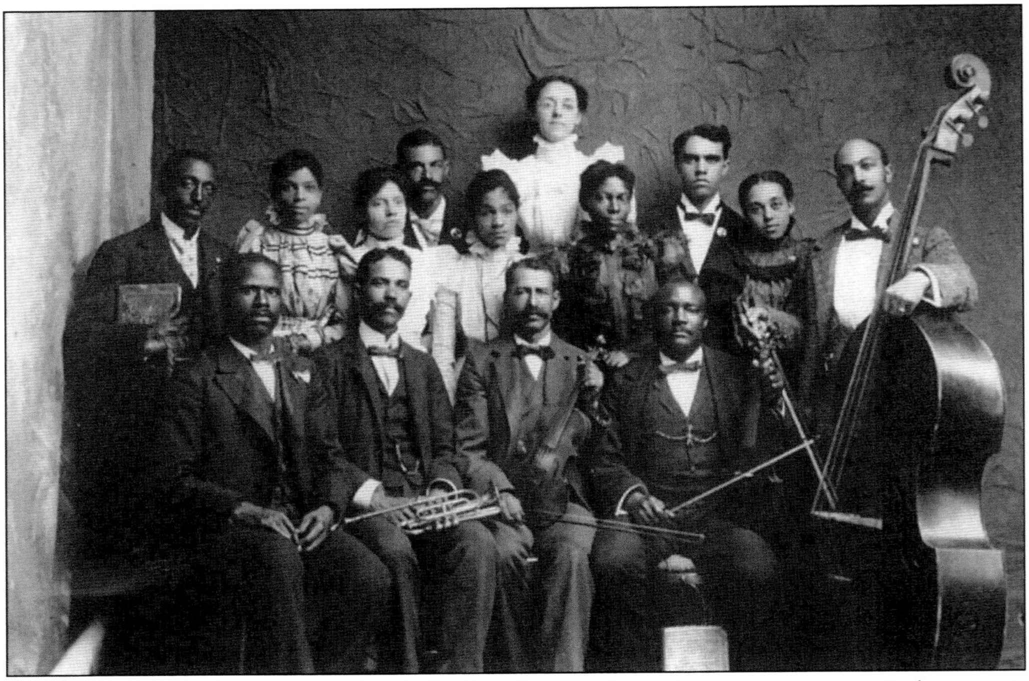

As a teenager, Sam Jones traveled with the Ringling Brothers circus as a trapeze artist but gave it up following a 15-foot fall. Jones later joined the Richards and Pringle Georgia Minstrels Group in 1884. (Courtesy Wichita–Sedgwick County Historical Museum.)

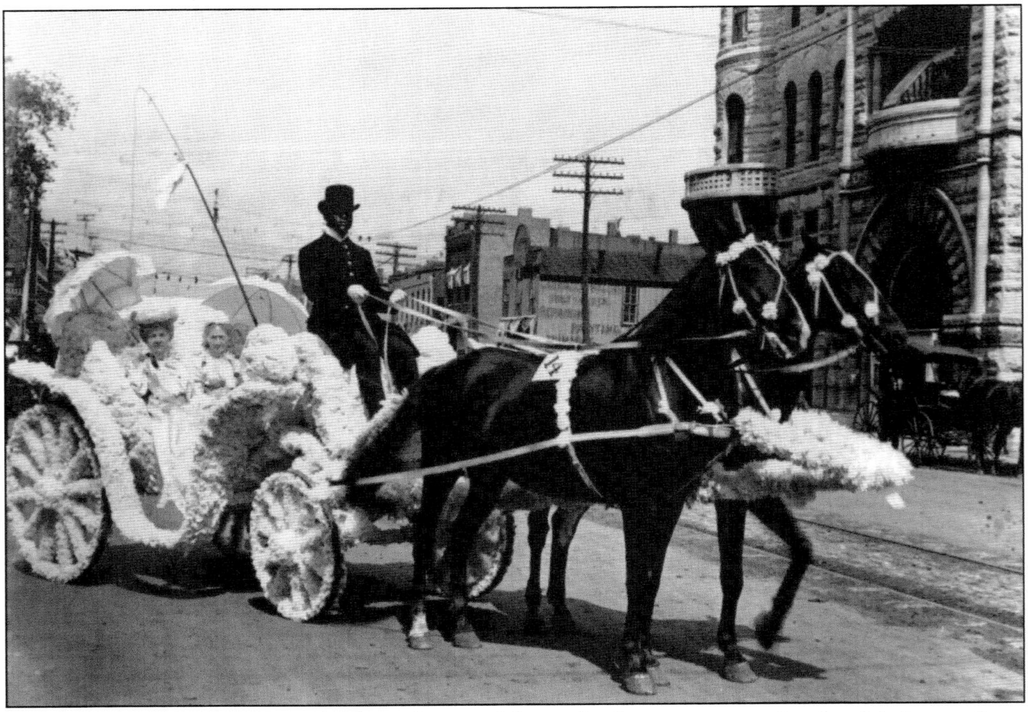

African Americans remained relatively invisible to the larger community. In this image from one of Wichita's annual flower parades, black citizens appear as footmen to the well-to-do white citizens in the carriage—a symbol of a social order assumed to be simply "the way things were."

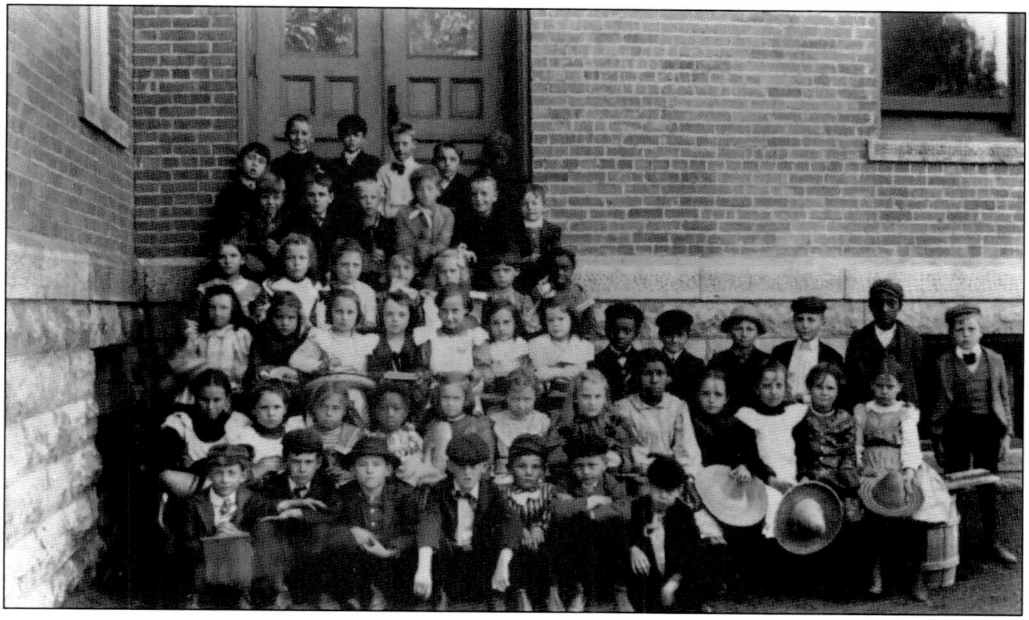

In these photographs, Carleton School's class of 1890 poses with the school's teachers. The school was located at the corner of Lewis and Lawrence (now Broadway) Avenues. Schools were integrated until Jim Crow laws began proliferating across the country in the 1890s. In 1893, when a school desegregation proposal arose, *The Wichita Eagle* reported "AN IMMENSE INDIGNATION MEETING HELD BY COLORED FOLKS. They Express Themselves Unmistakably on the Separate School Question." Massive protests delayed the board from implementing its unanimous 1906 decision to segregate Wichita's elementary schools through the eighth grade until 1911, when a bond issue funded the construction of two "colored" elementary schools: L'Ouverture at Thirteenth and Mosley Streets, and Douglass at 600 North Water Street. Elementary schools were segregated from 1912 to 1972. (Both, courtesy Wichita Public Library.)

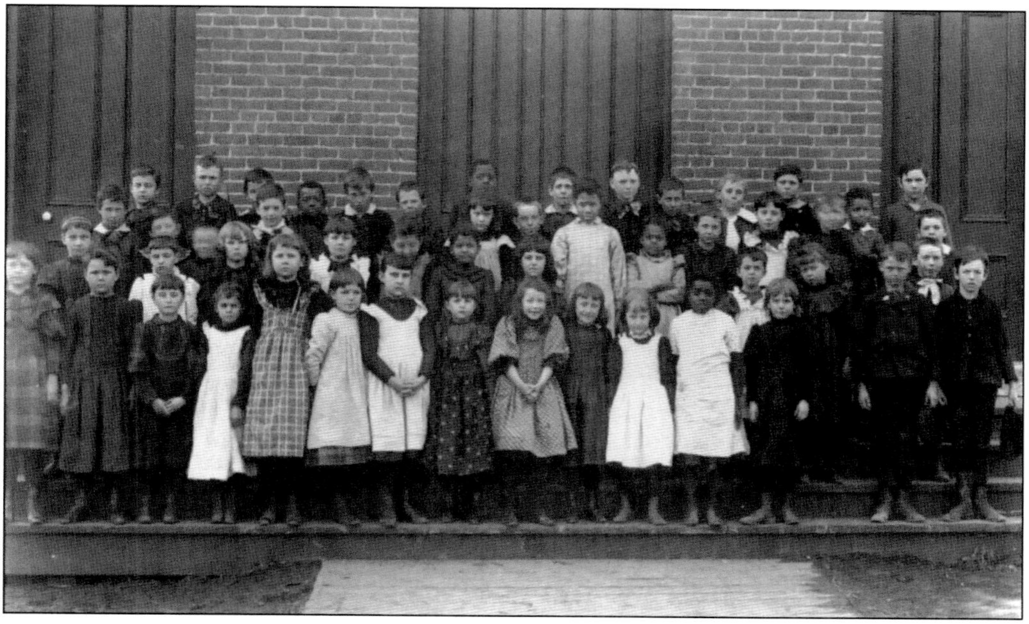

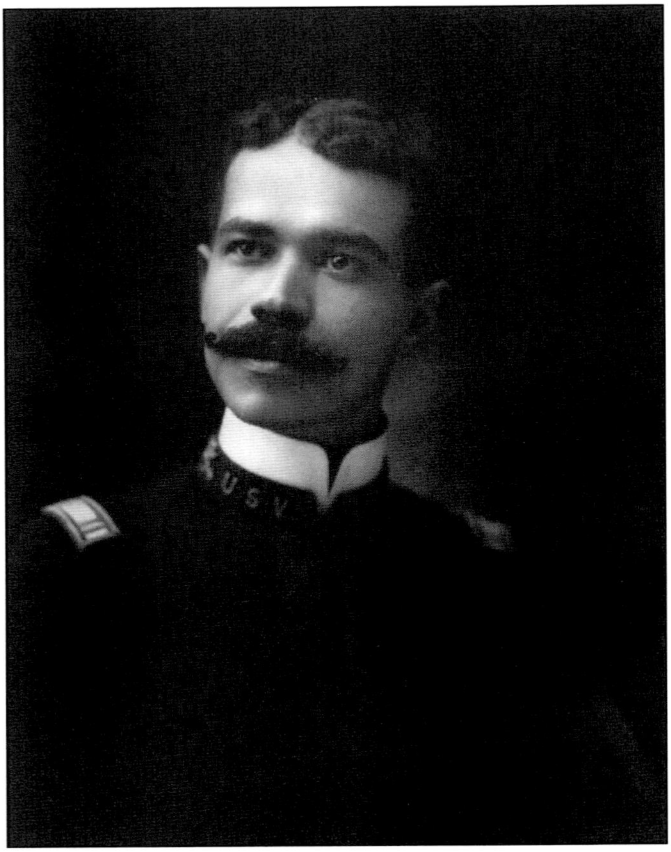

The Spanish American War saw three African American regiments serve in Cuba. One was the 23rd Regiment Kansas Volunteer Infantry. When forming the regiment in July 1898, Gov. John Leedy made the daring decision to have black officers as well as enlisted men. One of those officers was Sam Jones (left), who ended his service at the rank of captain. Another of the 49 black volunteers was Abraham McAfee, the son of Jacob. Stationed in the province of San Luis, the unit repaired roads and infrastructure until it returned to Kansas in 1899. (Left, courtesy Wichita–Sedgwick County Historical Museum.)

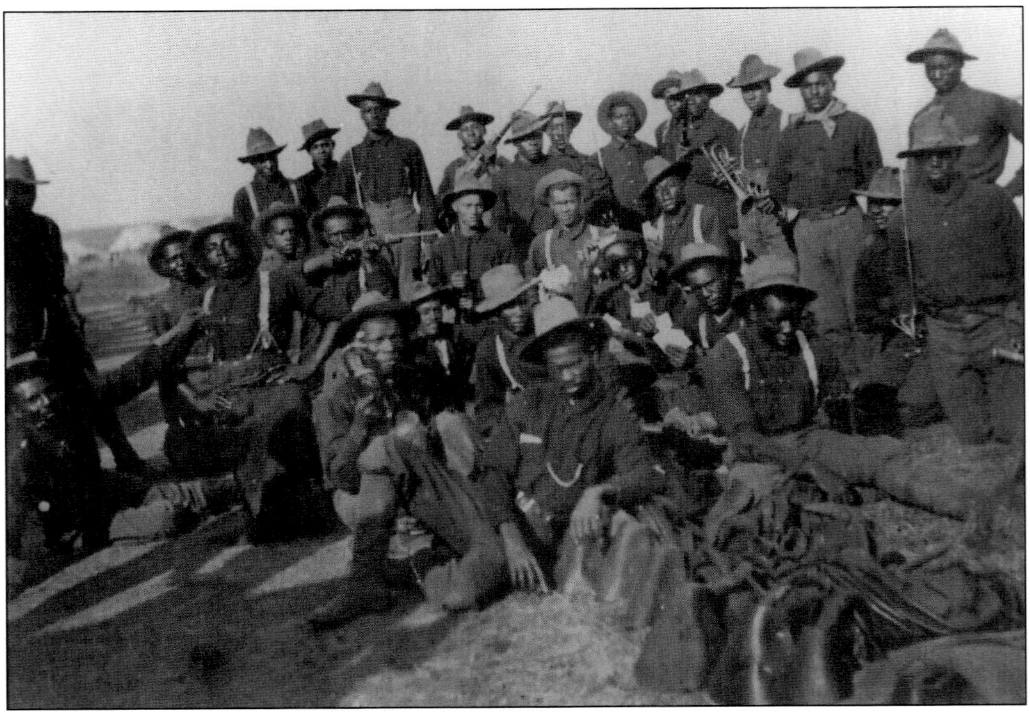

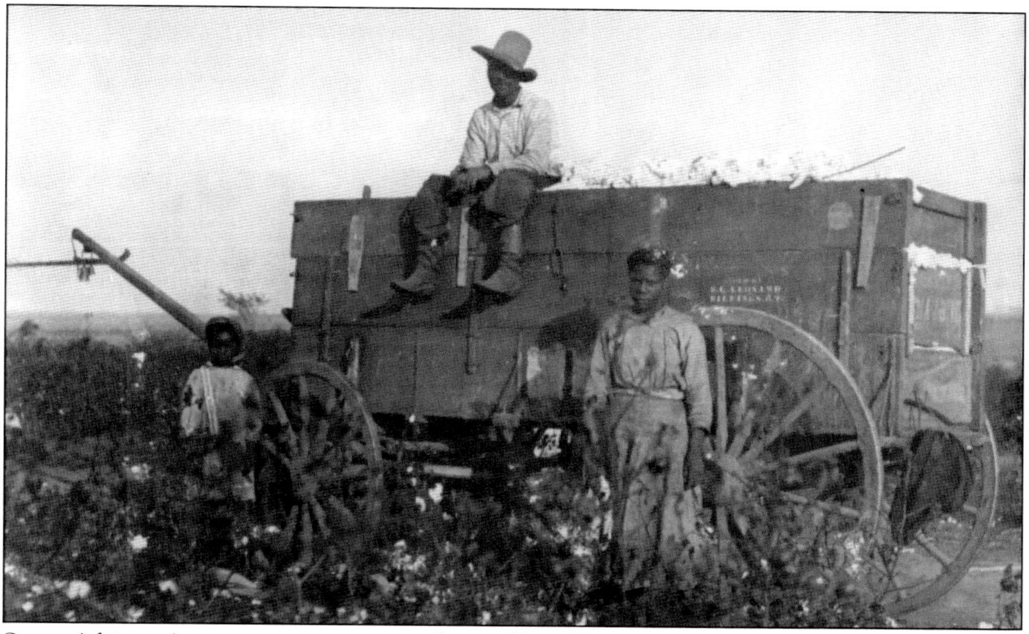

Some African Americans were among those affected by the forced removals of the Cherokee, Chickasaw, Choctaw, Creek, and Seminole from the southeastern United States between 1818 and 1848 as part of the Trails of Tears. In the 20th and 21st centuries, African American Cherokees have seen their tribal membership withdrawn by the tribe. One such person of mixed background was rodeo star Bill Pickett, seen here with his daughters.

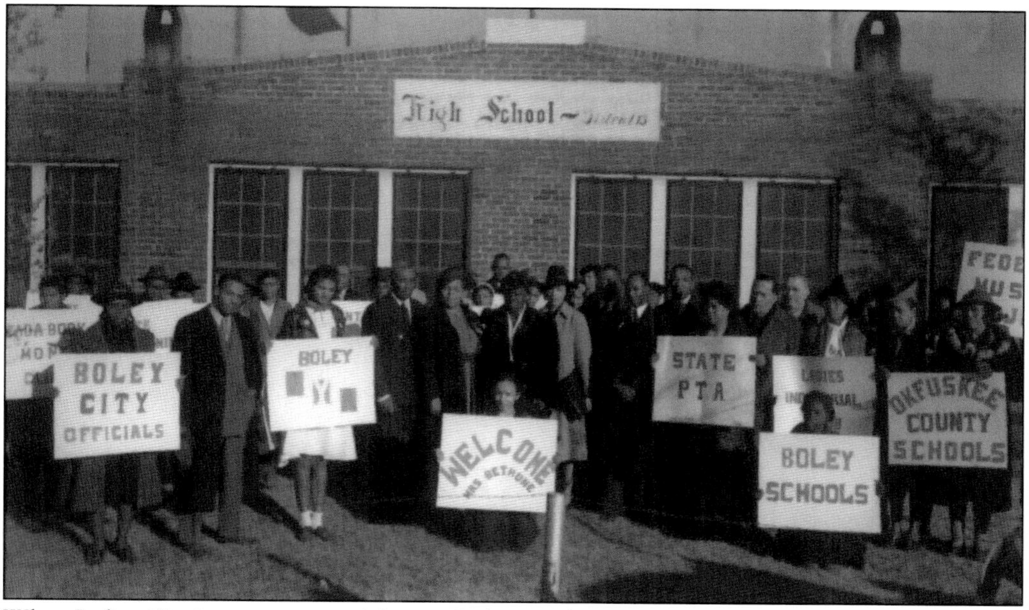

When Indian Territory was opened for non-Indian settlement in 1889, Wichita was a base for many of the 50,000 "Sooners" rushing to Oklahoma, which soon had 44 all-black towns. The community of Boley was constructed on land donated by Abigail Barnett McCormick, a Creek freedwoman, in 1903, and it fascinated many of the black leaders of the era. Booker T. Washington wrote about it being a place of great pride and industry. In this photograph, educator Mary McLeod Bethune (center) is seen visiting Boley High School. (Courtesy Mark E. McCormick.)

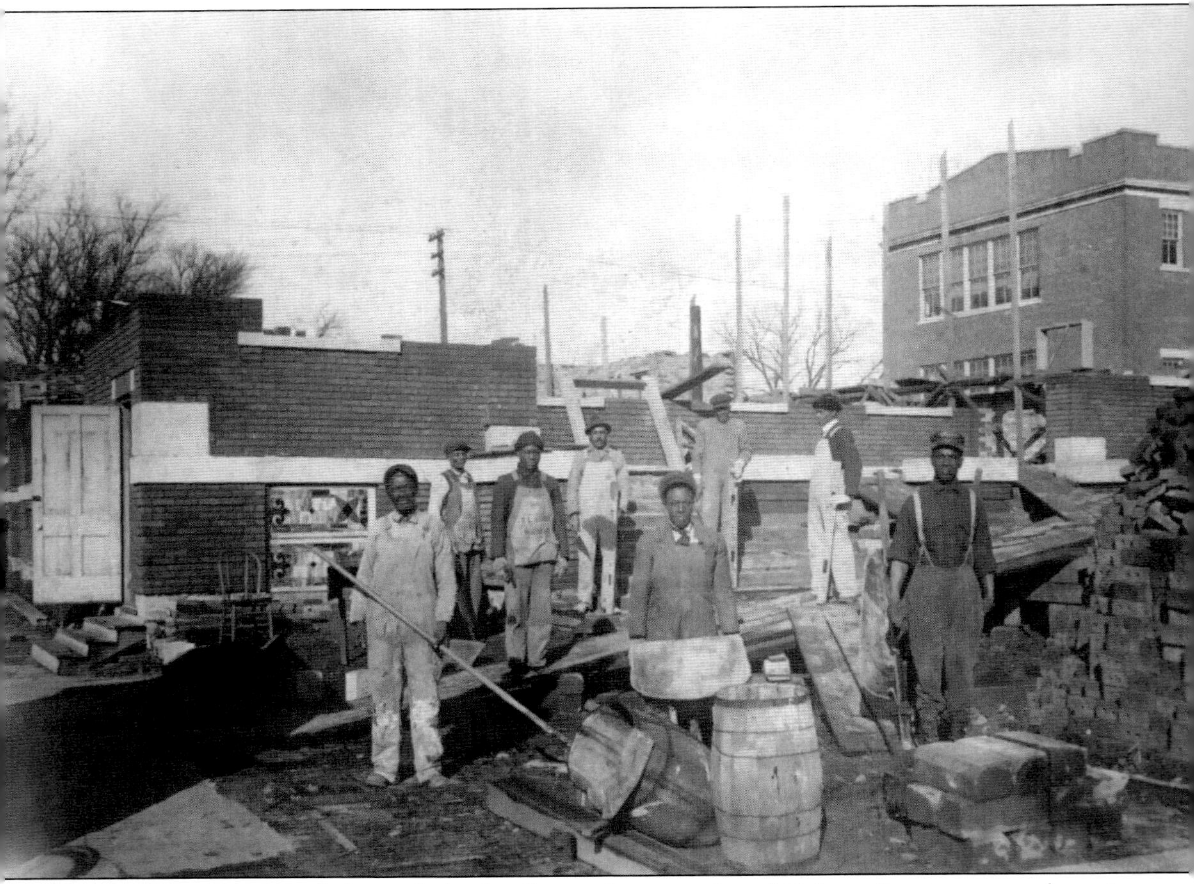

Building issues, including a lack of sufficient fire exits, forced Calvary Baptist to tear down its 1909 building and erect a new structure. This c. 1917 photograph looks west, showing that the foundation is nearly complete. While the building was erected, the congregation worshiped in the courthouse on Main Street. The structure on the right is the Frederick Douglass School.

Two

Creating a Community

A 1922 article in the *Wichita Beacon* proclaimed that, "the colored people of Wichita, records indicate, have made remarkable progress along all lines of endeavor last year." It went on to cite the efforts of H.T. Sims, who organized the Kansas Coal and Mercantile Company; Roscoe Robinson, who invested in a movie theater on North Main Street; and the prominence of groups such as the Excelsior Club and the New Hope Baptist Church choir. Although African Americans in Wichita could celebrate many accomplishments, they did so in the face of an increasingly segregated society and overt racial hostility.

World War I opened factory jobs to African Americans and started a major migration out of the South. At the same time, however, the Ku Klux Klan re-emerged and the state legislature enacted a law allowing cities to segregate schools. A strong sense of solidarity helped black Wichitans oppose local white hostility, and 50 to 100 came to school board meetings to oppose school segregation. Churches and the newly formed (1919) Wichita Chapter of the NAACP collected signatures on petitions and spoke out against segregating 5.6 percent of the city's population, and when Pres. Woodrow Wilson showed the racist film *The Birth of a Nation* at the White House, Wichita's NAACP joined chapters nationwide in telegraphing their protest to the president. In the 1920s, the city's black population was outnumbered by its 6,000 KKK members.

The city became the nation's air capital in the 1920s, producing one-fourth of the total commercial aircraft made in the United States by 1928, but African Americans were only hired to sweep floors, cook, and clean. In response, Wichita African Americans established a viable community in the downtown area, known by some as the "West End," which by the mid-1920s consisted of an array of businesses, churches, schools, Masonic organizations, and other community-based institutions. By the end of the decade, black Wichitans began an internal migration eastward, toward the McAdams neighborhood. On the eve of World War II, the center of black Wichita had moved from Central and Main Streets to Ninth Street and Cleveland Avenue.

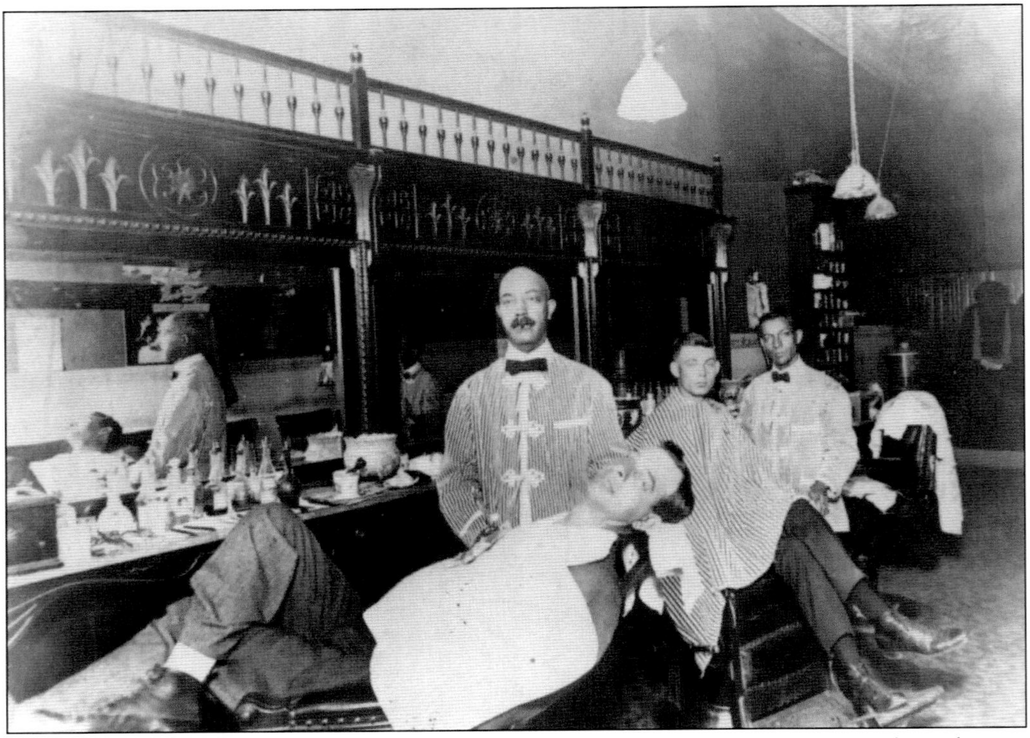

Masonic organizations were important social clubs for many African Americans. The Arkansas Valley Lodge of the Prince Hall Masons still stands today at 615 North Main Street. Above, the grand commander of Prince Hall Commandry, John T. Chinneth, poses in his barbershop at 117 West Douglas Avenue in August 1908. Below, members of the "Ark Valley Lodge"—established in 1885—gather around the lodge's cornerstone in 1910. (Both, courtesy Wichita Public Library.)

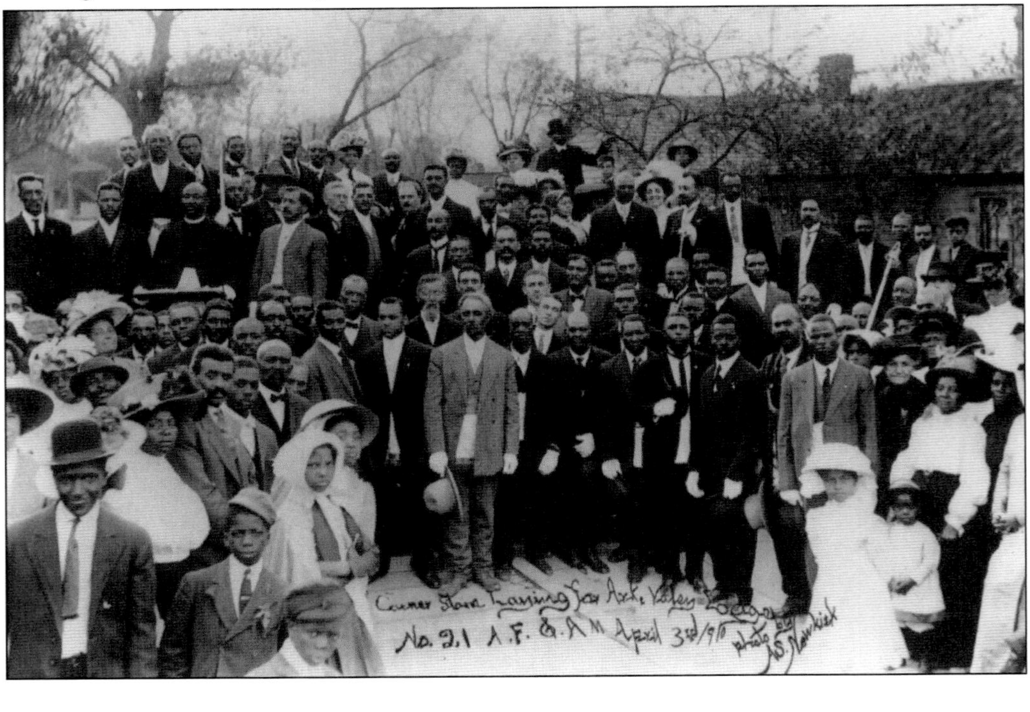

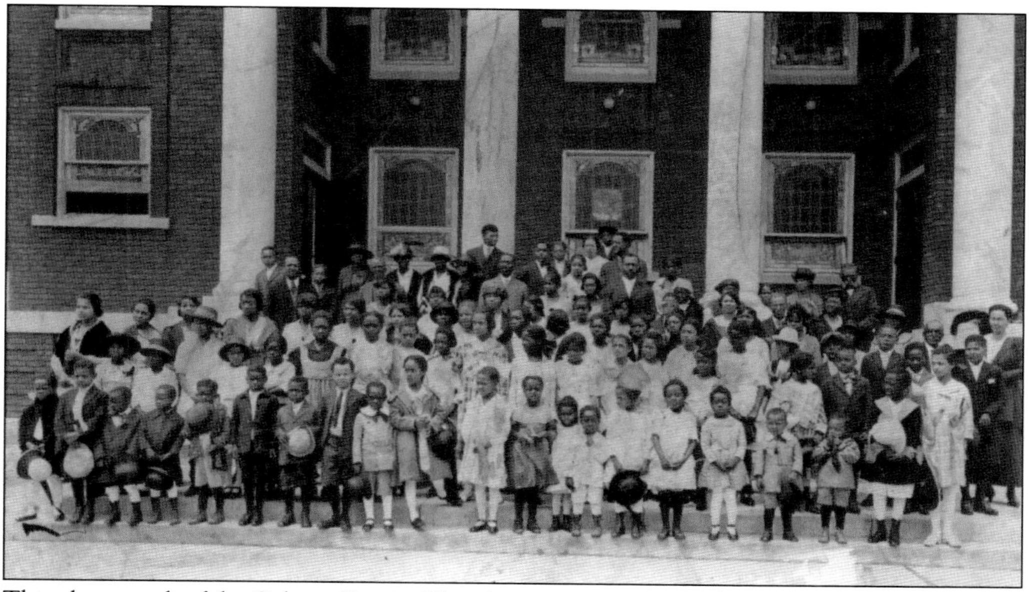

This photograph of the Calvary Baptist Church congregation was taken in 1943. Earlier that year, the $75,000 mortgage for the new church building was burned as the result of tireless fundraising efforts that began in 1916. That $75,000 would be equivalent to nearly $1.4 million today.

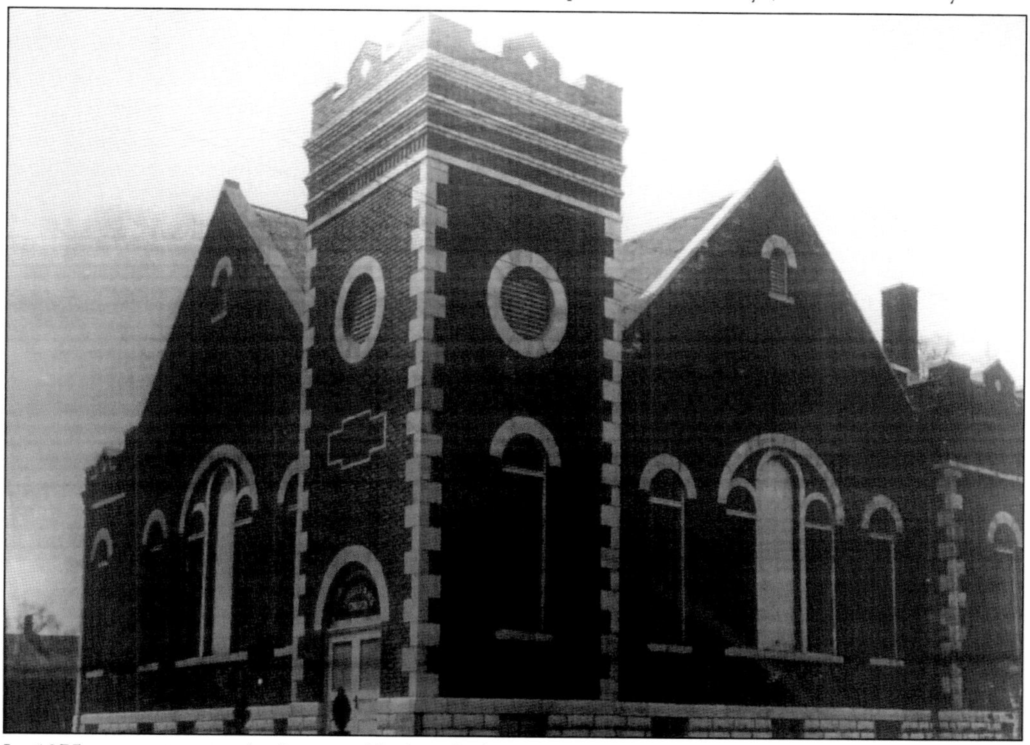

In 1875, a meeting in the home of Joshua Robinson resulted in the creation of St. Paul African Methodist Episcopal Church. The congregation met in rented quarters until they established their own church building on North Water Street in the 1880s. The congregation continued to expand and was noted locally for its choir. In 1914, the congregation laid the cornerstone for this structure, a fixture in the neighborhood until the 1950s. (Courtesy St. Paul AME)

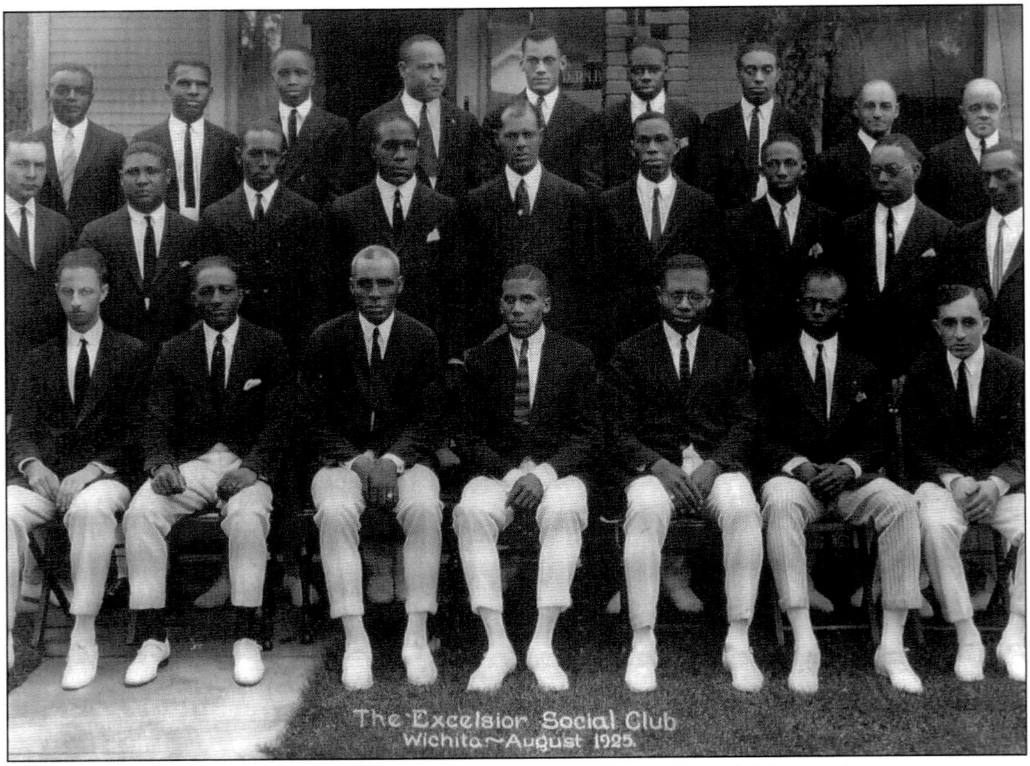

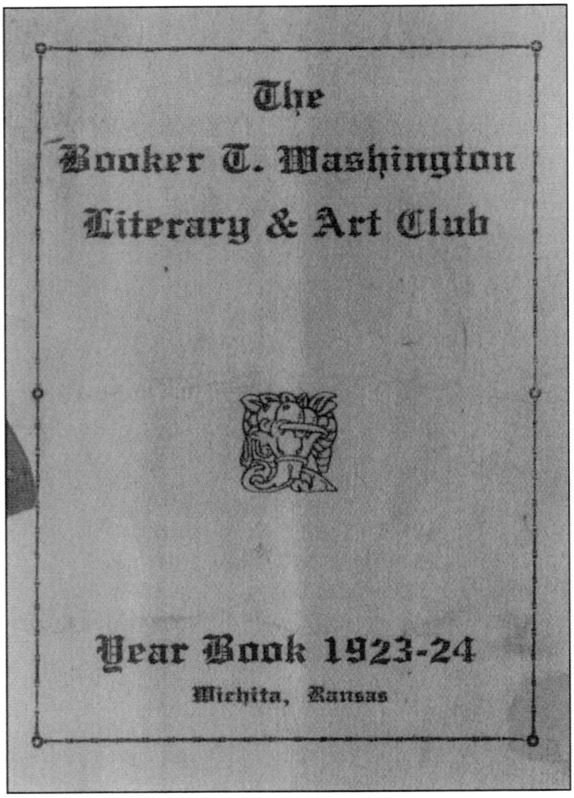
The
Booker T. Washington
Literary & Art Club

Year Book 1923-24
Wichita, Kansas

A number of African American clubs emerged in the early 1900s, in part to foster and build community but also because it was the heyday of such institutions. In 1900, black women's clubs in Kansas formed one of the first, statewide federations of women's clubs in the west. (Left, courtesy Yvette Harris.)

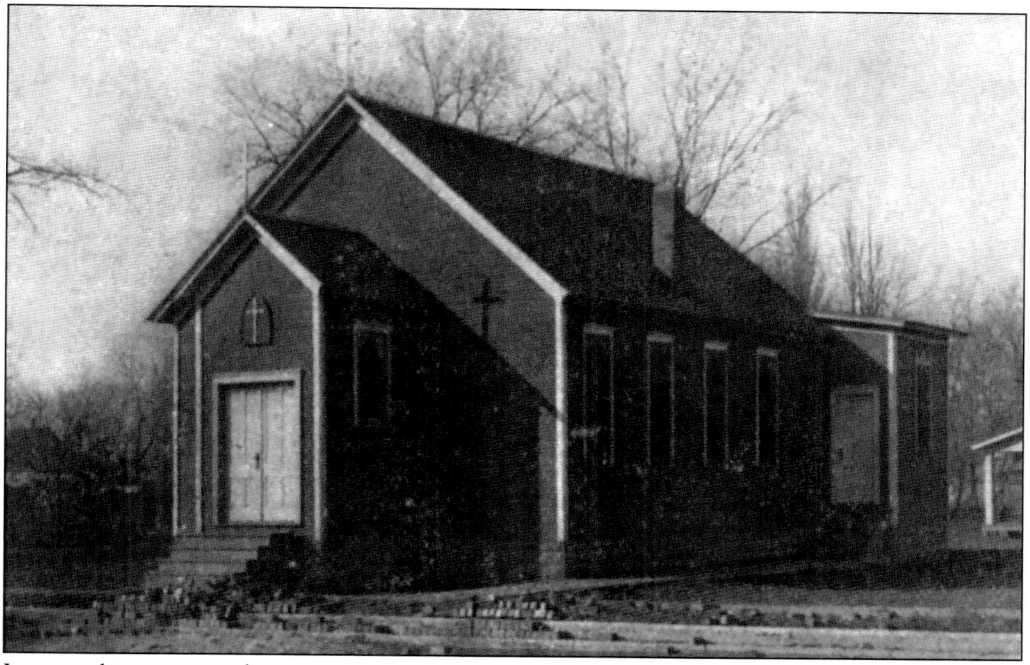

In several instances, white congregations created "colored missions" that were philanthropic but also ensured racially separate congregations. One was St. Augustine's Episcopal Church, which began in the 1910s as a mission of St. John's. Located at Ninth Street and Washington Avenue, the congregation began under the guidance of catechist Hugh Kimber (right) but had African American lay-leadership. (Both, courtesy St. John's Episcopal Church.)

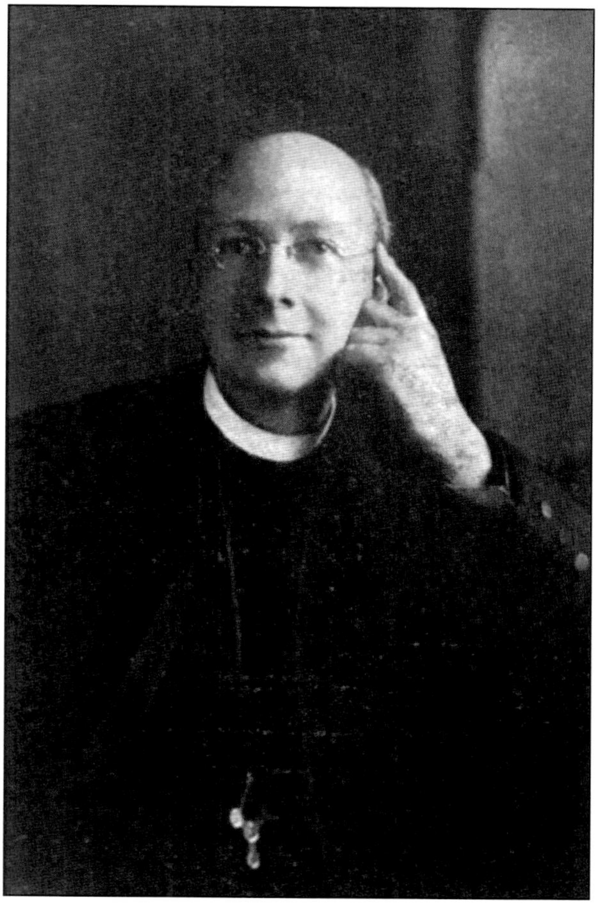

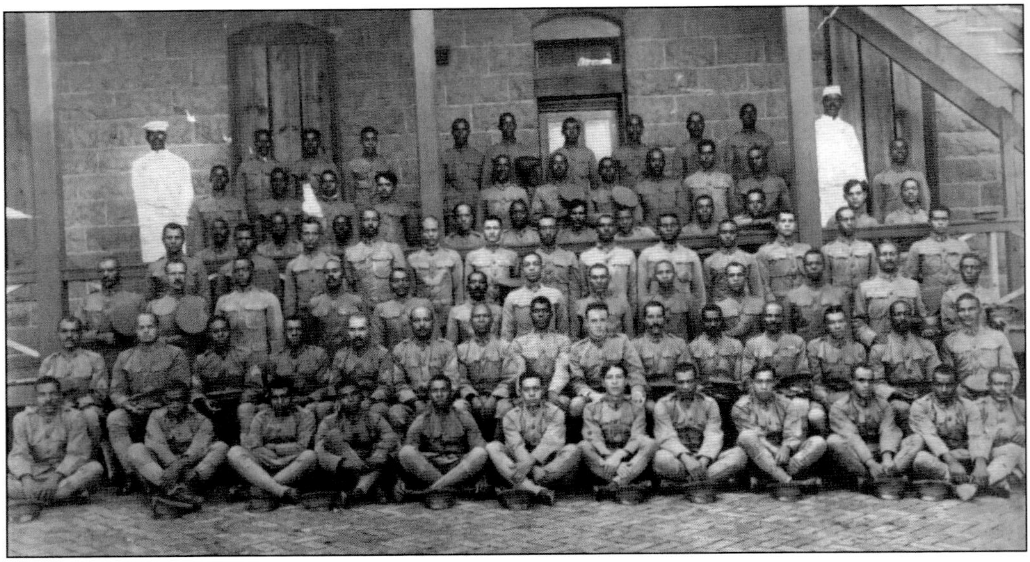

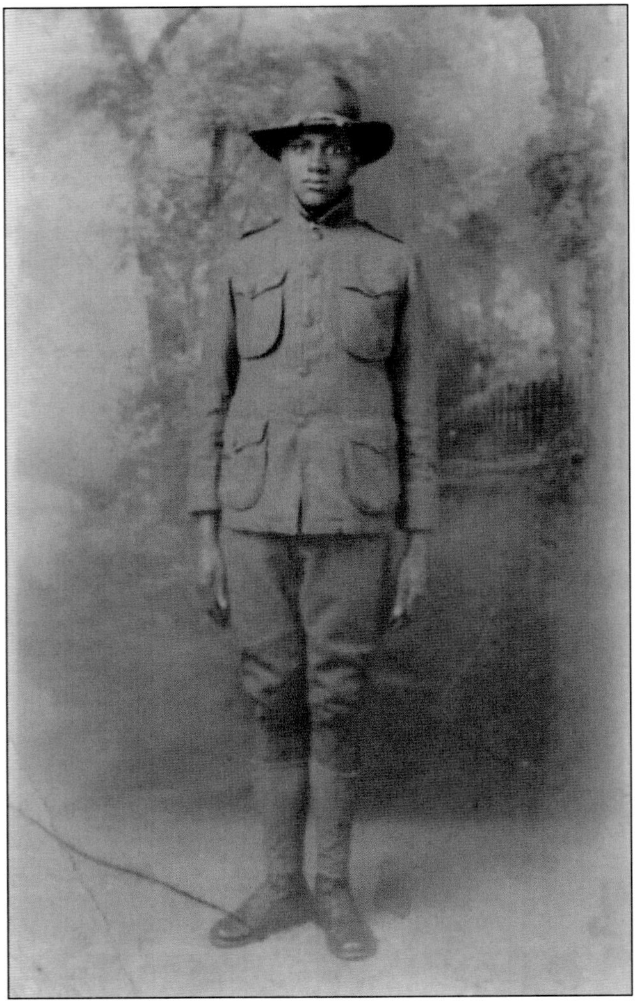

World War I broke out in 1914 and halted European immigration. The decreased availability of labor when American industrial production was surging to supply Europe with war materials forced a change in discriminatory hiring policies. Africans Americans were hired for factory work and began migrating by the thousands out of the South to northern cities—some half a million by 1920. Meanwhile, young black men volunteered to fight, and 370,000 were inducted into a segregated army—including the above members of Mounted Service School Detachment No. 2 from Fort Riley, Kansas. They fought beside French soldiers but were prohibited from fighting alongside white Americans. The army formed two black combat divisions and established a training camp for black officers that commissioned 639 officers. African American veterans returning to Wichita organized Arthur Gossett Post No. 273 of the American Legion in 1920. (Left, courtesy Butler County Historical Museum.)

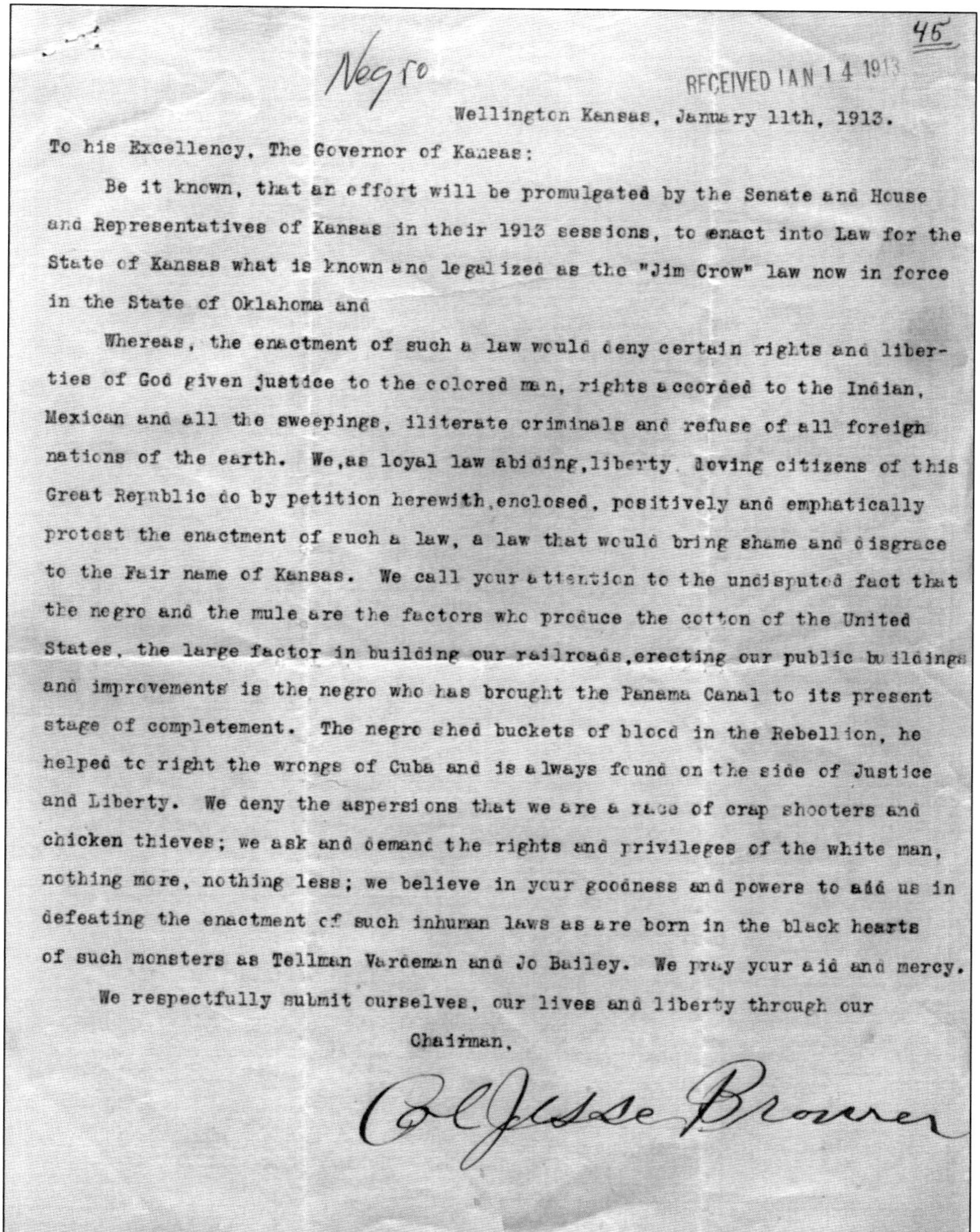

45

Negro

RECEIVED JAN 14 1913

Wellington Kansas, January 11th, 1913.

To his Excellency, The Governor of Kansas:

Be it known, that an effort will be promulgated by the Senate and House and Representatives of Kansas in their 1913 sessions, to enact into Law for the State of Kansas what is known and legalized as the "Jim Crow" law now in force in the State of Oklahoma and

Whereas, the enactment of such a law would deny certain rights and liberties of God given justice to the colored man, rights accorded to the Indian, Mexican and all the sweepings, iliterate criminals and refuse of all foreign nations of the earth. We,as loyal law abiding,liberty loving citizens of this Great Republic do by petition herewith,enclosed, positively and emphatically protest the enactment of such a law, a law that would bring shame and disgrace to the Fair name of Kansas. We call your attention to the undisputed fact that the negro and the mule are the factors who produce the cotton of the United States, the large factor in building our railroads,erecting our public buildings and improvements is the negro who has brought the Panama Canal to its present stage of completement. The negro shed buckets of blood in the Rebellion, he helped to right the wrongs of Cuba and is always found on the side of Justice and Liberty. We deny the aspersions that we are a race of crap shooters and chicken thieves; we ask and demand the rights and privileges of the white man, nothing more, nothing less; we believe in your goodness and powers to add us in defeating the enactment of such inhuman laws as are born in the black hearts of such monsters as Tellman Vardeman and Jo Bailey. We pray your aid and mercy.

We respectfully submit ourselves, our lives and liberty through our

Chairman,

Col Jesse Browner

Black Kansans from Wichita and nearby communities protested growing anti-black hostility, which was evident in bills and legislature that legalized racial discrimination and denied blacks rights accorded to Native Americans, Mexicans, criminals, and "the refuse of foreign nations." This letter to the governor reminds him that African Americans built the railroads, farmed the cotton, built the Panama Canal and public buildings (like the United States Capitol), and died fighting in the Civil War and in Cuba during the Spanish American War. (Courtesy Kansas State Historical Society.)

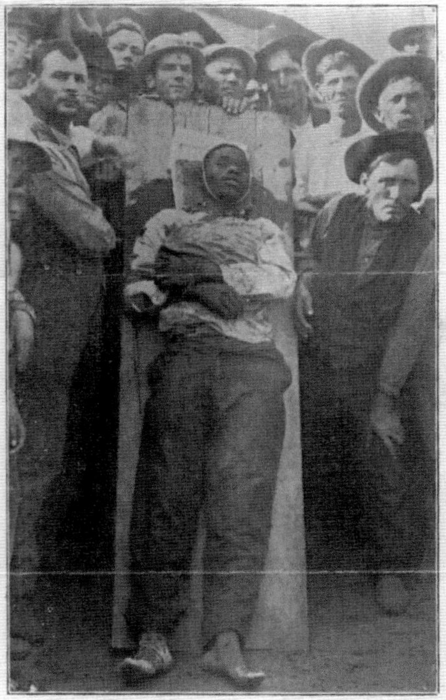

At Durant, Okla., Aug. 13, 1911, this photograph was made. It is now the property of The Topeka PLAINDEALER, the peerless Newspaper.

The community distributed flyers that protested lynchings with vivid photos like the one at left. On the reverse side (below) is condemnatory text. When the peace came in 1919, there were 23 white-on-black race riots in the United States, which devastated black communities. Protests from black communities included this from Winfield: "We the colored people of Winfield . . . have proven our loyalty, fidelity, and courageous manhood and womanhood in answering the call of the nation [even though the government does not protect our rights as citizens] . . . have given you [our] loyal support throughout your gubernatorial campaign . . . We appeal to you to use your influence in bringing about a readjustment of the aforesaid conditions [lynching, mob violence, Jim-Crowism] affecting fifteen million Negroes." (Both, courtesy Kansas State Historical Society.)

Do You Endorse Murder?

THESE MEN

Kill a Defenseless Unknown Negro in a Running Fight, Pose for a Photograph, then Burn the Body! —Do you Picture This?

WHAT OF OUR LAW?

The Law Claims That it is Impossible to Find

A Single Soul Connected with the CRIME!...

Let China Alone; Christianize America

How Long Shall We Sleep? The World Points a Finger of SCORN at our JUSTICE

Look at the picture, it needs no further recommendation—it "speaks" loudly for itself

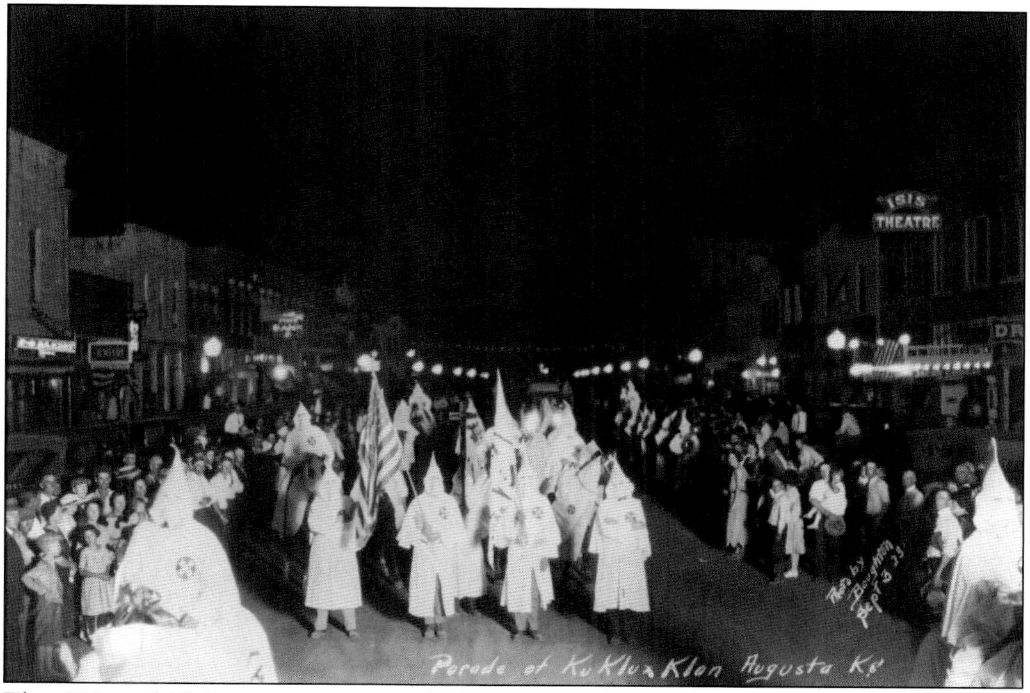

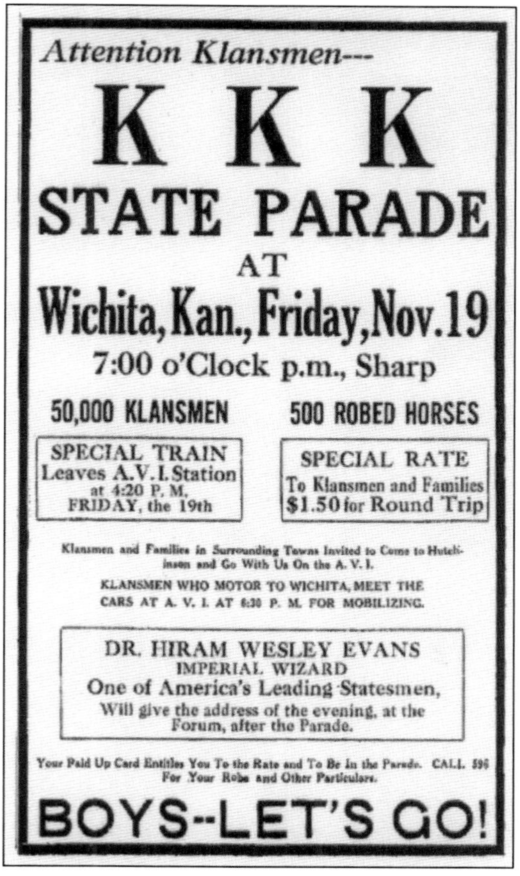
Attention Klansmen---

KKK

STATE PARADE

AT

Wichita, Kan., Friday, Nov. 19

7:00 o'Clock p.m., Sharp

50,000 KLANSMEN

500 ROBED HORSES

SPECIAL TRAIN
Leaves A.V.I. Station
at 4:20 P. M.
FRIDAY, the 19th

SPECIAL RATE
To Klansmen and Families
$1.50 for Round Trip

Klansmen and Families in Surrounding Towns Invited to Come to Hutchinson and Go With Us On the A. V. I.

KLANSMEN WHO MOTOR TO WICHITA, MEET THE CARS AT A. V. I. AT 6:30 P. M. FOR MOBILIZING.

DR. HIRAM WESLEY EVANS
IMPERIAL WIZARD
One of America's Leading Statesmen,
Will give the address of the evening, at the Forum, after the Parade.

Your Paid Up Card Entitles You To the Rate and To Be In the Parade. CALL 596 For Your Robe and Other Particulars.

BOYS--LET'S GO!

The 1910s and 1920s saw a major revival of the Ku Klux Klan that tapped into nativist and racist sentiments in the country. Although the movie *Birth of a Nation* was initially banned in Kansas at the insistence of the NAACP, and Gov. Henry J. Allen of Wichita worked to restrict the organization, the Klan had large followings across the state. By the early 1920s, an estimated 60,000 Kansans were members. There was a particularly strong presence in south central Kansas. In Wichita, some city leaders were members, and in El Dorado and Augusta the KKK held large rallies. (Above, courtesy Augusta Historical Museum; right, courtesy Kansas State Historical Society.)

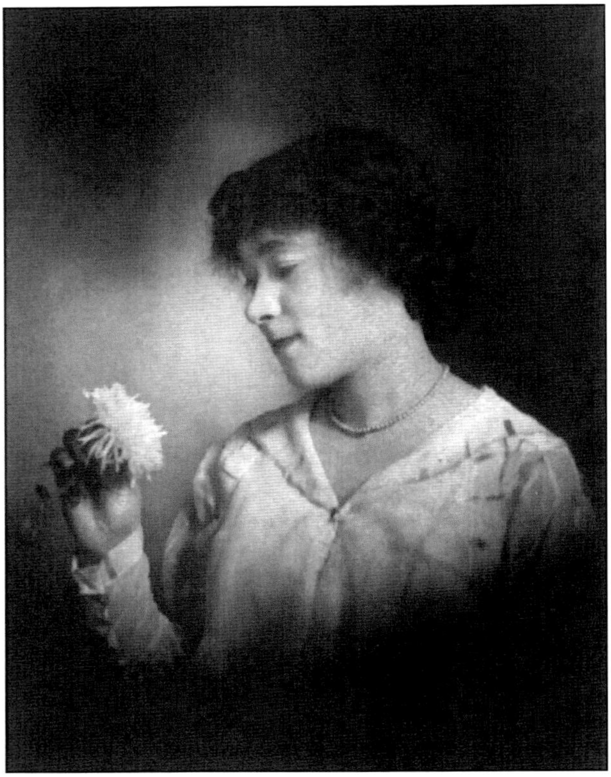

Raised in Wichita, Myrtle "Mickey" Hurst attended the Tuskegee Institute and returned in 1912 to become the first black teacher hired by the Wichita Board of Education. She taught for 47 years at L'Ouverture, serving as a mentor to generations of African American Wichitans. Black schools benefitted from a cohort of very strong teachers, in part because educated black persons could often not find employment in the rest of the school system or at other institutions. In a 1972 *Wichita Times* editorial, Jo Gardenhire recalled that "long before most of us were into a black thing, Mickey was out there preaching racial pride, encouraging us to read, to learn, to understand from whence we came. Years ahead of her time, she was." (Left, courtesy Charles McAfee; below, courtesy Gretchen Eick.)

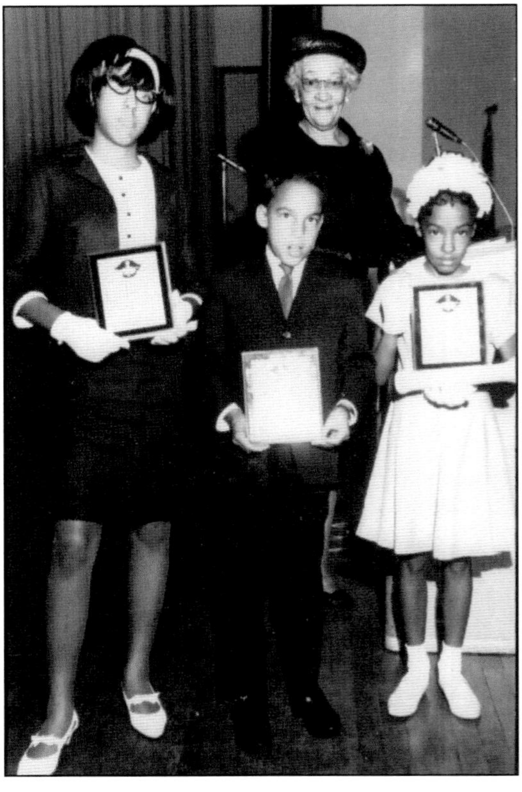

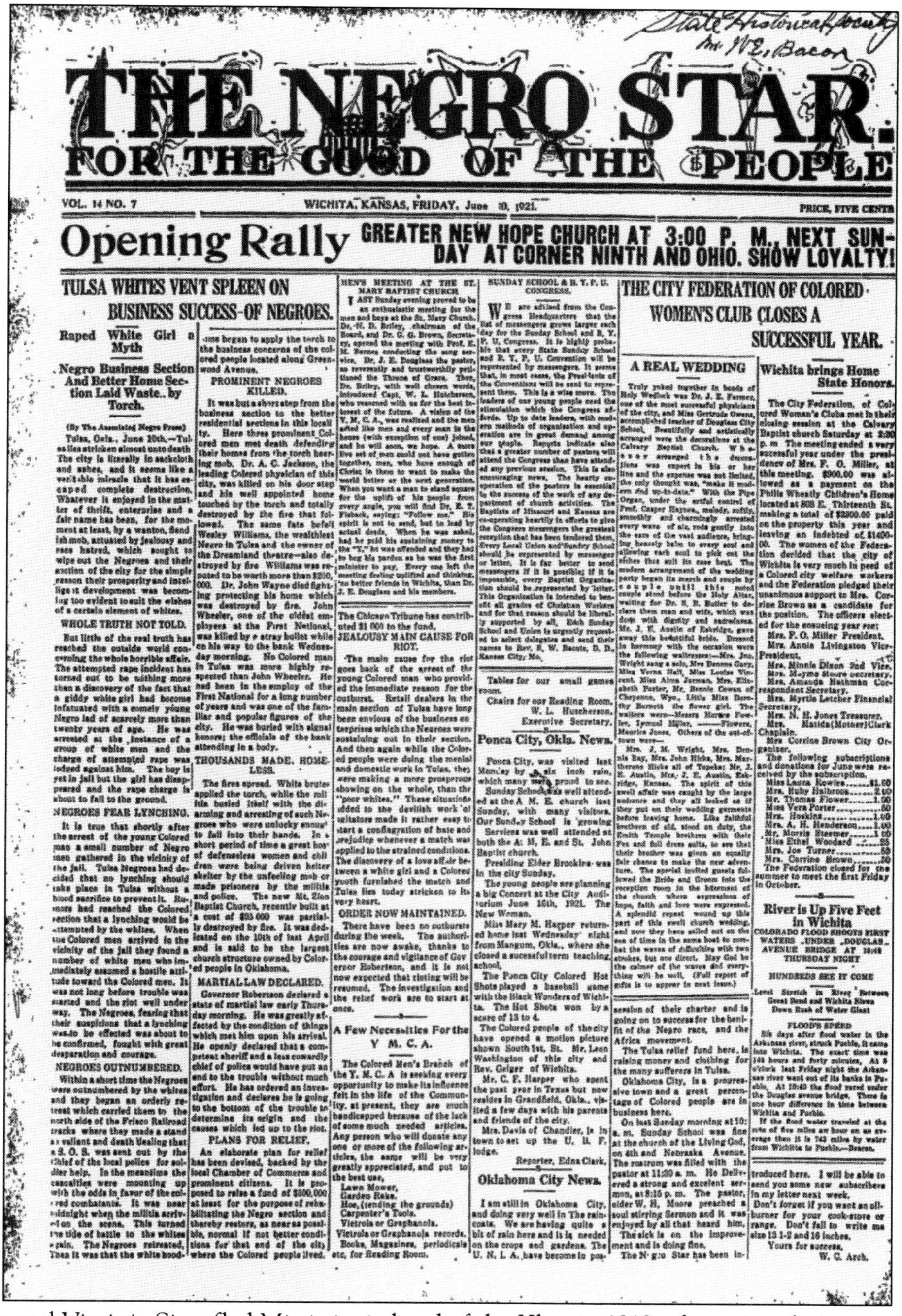
THE NEGRO STAR.
FOR THE GOOD OF THE PEOPLE

VOL. 14 NO. 7 — WICHITA, KANSAS, FRIDAY, June 10, 1921. — PRICE, FIVE CENTS

Opening Rally — GREATER NEW HOPE CHURCH AT 3:00 P. M., NEXT SUNDAY AT CORNER NINTH AND OHIO. SHOW LOYALTY!

TULSA WHITES VENT SPLEEN ON BUSINESS SUCCESS OF NEGROES.

Raped White Girl a Myth

Negro Business Section And Better Home Section Laid Waste.. by Torch.

(By The Associated Negro Press)

Tulsa, Okla., June 10th.—Tulsa lies stricken almost unto death. The city is literally in sackcloth and ashes, and it seems like a veritable miracle that it has escaped complete destruction. Whatever it enjoyed in the matter of thrift, enterprise and a fair name has been, for the moment at least, by a wanton, fiendish mob, actuated by jealousy and race hatred, which sought to wipe out the Negroes and their section of the city for the simple reason their prosperity and intelligent development was becoming too evident to suit the wishes of a certain element of whites.

WHOLE TRUTH NOT TOLD.

NEGROES FEAR LYNCHING.

NEGROES OUTNUMBERED.

PROMINENT NEGROES KILLED.

THOUSANDS MADE HOMELESS.

MARTIAL LAW DECLARED.

PLANS FOR RELIEF.

MEN'S MEETING AT THE ST. MARY BAPTIST CHURCH

The Chicago Tribune has contributed $1000 to the fund. JEALOUSY MAIN CAUSE FOR RIOT.

ORDER NOW MAINTAINED.

A Few Necessities For the Y. M. C. A.

SUNDAY SCHOOL & B. Y. P. U. CONGRESS.

Ponca City, Okla. News.

Oklahoma City News.

THE CITY FEDERATION OF COLORED WOMEN'S CLUB CLOSES A SUCCESSFUL YEAR.

A REAL WEDDING

Wichita brings Home State Honors.

River is Up Five Feet in Wichita

Hollis and Virginia Sims fled Mississippi ahead of the Klan in 1919, after using their newspaper to commend African American troops for their contributions during World War I. In Wichita, they opened *The Negro Star* and kept it going for 30 years. This edition describes the destruction of Tulsa's Greenwood community in 1921. Hollis's sister Dorothy Sims Winston, the first black graduate of Wichita University, opened the Coleridge-Taylor School of Music in Wichita in 1925—probably the first business owned by an African American female—and corresponded with W.C. Handy and other nationally prominent musicians. Brother Hugh Sims, a dentist, was elected to the school board from 1949 to 1961. (Courtesy Newsbank.)

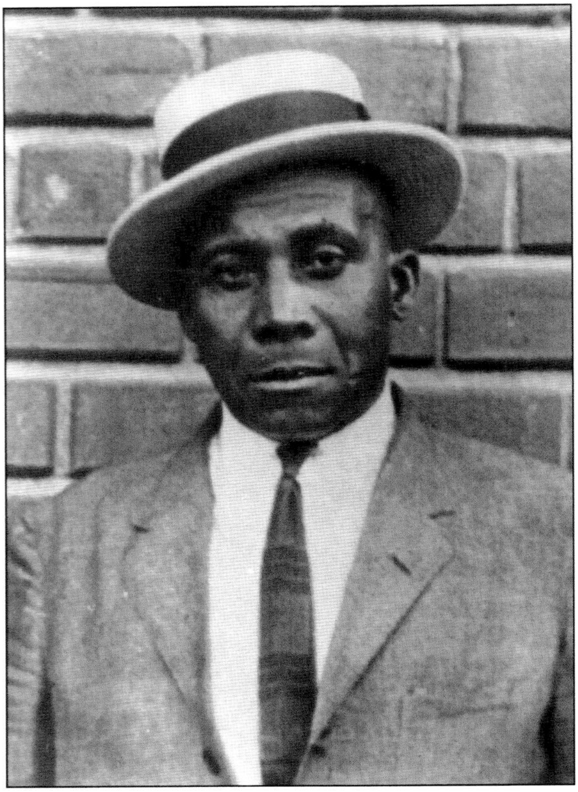

In 1902, Jeff Thompson became the first black detective on the Wichita police force. Black officers worked in what was known as the "black belt" area, which ran from Central Street to Eighth and Wichita Streets to Main Street. Unable to arrest white offenders, black officers could only detain them until a white officer came to the scene. Thompson remained on the police force until 1941.

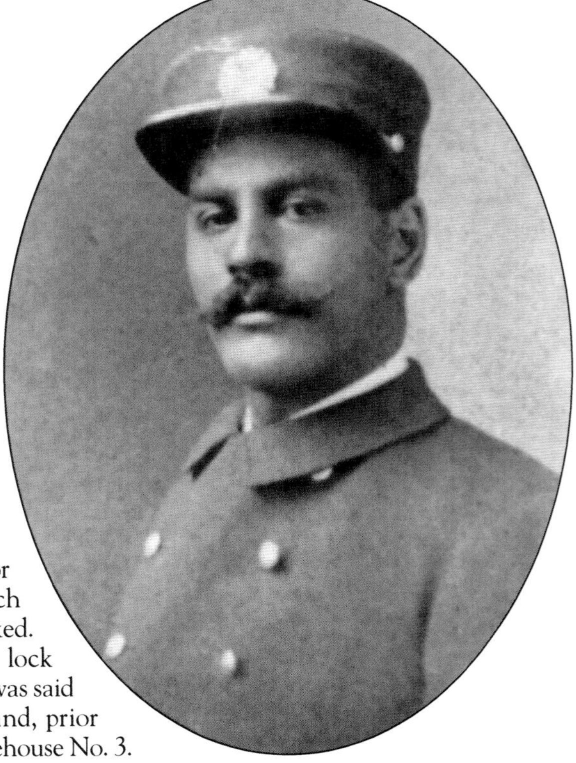

On August 16, 1927, Frank Hill, a jailer for the county, was serving a prisoner his lunch and mistakenly left the other cells unlocked. Three inmates escaped before Hill could lock the cells, and he was shot and killed. Hill was said to have been active in the community and, prior to working in the jail, was a member of Firehouse No. 3.

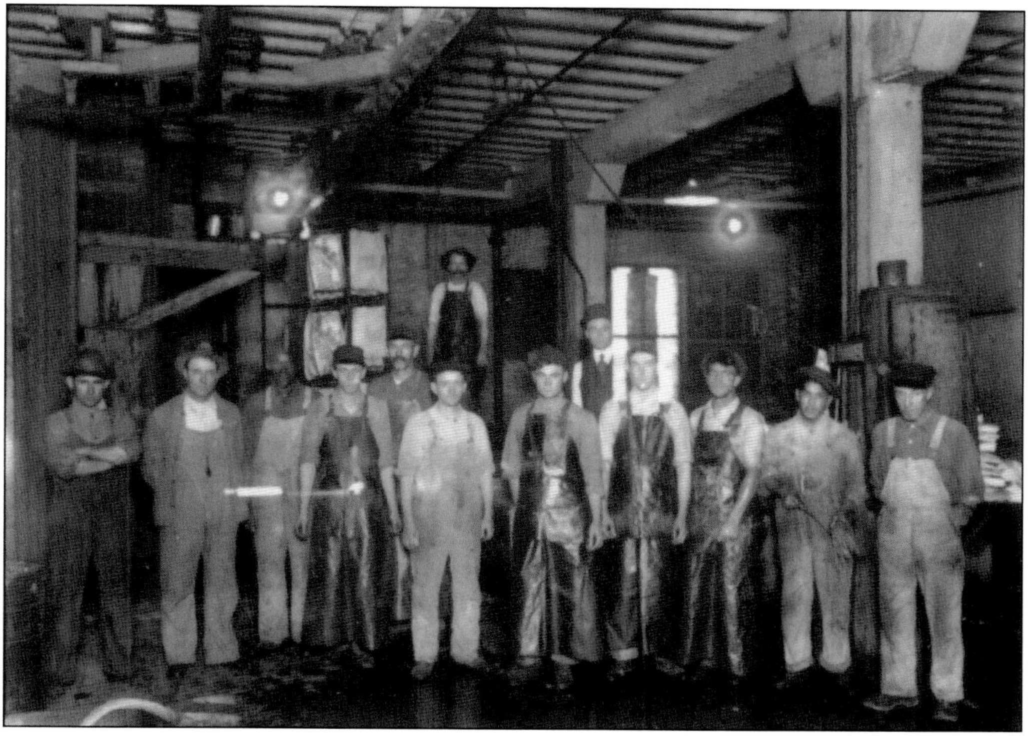

Wichita's meatpacking industry had a diverse workforce, including Latinos and African Americans, as can be seen in this image from the Cudahy plant around 1915. Employment in these plants on the city's northern edge resulted in a modest African American population living in the vicinity of Eighteenth and Mosley Streets. (Courtesy Wichita–Sedgwick County Historical Museum.)

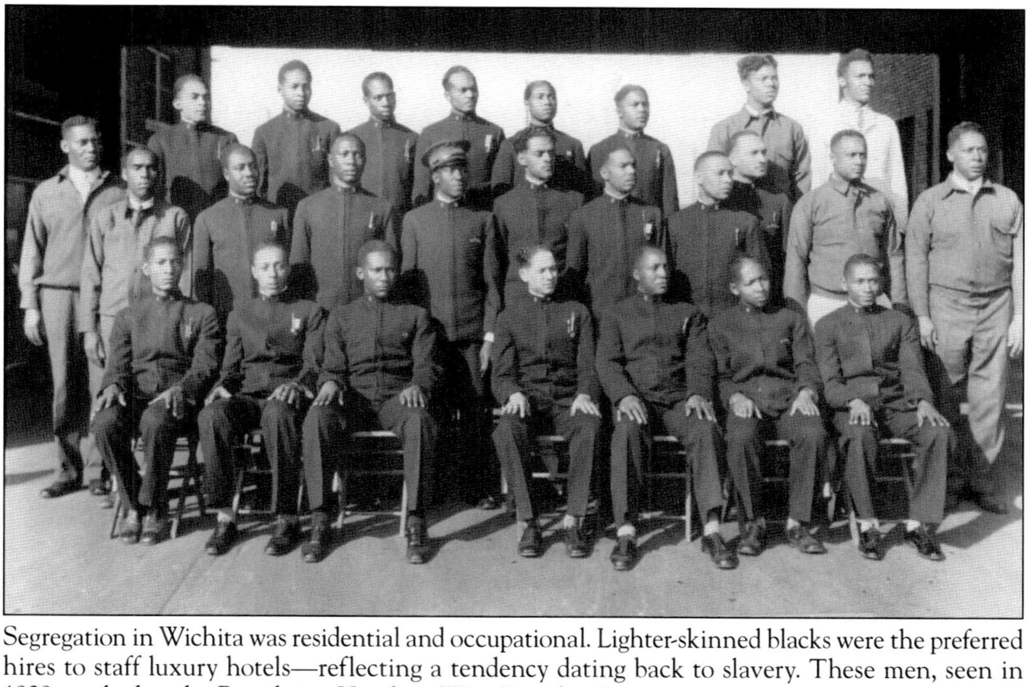

Segregation in Wichita was residential and occupational. Lighter-skinned blacks were the preferred hires to staff luxury hotels—reflecting a tendency dating back to slavery. These men, seen in 1929, worked at the Broadview Hotel on West Douglas Avenue.

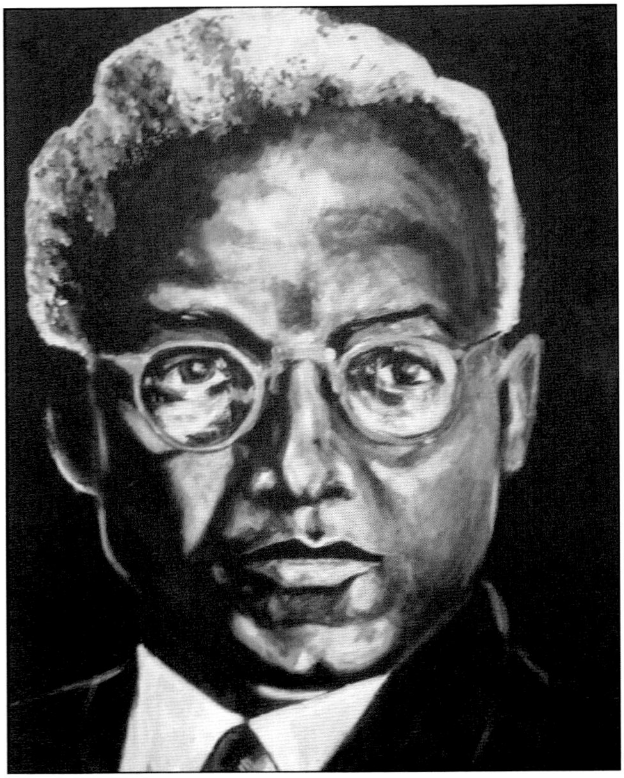

In 1926, Abner B. Jackson Sr. began an ambulance service for the African American community, a venture that was the start of Jackson Mortuary—one of the community's most prominent institutions. The image below shows Jackson Mortuary's second home, located at 703 North Water Street. Jackson's son, Abner B. Jackson Jr., began as a partner, later became manager, and finally assumed ownership of the business in 1950. These paintings by the late Tevis Mike, himself a descendant of the Van Leu family, now hang at Jackson Mortuary. (Both, courtesy Jackson Mortuary and Pam Thompson.)

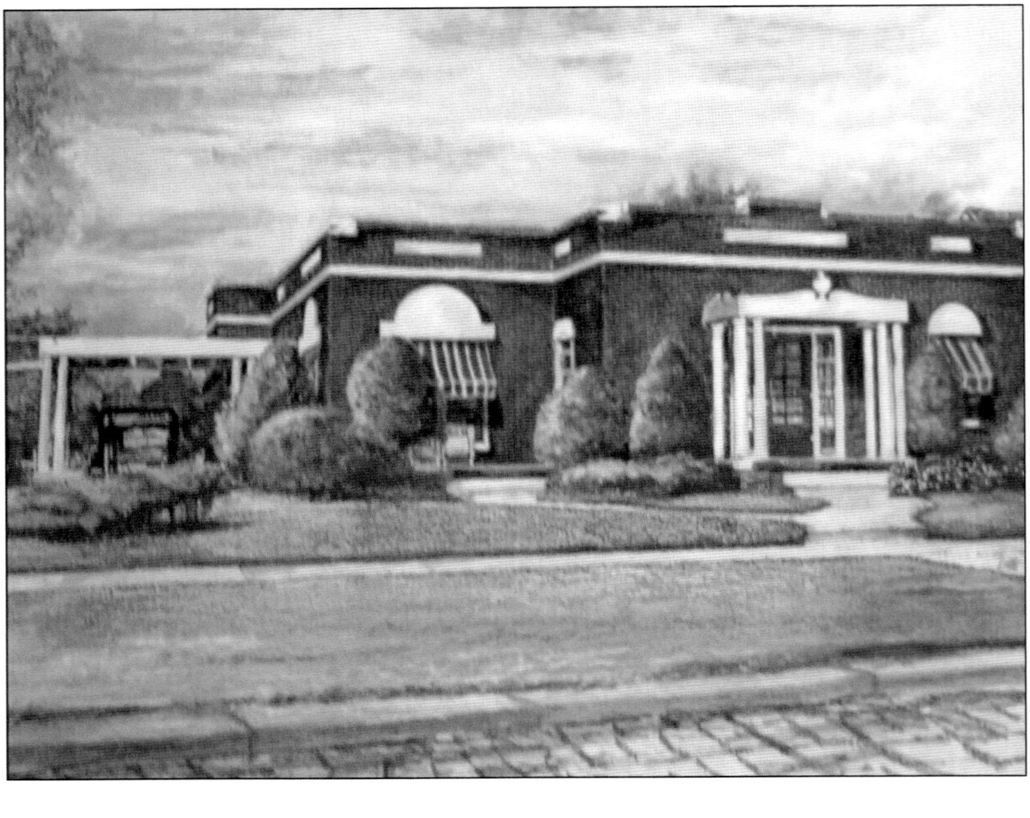

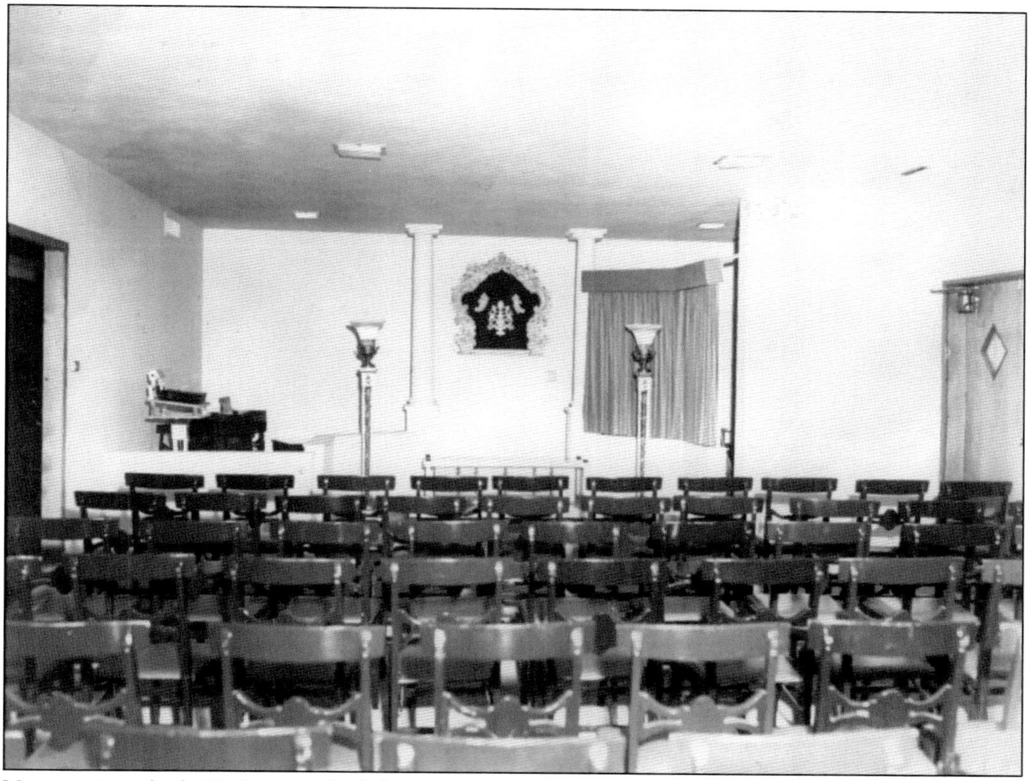

Victoria Murdoch-Hightower (right) was the first African American funeral director in Kansas. She also owned the Hightower Funeral Home in Coffeyville. She was the first licensed female African American funeral director and embalmer, operating out of the Citizens Funeral Home in Wichita. Victoria died in 1942. Her daughter Xavia Earline Hightower also obtained her funeral director and embalmer's licenses. (Above, courtesy Kansas State Historical Society.)

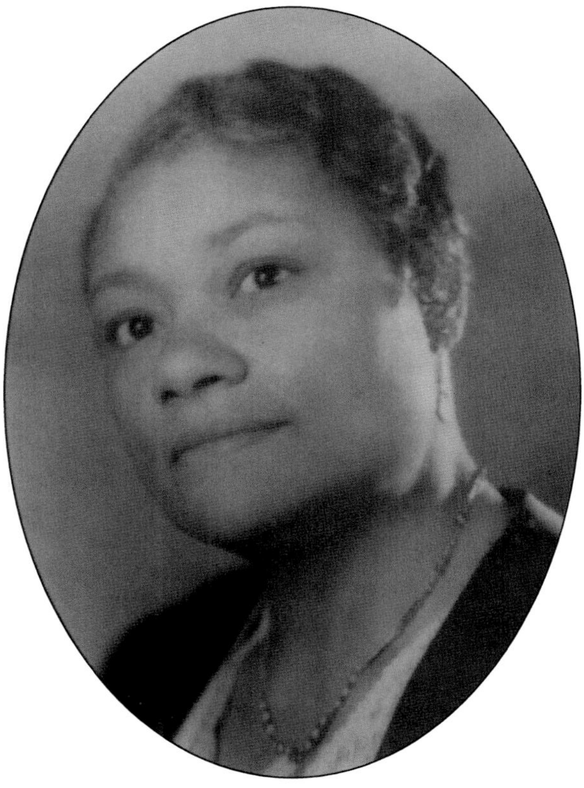

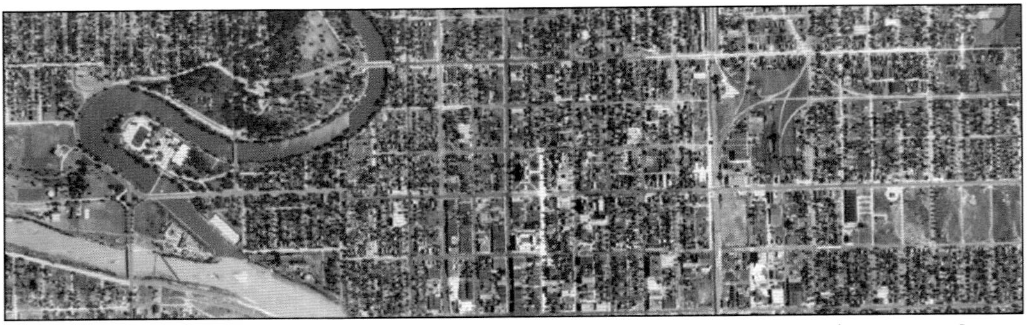

This aerial photograph from 1938 shows the African American business district along Water Street, north of Central Street. The Sedgwick County Courthouse is at center. To its left, along Water and Main Streets—in the old West End community—was a hub of black-owned commercial enterprises that at one time included 12 restaurants, 5 grocery stores, 8 barbershops, 7 billiard parlors, and a taxi service. Occupations in black Wichita ranged from professionals such as physicians, lawyers, and dentists to workers in the meatpacking plants, government employees, tailors, dressmakers, hairdressers, janitors, porters, and laborers. (Courtesy Wichita City Planning.)

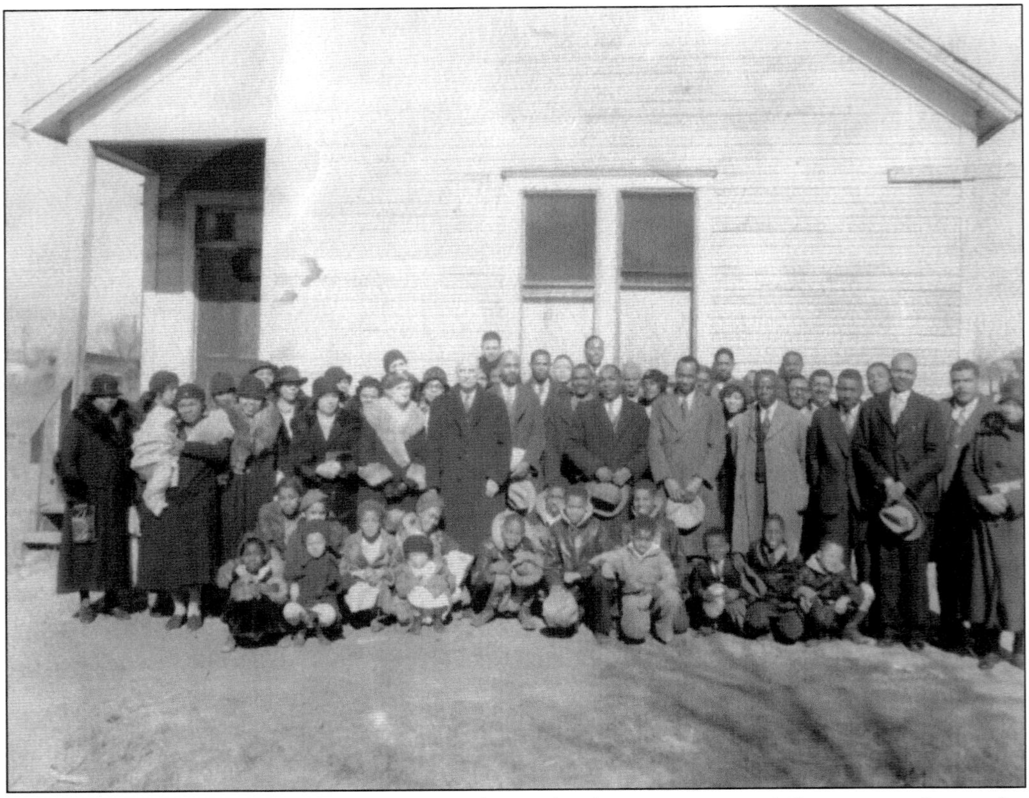

African Americans did not live exclusively in the downtown area. This image shows the congregation of what is now Chisholm Trail Church of Christ at its home on Wabash Street, east of downtown along what was once Chisholm Creek and has since become a drainage canal. (Courtesy Yvette Harris.)

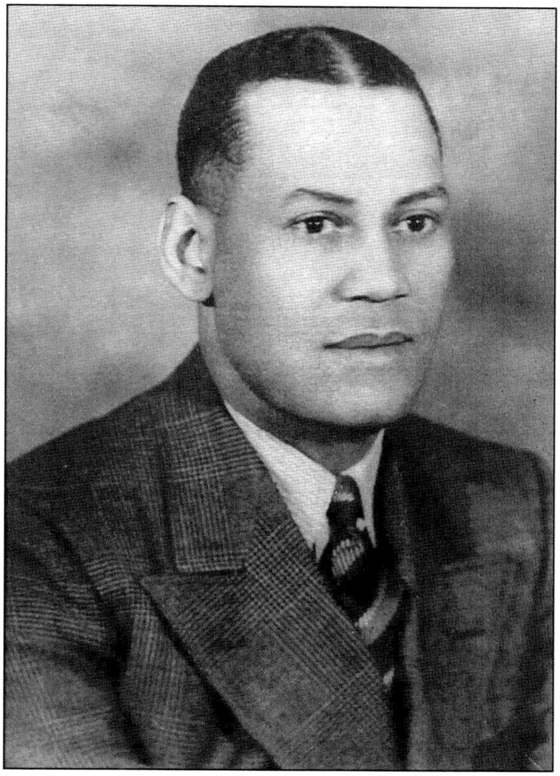

The community included several veterinarians, including Donald Jackson, Monroe Balton, T.E. McDonald, and Othello Curry. Another was Dr. G.T. Bronson, pictured at right. Thomas G. Perry, below, opened the area's first small animal hospital, at 1325 Cleveland Avenue, in 1921 after receiving his DVM from Kansas State Agricultural College (now Kansas State University). After retiring in the mid-1940s, he joined the faculty of the Tuskegee Institute in Alabama—one of several KSU alumni who did so.

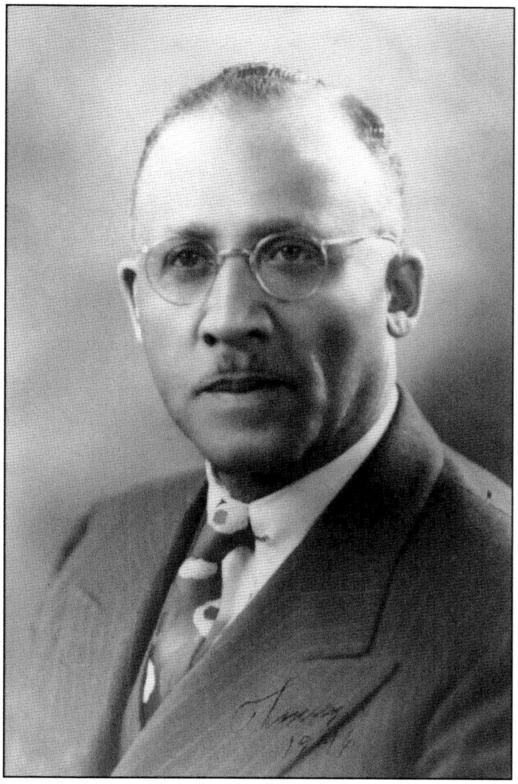

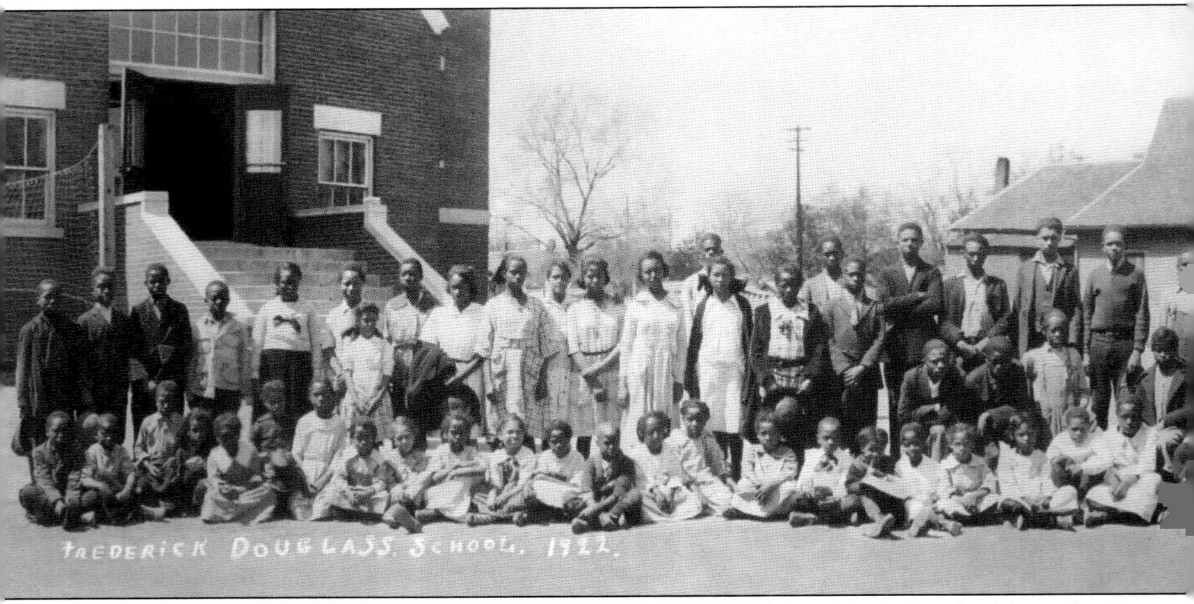

During the 1800s, Wichita's schools were integrated. By 1912, however, Wichita had four schools designated for African American children: Frederick Douglass at 615 North Water Street, Toussaint L'Ouverture at Thirteenth and Mosley Streets, Grand at 1447 South Mosley Street,

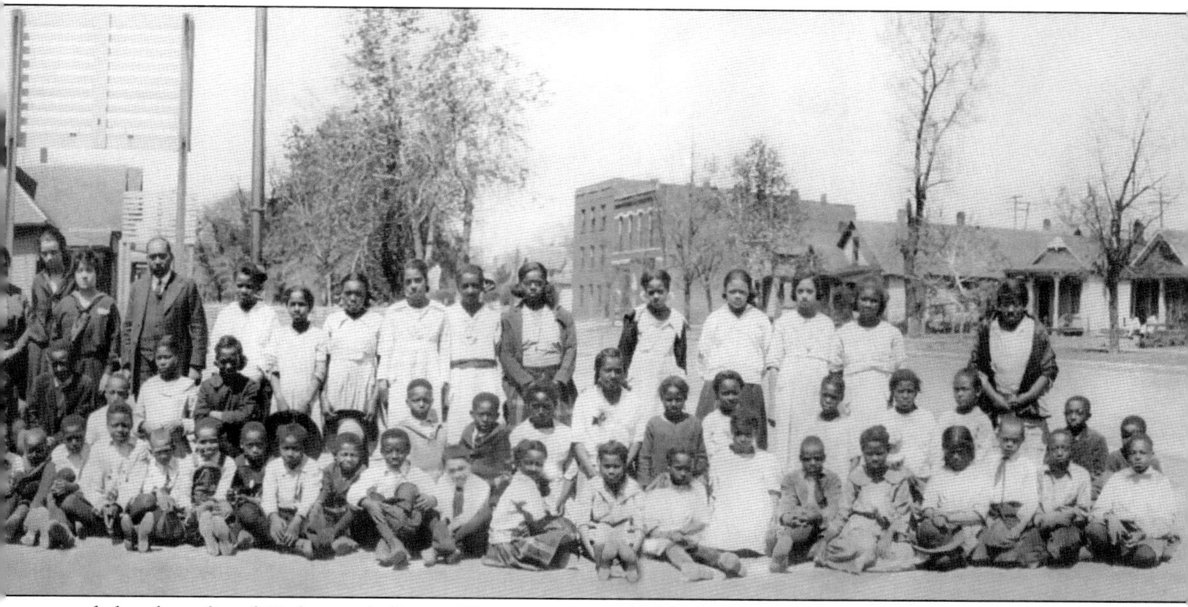

and the short-lived Eighteenth Street Elementary at 1905 North Heiserman Avenue. This image shows the students at Frederick Douglass, located next to Calvary Baptist Church and the Water Street neighborhood. The Murdock Hotel is in the background.

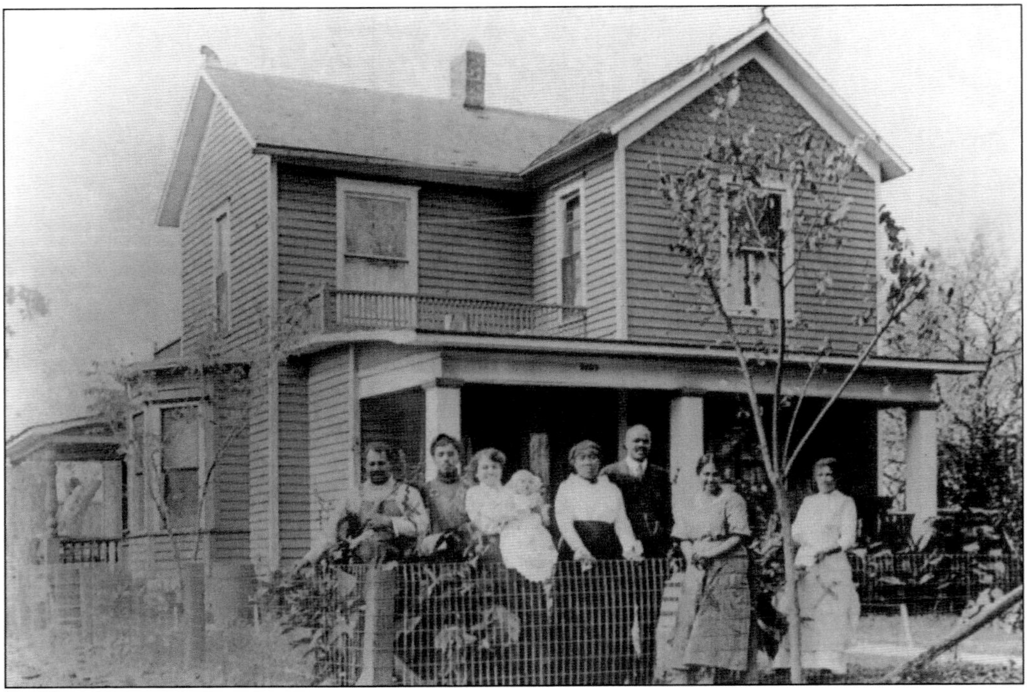

The *Wichita Colored Directory 1927-8* proclaimed proudly: "did you know that Greater Wichita has over 7,000 Negroes? That 65% own or are buying their own homes and property representing over $995,850.00? That we have 15 churches with over 3100 members, 1 Y.M.C.A., 1 Y.W.C.A., 1 N.A.A.C.P. with over 200 members, the strongest and only (African American) American Legion in the state with 84 members, 24 fraternal organizations, one orphan's home, three public school(s), employing 25 teachers, with almost 3,000 students . . ." Shown here are examples of black home ownership from this period. (Below, courtesy Yvette Harris.)

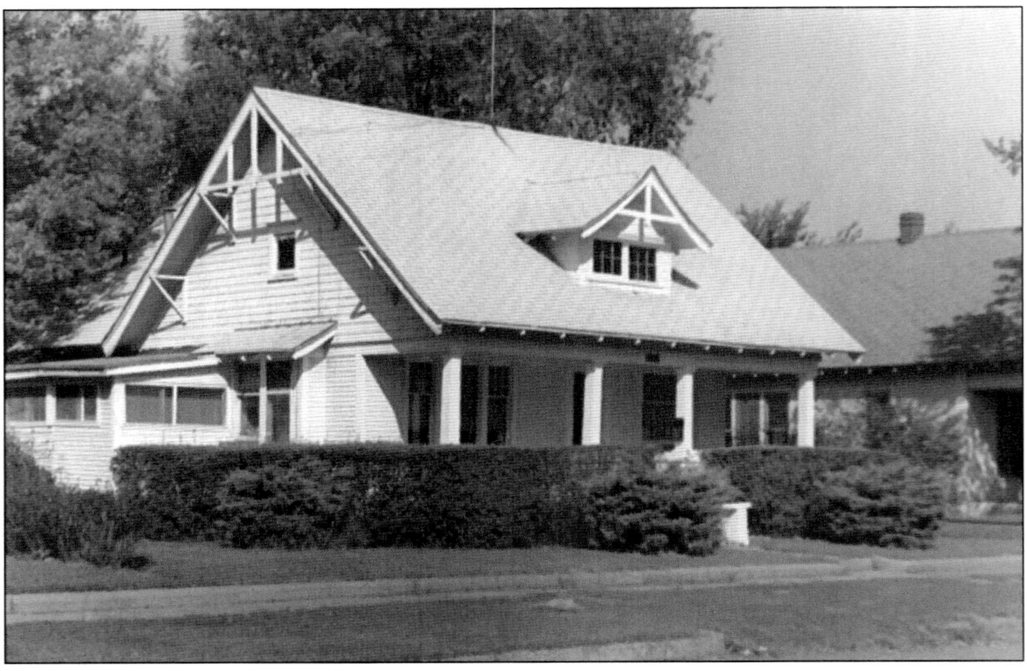

Solomon "Sol" Butler set records in track and field, quarterbacked the Dubuque (Iowa) College football team, and competed in the 1920 Olympics in Antwerp, Belgium. After joining the Army, Sol traveled to France as part of the American military team for the Inter-Allied Games of 1919. He won the gold medal in the broad jump and was knighted by King Nicholas I of Montenegro. He is buried in Maple Grove Cemetery. (Courtesy Reno County Historical Museum.)

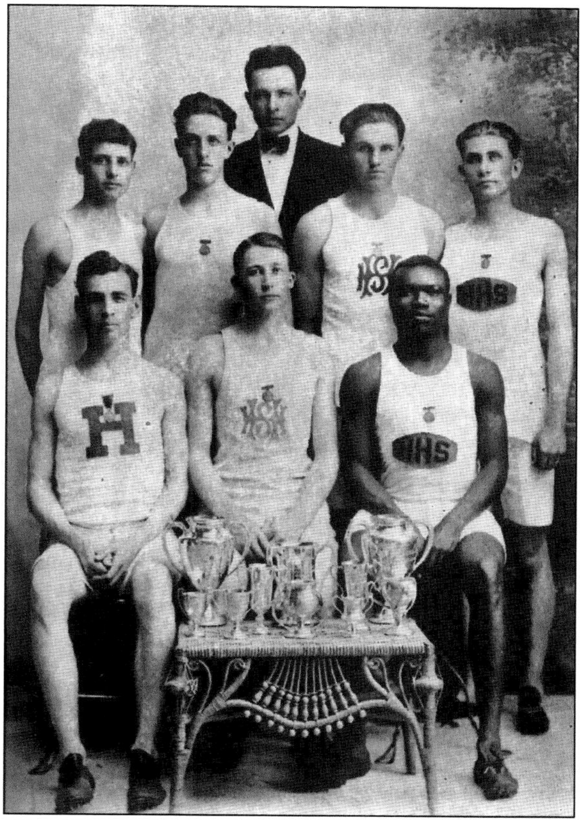

In 1909, African Americans created their own YMCA at 525 North Water Street. This photograph, taken in 1923, shows Walter L. Hutcherson in white trousers. He was the YMCA's executive secretary during the move to a larger facility across the street. The site was donated to the YMCA largely due to the friendship of Hutcherson and A.A. Hyde, owner and founder of the Mentholatum Industry. (Courtesy Wichita–Sedgwick County Historical Museum.)

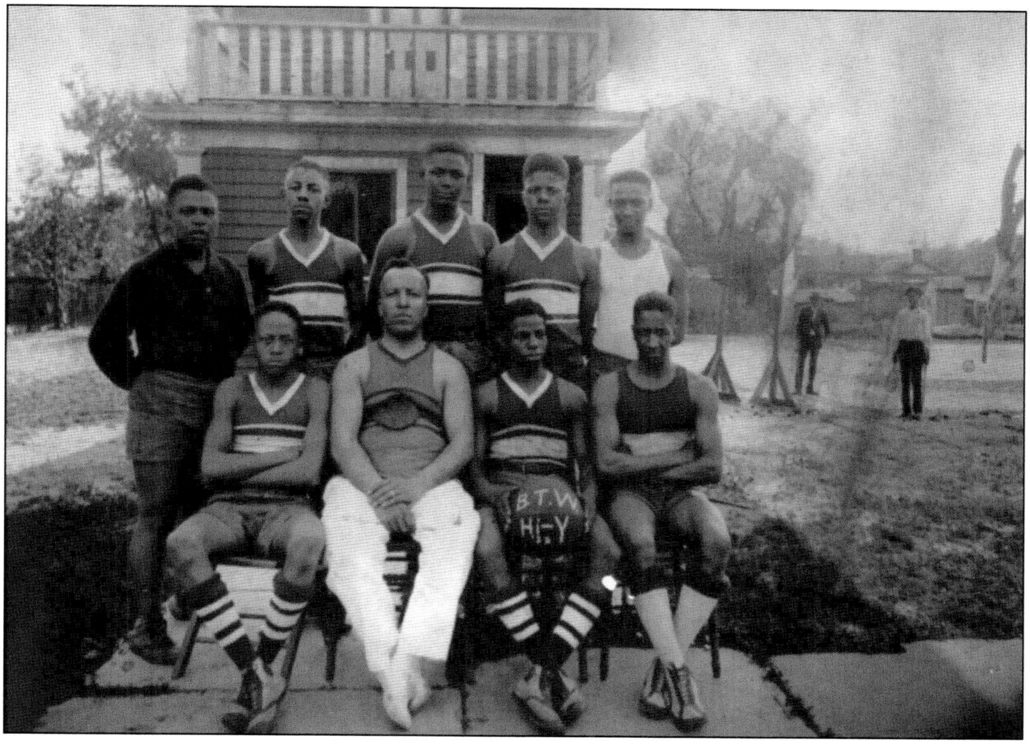

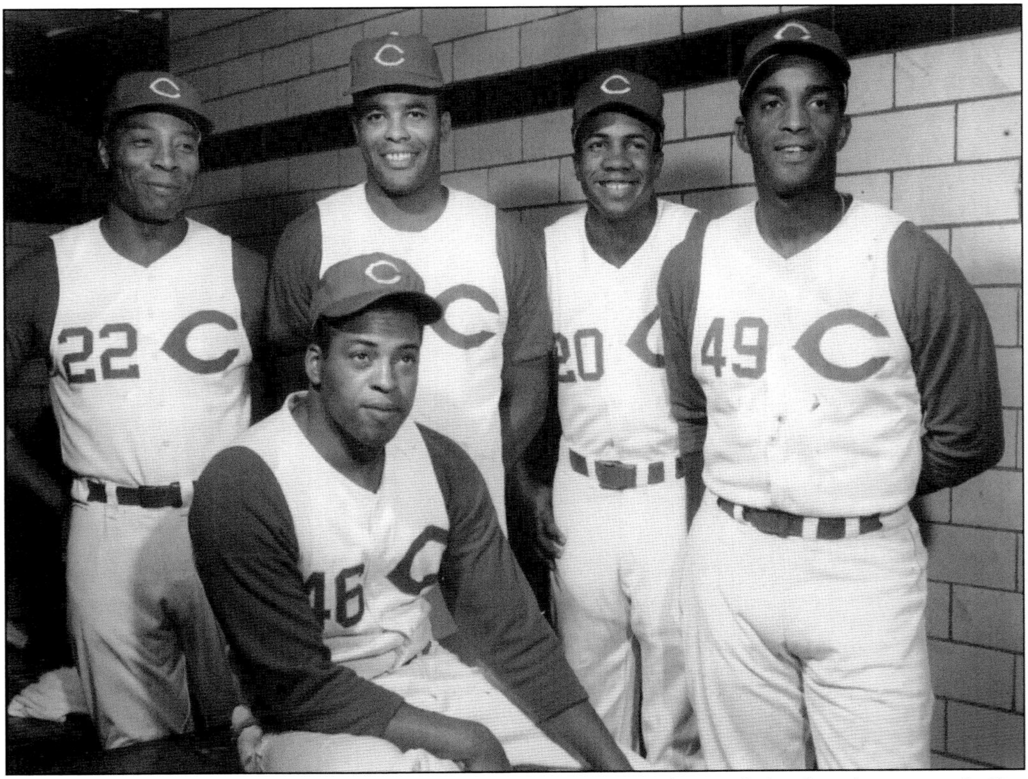

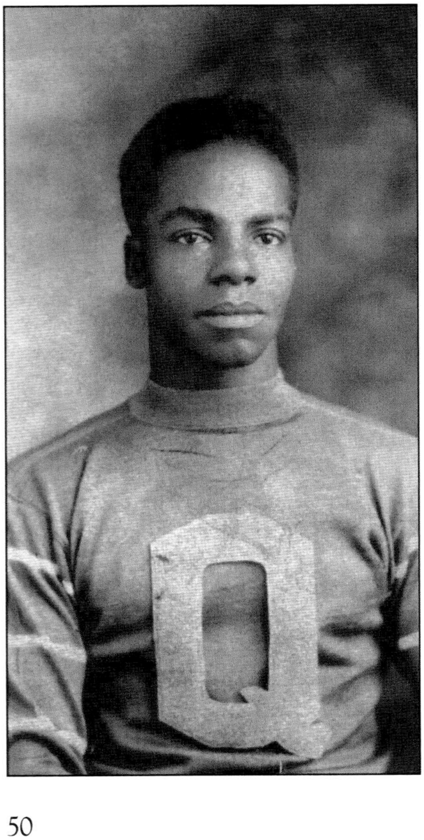

Bob Thurman, standing at left, played semi-pro ball with the Negro Leagues in the Wichita area and, at the end of his career, in the Major Leagues with the Cincinnati Reds. Like a lot of Negro Leaguers, he played in the winter league in Puerto Rico, where he was a star. He was voted into the Puerto Rican Baseball Hall of Fame and, after retirement, settled in Wichita. (Courtesy Charles McAfee.)

Wendell Van Leu, son of Rev. Henry Van Leu, was the first black student to graduate from Friends University. This image appeared in the *Negro Star* on June 11, 1926.

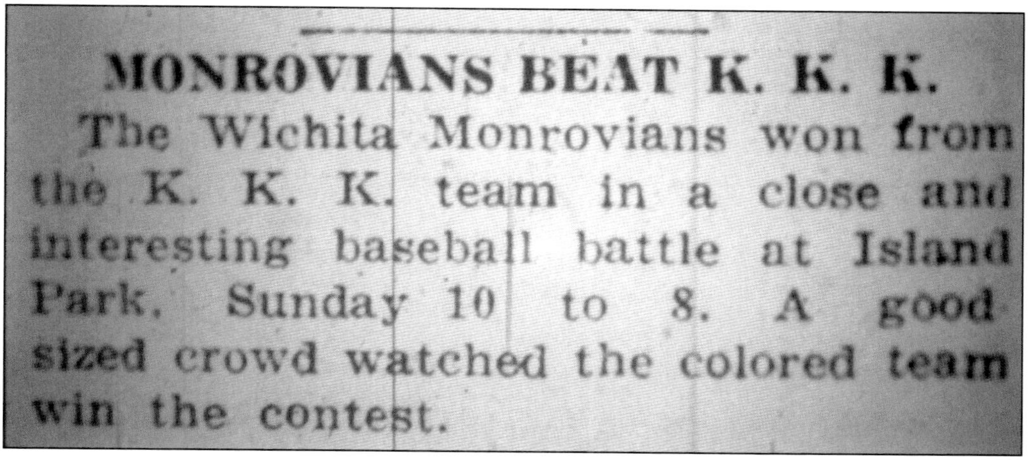
MONROVIANS BEAT K. K. K.

The Wichita Monrovians won from the K. K. K. team in a close and interesting baseball battle at Island Park, Sunday 10 to 8. A good sized crowd watched the colored team win the contest.

Baseball, like so much of life in Wichita, involved separate institutions for black people and white people. Black teams included Cudahy Rex, which was sponsored by the Cudahy meatpacking company. The Monrovians, however, were the city's best known team. Part of their fame came from a show game they played in June 1925, against the team of Wichita Klan No. 6. White Catholics served as umpires. The above clipping from *The Wichita Eagle* from June 22, 1925, shows that the Monrovians won. The photograph below shows the Island Park stadium where this game took place. (Above, courtesy *The Wichita Eagle*; below, courtesy Wichita Public Library.)

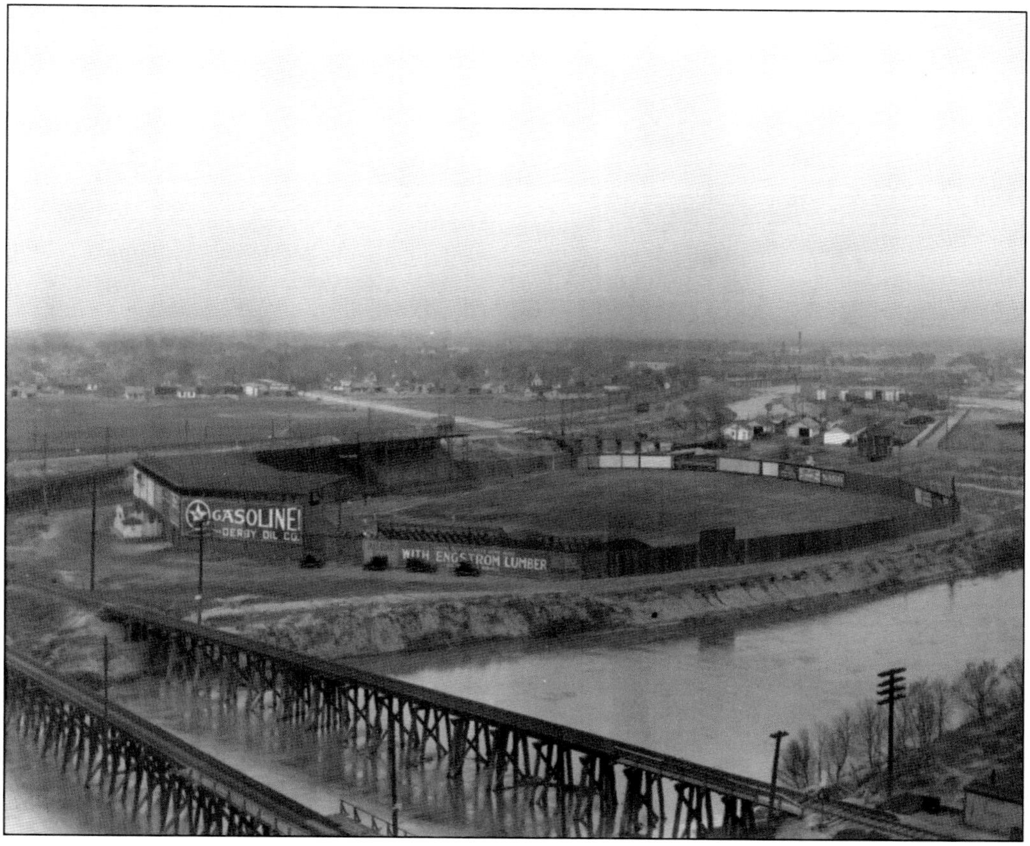

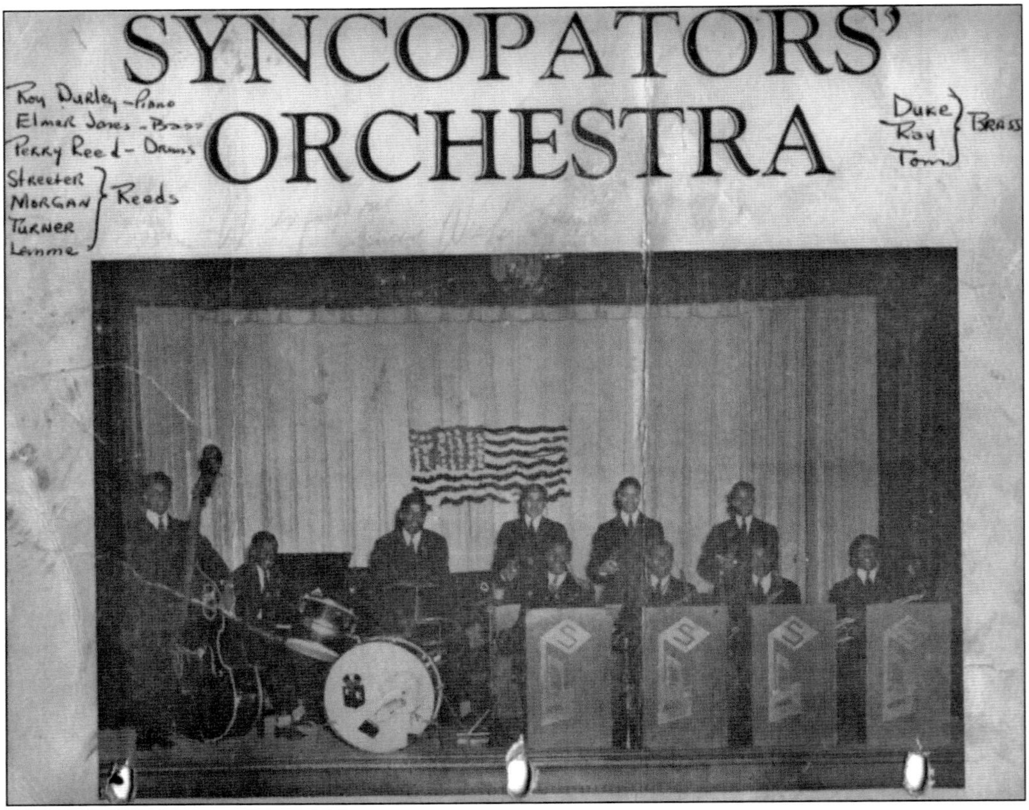

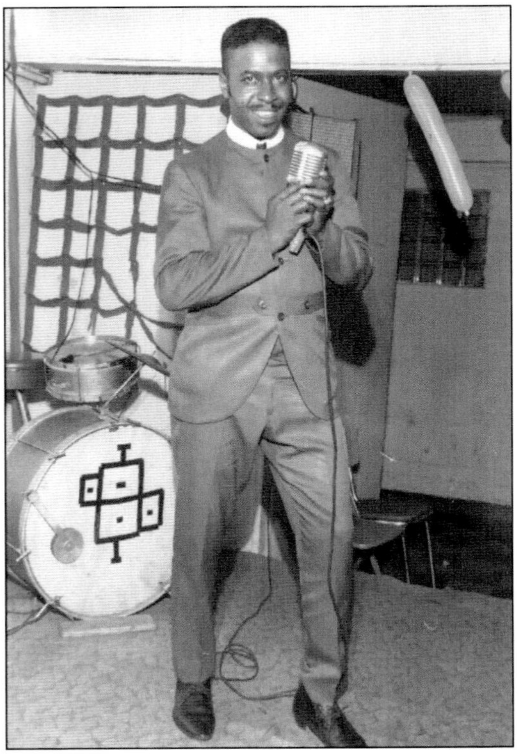

Wichita was home to a number of local musicians, including blues artist Homer Osborne, Junior Johnson, Ernie Fields, Clarence Love, Red Perkins, and the Syncopators, which was composed of local high school students. Black musicians faced numerous challenges, and African Americans were initially prohibited from joining the local musicians union. Venues allowed musicians of color to play, but during breaks, they had to go outside while their white counterparts could stay indoors.

Musicians who came of age in the mid-20th century inspired the children who shaped the sound of the early 21st. Following in his mother's musical footsteps was Charlie "Harmonica Chuck" Phillips. Born in Oklahoma, Phillips moved to Wichita in 1953 and began creating a following around Kansas with his harmonica skills. In 1965, he became manager of the 904 Club at Fifteenth and Mosley Streets, which later moved to 2418 East Ninth Street.

The *Colored Directory, Wichita, Kansas, 1927-8* states: "Dr. H.H. Wilson practiced medicine in Wichita for several years. He came here from Salina. Dr. Wilson finished his medical degree at Shaw University, Raleigh, N.C., before coming to Kansas and had an extensive practice in the city."

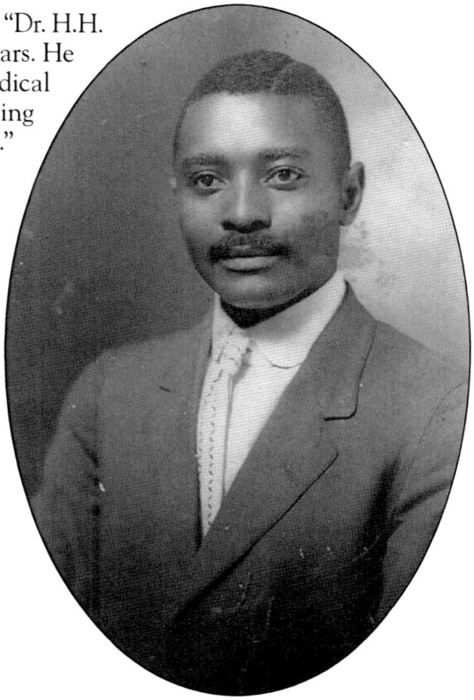

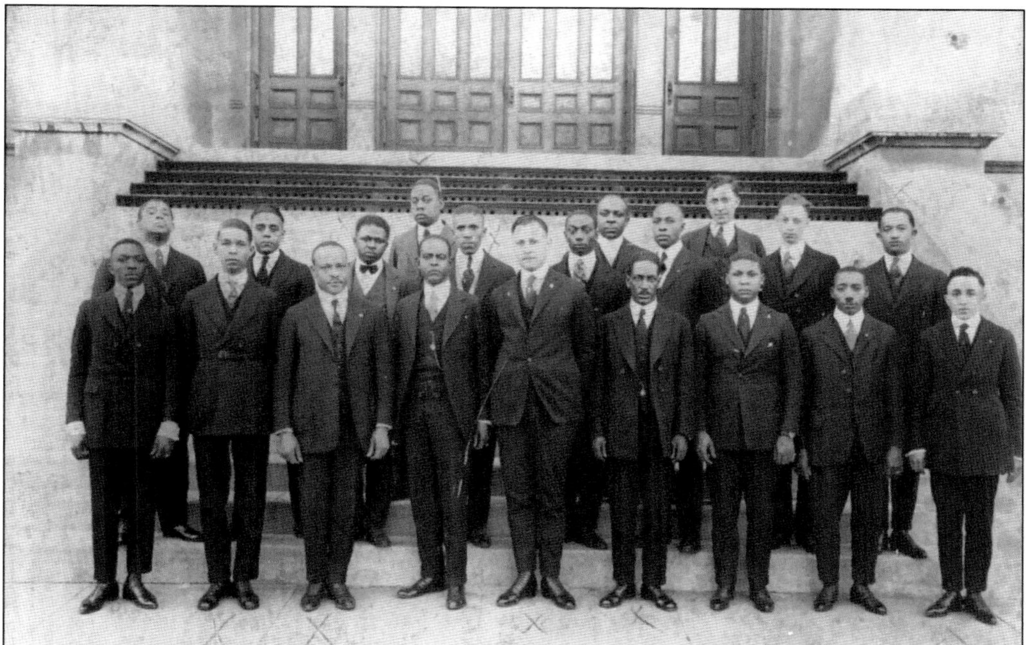

Here, several African American medical students are gathered in front of the Sedgwick County Courthouse. Among them is Dr. P.M. Bell (front row, third from left). Dr. Bell was a member of the medical staffs at St. Francis, Wesley, and County Hospitals; was an active member of the YMCA, the Sigma Phi Alpha, and the NAACP; and was a 32nd degree Mason.

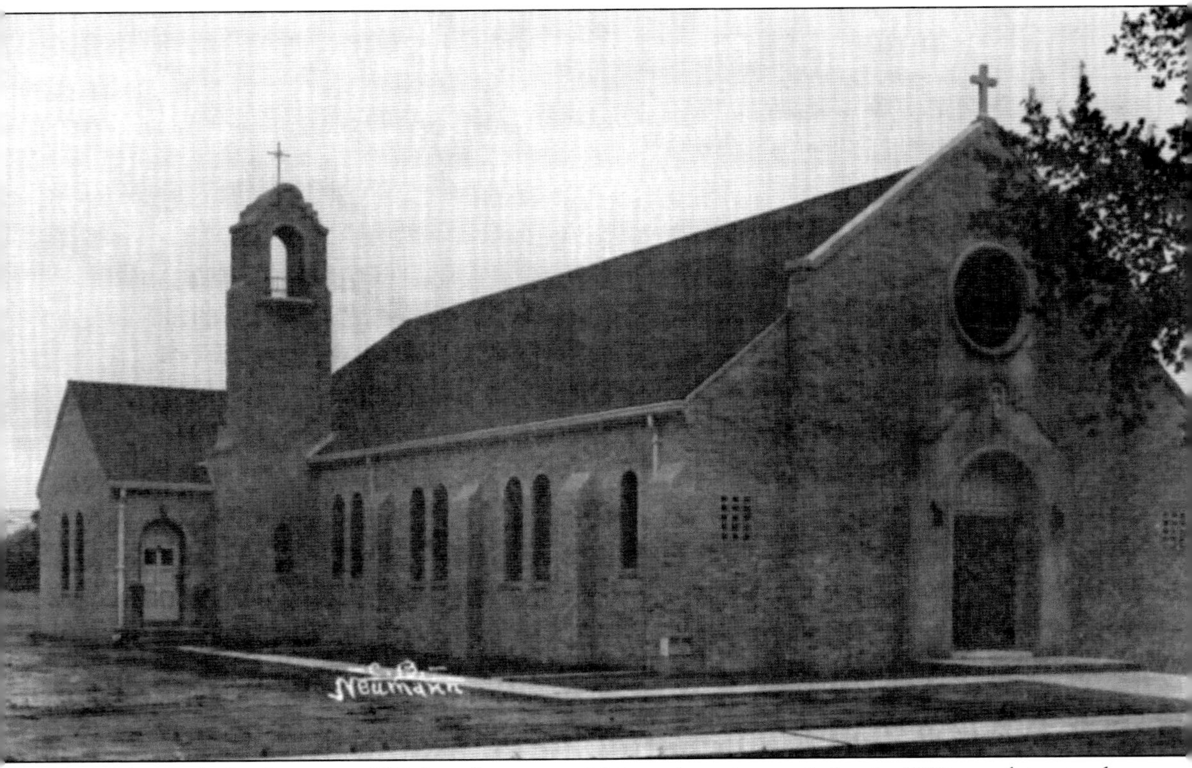

The Catholic Diocese of Wichita began an African American mission in 1930, resulting in the creation of the parish of St. Peter Claver. The congregation initially met in a converted pool hall, but moved to a permanent church building at Eleventh and Indiana Streets in September 1940. Led by an activist white priest, Fr. Leon A. McNeill, St. Peter Claver became an important institution in civil rights efforts and was a home of the NAACP youth council in the 1950s. (Courtesy Adorers of the Blood of Christ.)

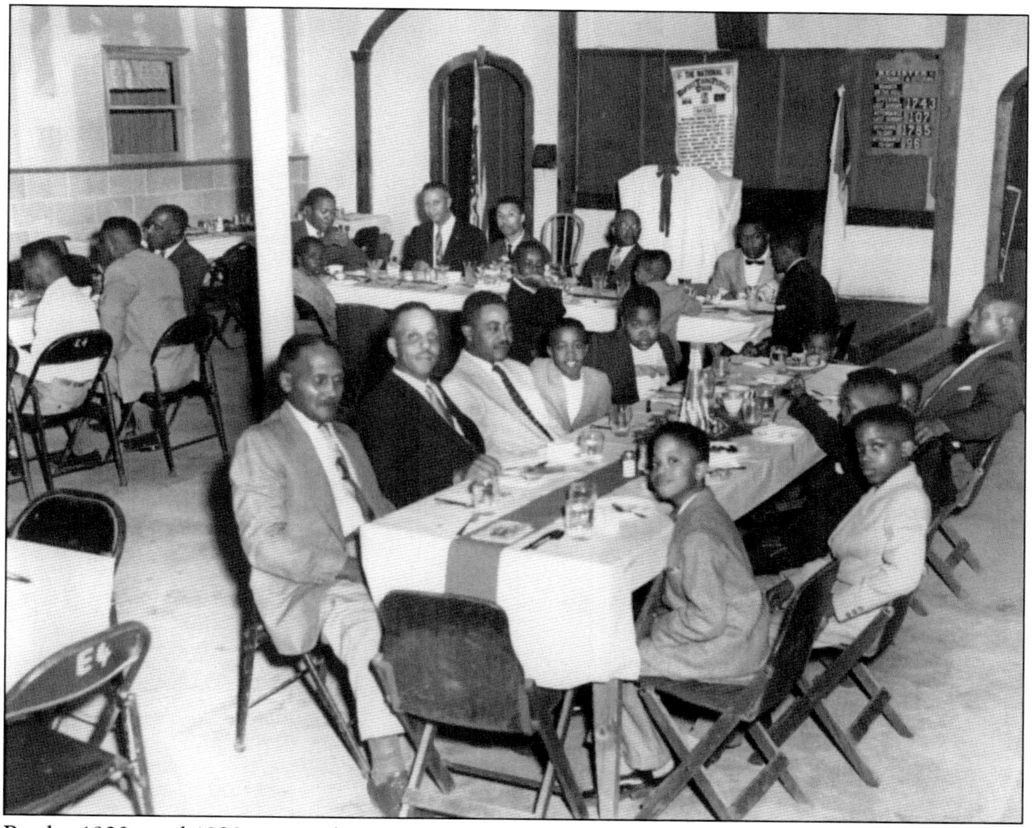

By the 1920s and 1930s, a number of families were starting to buy houses along several streets between the main railroad tracks and the Chisholm Creek canal: Wabash, Indiana, Mathewson, Ohio, Pennsylvania, and New York Streets. As the African American community moved eastward, they erected new institutions, including churches. In the 1930s, Baptists on the east side formed New Hope Baptist on Ohio Street. At right, Arthur McAfee, grandson of Jacob McAfee and one of the founders of New Hope, gives an address to the assembled congregation. (Both, courtesy Charles McAfee.)

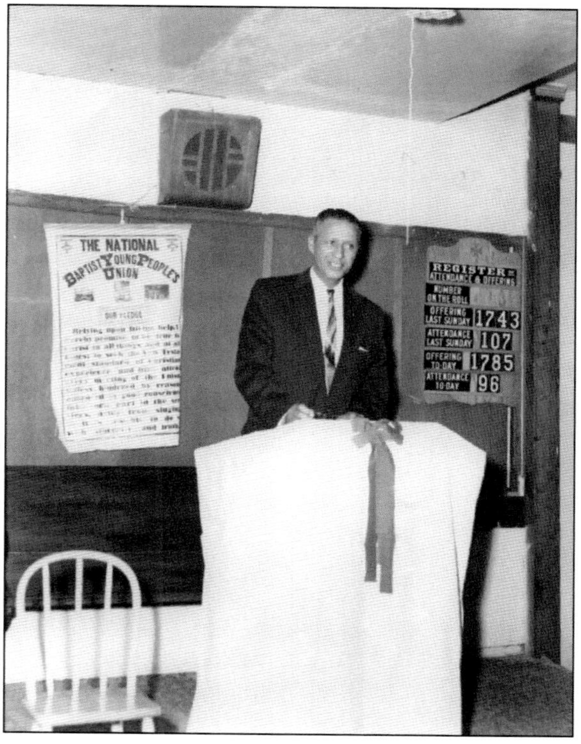

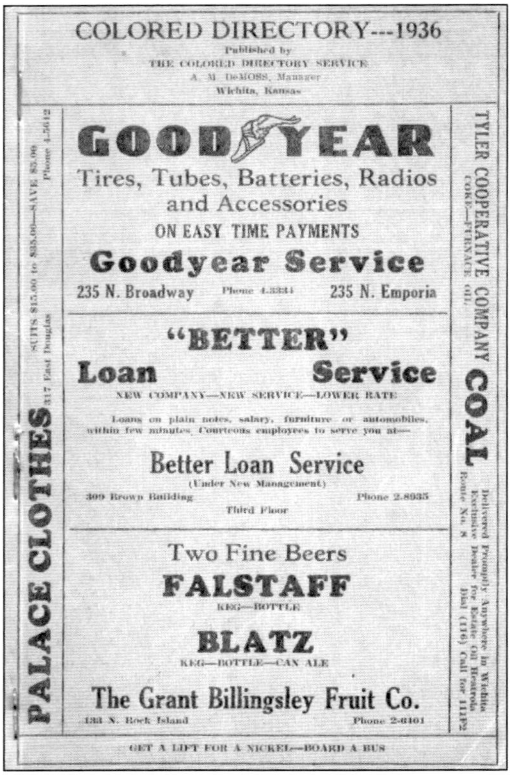

COLORED DIRECTORY---1936

Published by

THE COLORED DIRECTORY SERVICE

A. M. DeMOSS, Manager

Wichita, Kansas

GOODYEAR

Tires, Tubes, Batteries, Radios and Accessories

ON EASY TIME PAYMENTS

Goodyear Service

235 N. Broadway Phone 4.3334 235 N. Emporia

"BETTER" Loan Service

NEW COMPANY—NEW SERVICE—LOWER RATE

Loans on plain notes, salary, furniture or automobiles, within few minutes. Courteous employees to serve you at—

Better Loan Service

(Under New Management)

309 Brown Building Phone 2.8935

Third Floor

Two Fine Beers

FALSTAFF

KEG—BOTTLE

BLATZ

KEG—BOTTLE—CAN ALE

The Grant Billingsley Fruit Co.

133 N. Rock Island Phone 2-6401

PALACE CLOTHES 317 East Douglas

SUITS $15.00 to $35.00—SAVE $5.00 Phone 4-5612

TYLER COOPERATIVE COMPANY COAL

COKE—FURNACE OIL

Delivered Promptly Anywhere in Wichita

Exclusive Dealer for Estate Oil Heatrola

Route No. 8 Dial (116) Call for 111P2

GET A LIFT FOR A NICKEL—BOARD A BUS

During the 1920s and 1930s, several ethnic and racial groups had their own directories that listed residents, businesses, and community institutions. They were also booster publications, celebrating the success of community leaders and extolling the ways in which the particular group contributed to the larger community.

In the 1930s, at the height of the Great Depression, classes in Wichita taught young African Americans skills like typing as part of the federal WPA program. (Courtesy Kansas State Historical Society.)

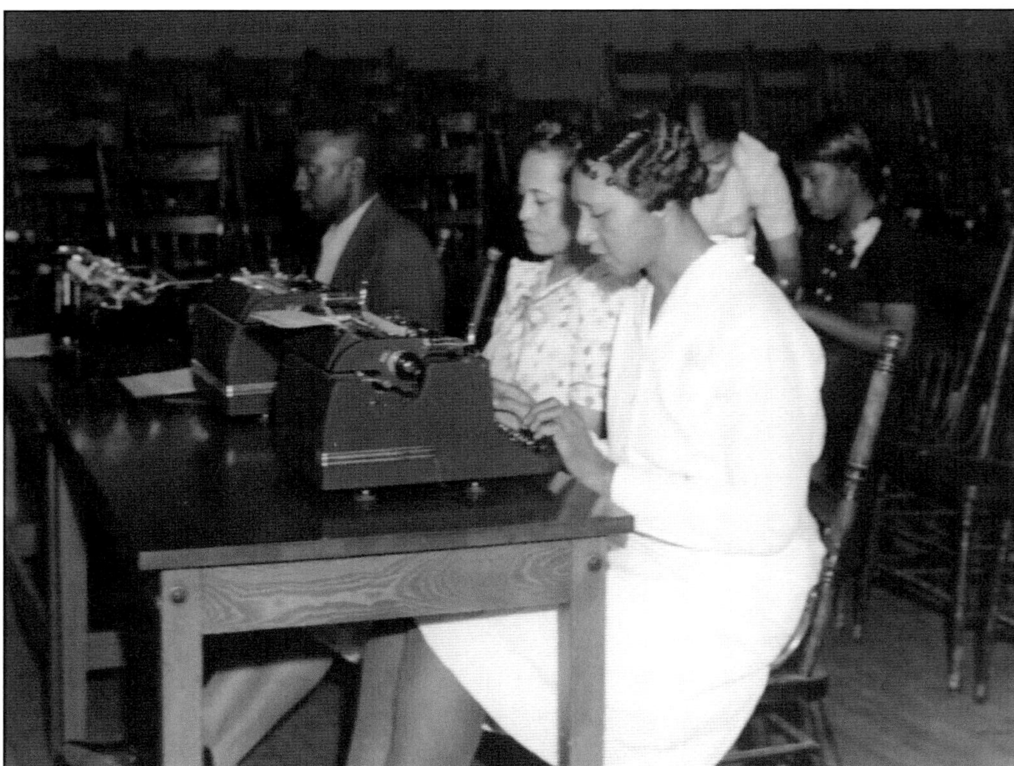

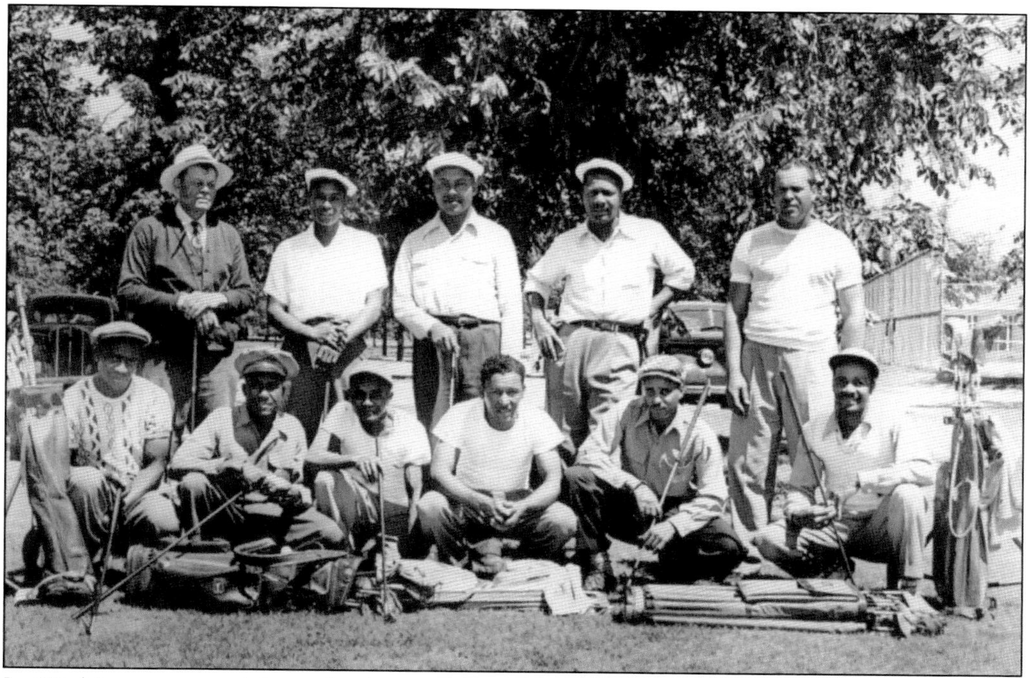

In Wichita, country clubs and other social organizations restricted African Americans, Jews, Syrians, and others from membership. These communities responded by establishing their own venues. For African Americans, the McKinley Golf Club—later renamed the McAdams Golf Club, for Emerson McAdams—was *the* place to golf.

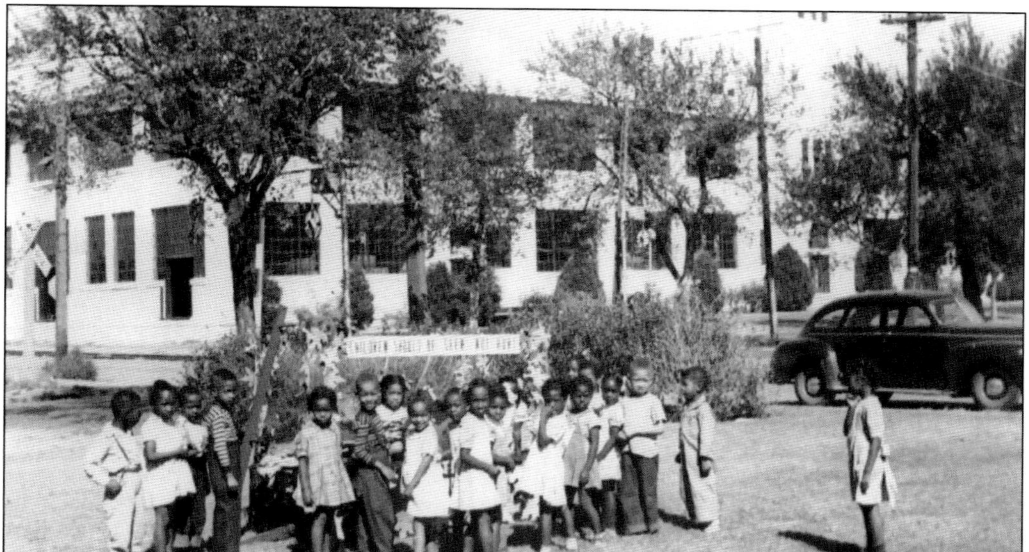

Through eighth grade, schools were segregated by policy until 1952. This was further achieved until 1972 by redrawing boundary lines to match the racial makeup of neighborhoods. In 1927, the former Ingalls Elementary became the all-black Dunbar Elementary School. Most African Americans attended Horace Mann or Central Junior High before Mathewson was built. Local high schools were never segregated. (Courtesy Wichita–Sedgwick County Historical Museum.)

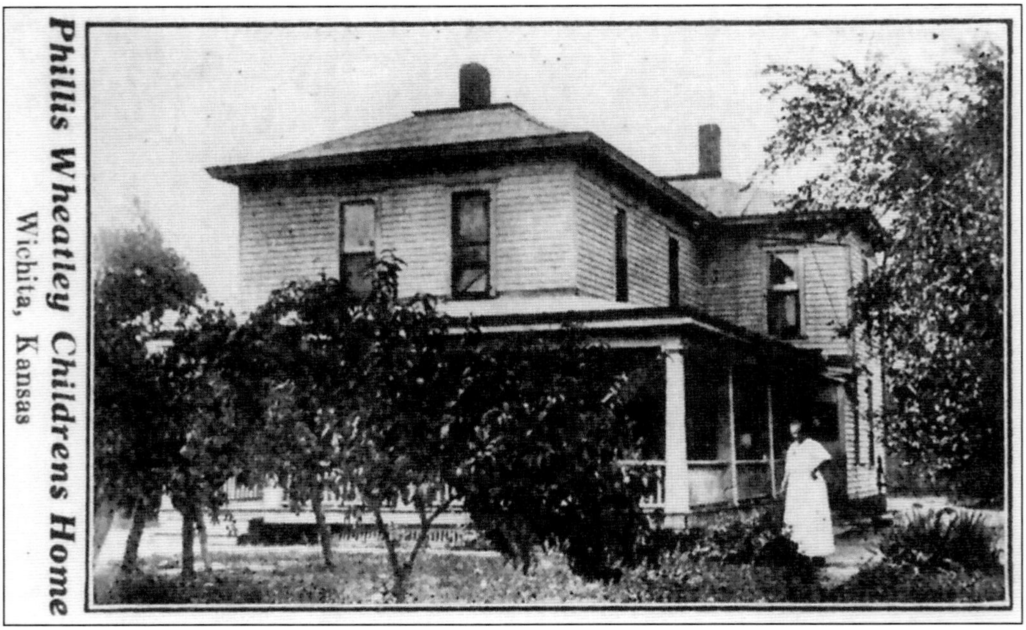

Phyllis Wheatley homes were part of a national movement to provide settlement house services to African Americans moving to Northern and Midwestern cities as part of the post-1910 Great Migration. Some were affiliated with the YWCA, while others—like this one—were independently run. In Wichita, the Wheatley Home provided a temporary place to live, classes, childcare, and an orphanage. By the late 1920s, over 45 children were in residence. The brick building below was built in 1932 and was located at Ninth and Mathewson Streets.

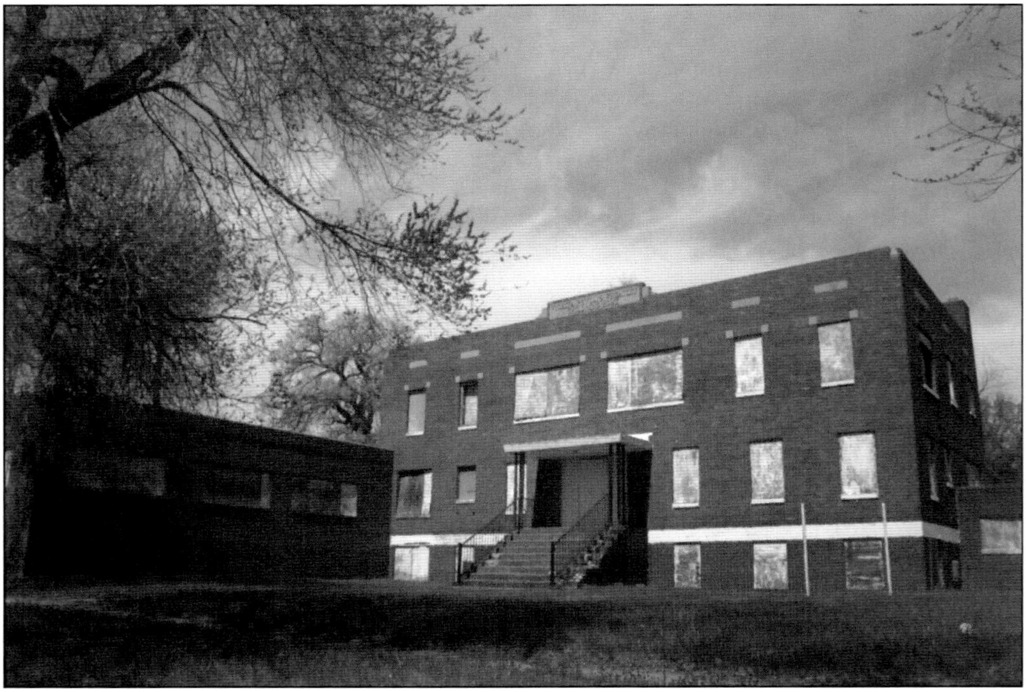

Born in Wichita, Hattie McDaniel performed in vaudeville, minstrel shows, and films while cleaning homes to pay her bills. In 1940, she won an Academy Award for Best Supporting Actress for her portrayal of Mammy in *Gone with the Wind*. She was the first African American to win an Oscar, but was barred from attending the film's Atlanta premier.

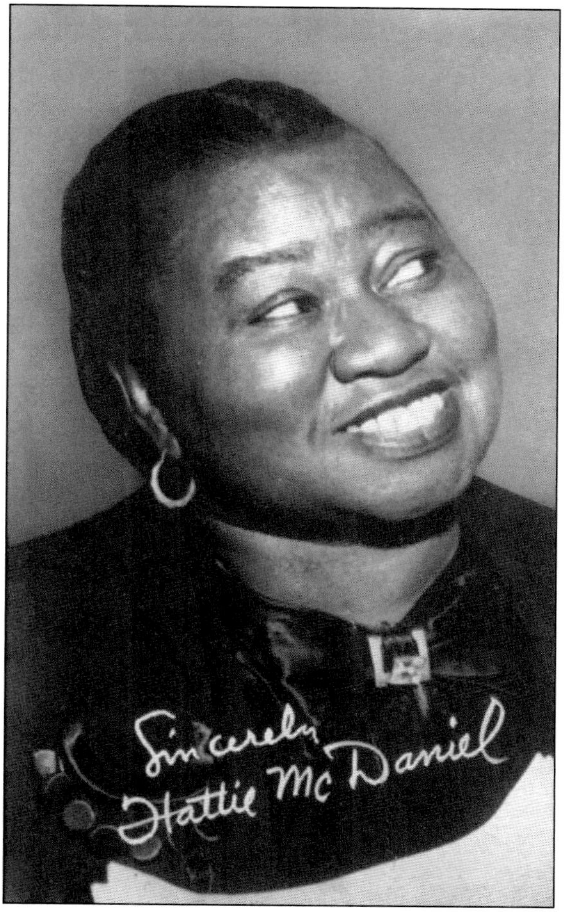

While movies such as *Gone with the Wind* depicted African Americans as servants or comic relief, many African American families like the Dandridges—seen here at Thanksgiving—worked to convey a sense of respectability and sophistication. (Courtesy Deborah Dandridge and University of Kansas.)

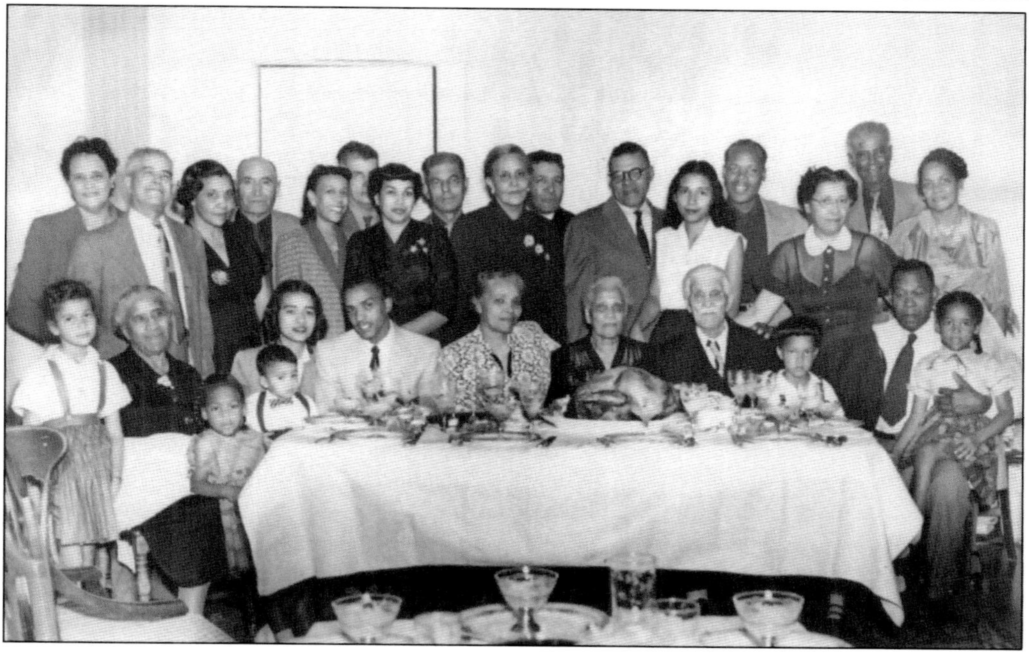

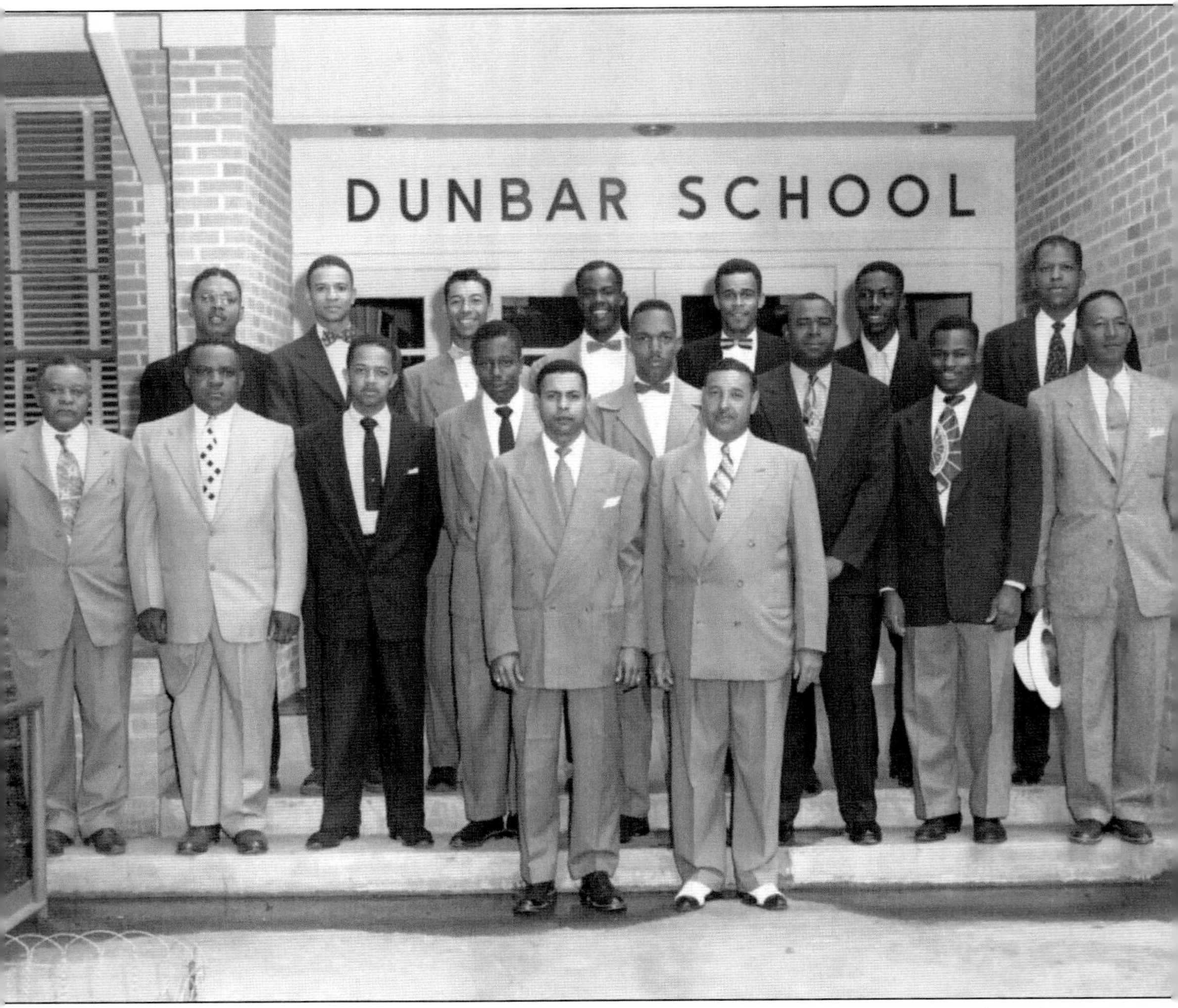

The men in this 1952 photograph were members of Kappa Alpha Psi fraternity and later became some of the most significant leaders in the community. Pictured from left to right are, (first row) Howard University graduate Dr. Val Brown and Tom Green; (second row) Dr. H.H. Wilson, Luther Harris, Jesse Merida, Perry Lee, Wichita State football icon Linwood Sexton, Emerson McAdams (for whom the McAdams Park and neighborhood are named), Herb Edington, and James Anderson Sr.; (third row) James Easter, Tuskegee airman and veterinarian Donald Jackson, noted architect Charles McAfee, James Harris, Curtis Hightower, trailblazing educator Sam Spaght, and lawyer and Wichita's first black appointed mayor A. Price Woodard. (Courtesy Charles McAfee.)

Three

PARALLEL WORLDS

By the 1940s, the African American community was shifting from a hub along Water Street—also known as the West End—to a new business district at Ninth Street and Cleveland Avenue, and in many ways, the community was self-sufficient. Production for World War II created employment opportunities, bringing white and black migrants from the South to Wichita for jobs. During the 1940s and 1950s, African Americans came to Wichita to work in the aircraft plants, packing plants, downtown warehouses, hotels, and other businesses that benefited from the economic growth of the era. This allowed families to afford houses, cars, and the other amenities of postwar life. Segregation, however, remained. Black Wichitans could not eat in downtown establishments. Hospitals were segregated until Chester Lewis threatened a suit in the 1950s. Through it all, people fought back by developing black institutions and patronizing them—black-owned beauty schools, cleaners, groceries, taxi companies, contractors, an ice plant, and other enterprises. The booming economy that needed black labor empowered protests against police aggression and school and housing segregation, led by the Congress of Racial Equality (CORE) and, later, Rev. J.C. Douglass—president of the NAACP. When black veterans returned home from war, they and other African Americans were frustrated by the continuation of real estate practices that restricted them to "Negro areas" and by employers hiring blacks only for unskilled jobs. Black activism expanded during the 1950s—often led by veterans and college educated stay-at-home moms. Following a historic local student sit-in in 1958, the NAACP's Jo Gardenhire, Billy McCray, and Chester I. Lewis Jr. organized five years of protests, including a "Don't Shop Where You Can't Work" campaign. African American doctors' wives ran up bills for clothing purchased at upscale stores that would not allow them to try on clothing before purchasing it. Upon receiving the bills, the women called the stores to say they would be paid once they were allowed to try on clothing in the stores. These same women refused dental appointments on Thursdays once they learned that white dentists would see black patients only on Thursdays. As protests escalated, policies slowly changed.

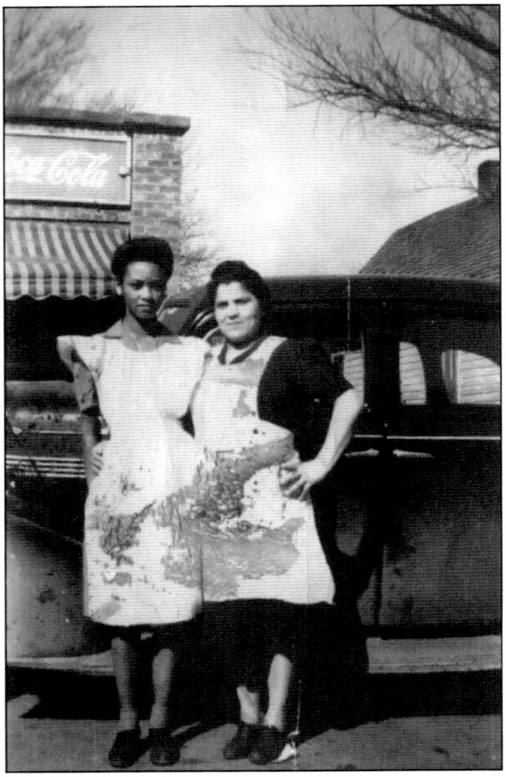

In 1943, Ethel Daniels left Boley, Oklahoma, to attend school in Wichita. She found work at the Namee neighborhood grocery store and is seen here with Mrs. Thelma Namee. The Namees were one of several Lebanese families who operated grocery stores in the African American community. They considered Ethel part of the family.

Lake Anderson Jr. was a bellhop for the Eaton Hotel, and could recall colorful stories about escorting prostitutes to the rooms of guests. Later on, he transitioned into landscaping in upscale neighborhoods like Crown Heights. These efforts allowed him to erect a modest home on New York Street, in what was becoming a new center for the African American community. (Courtesy Yvette Harris.)

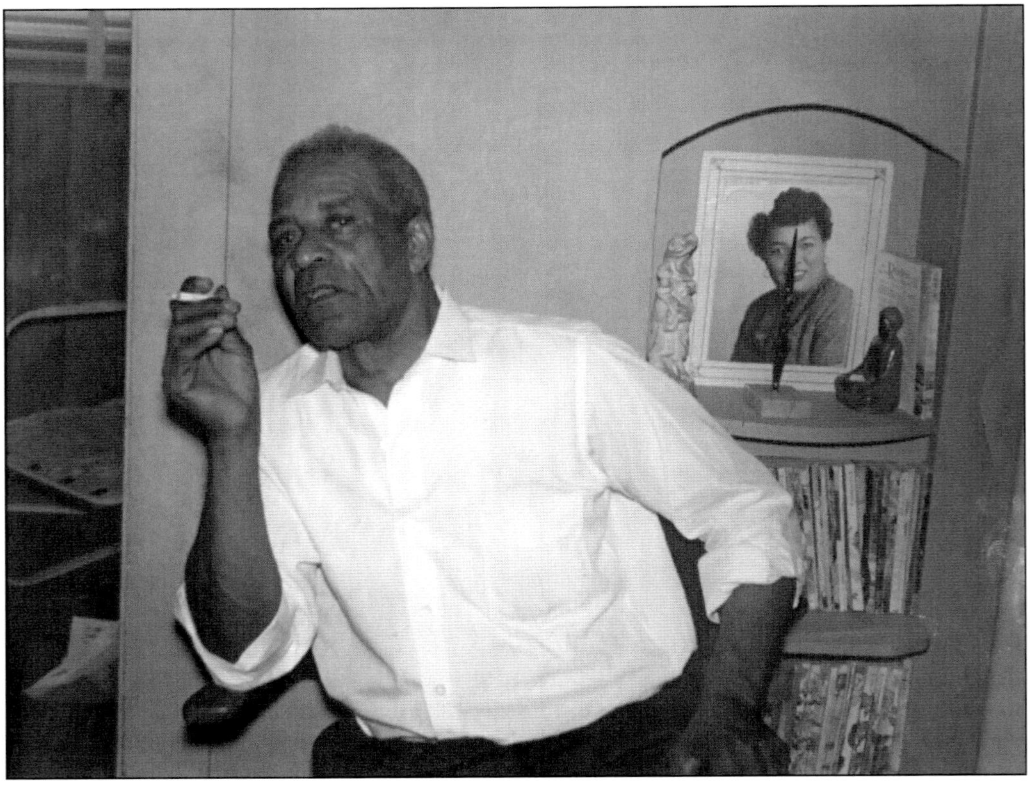

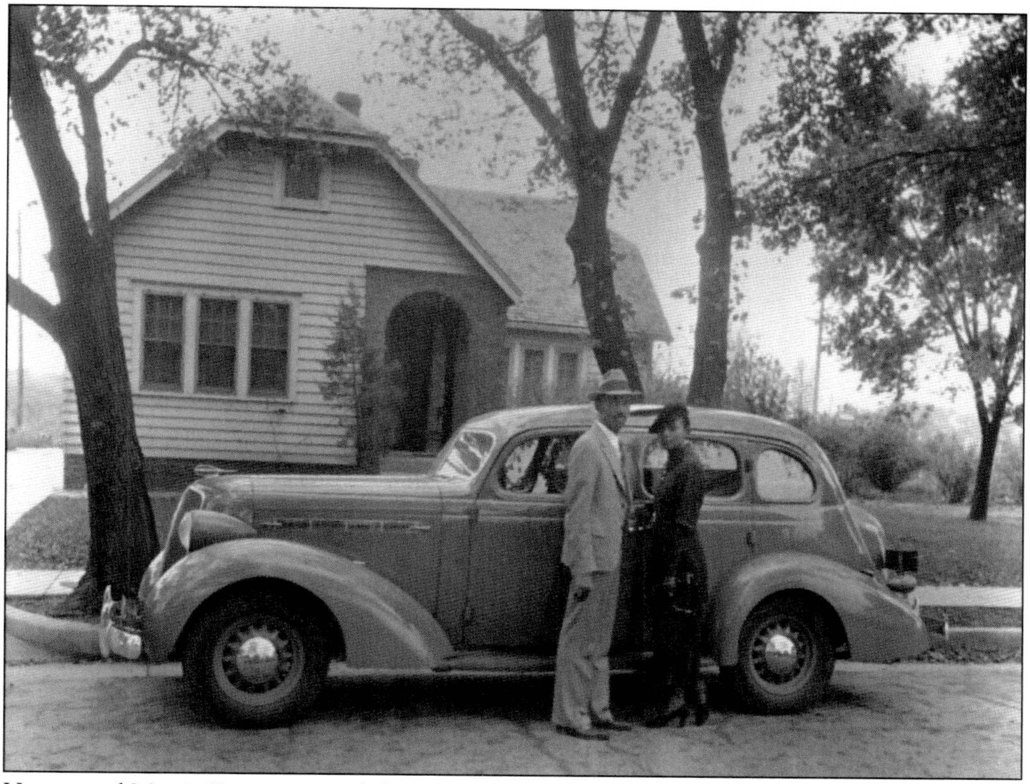

Homer and Mattie Perry, pictured above in 1940 at their home at 1314 North Cleveland Avenue, were part of Wichita's black middle class. Mattie was a schoolteacher, and Perry was a 33rd degree member of the Albert Hall Lodge, Western Star Consistory No. 18. At right are his apron and 33rd degree hat, kept safe in a tambourine case.

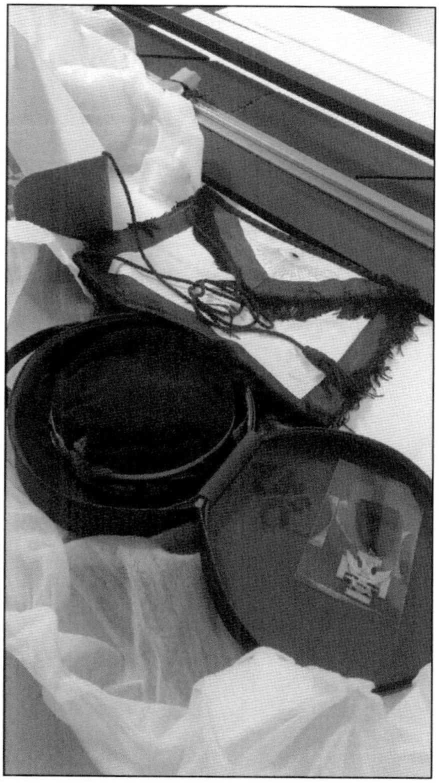

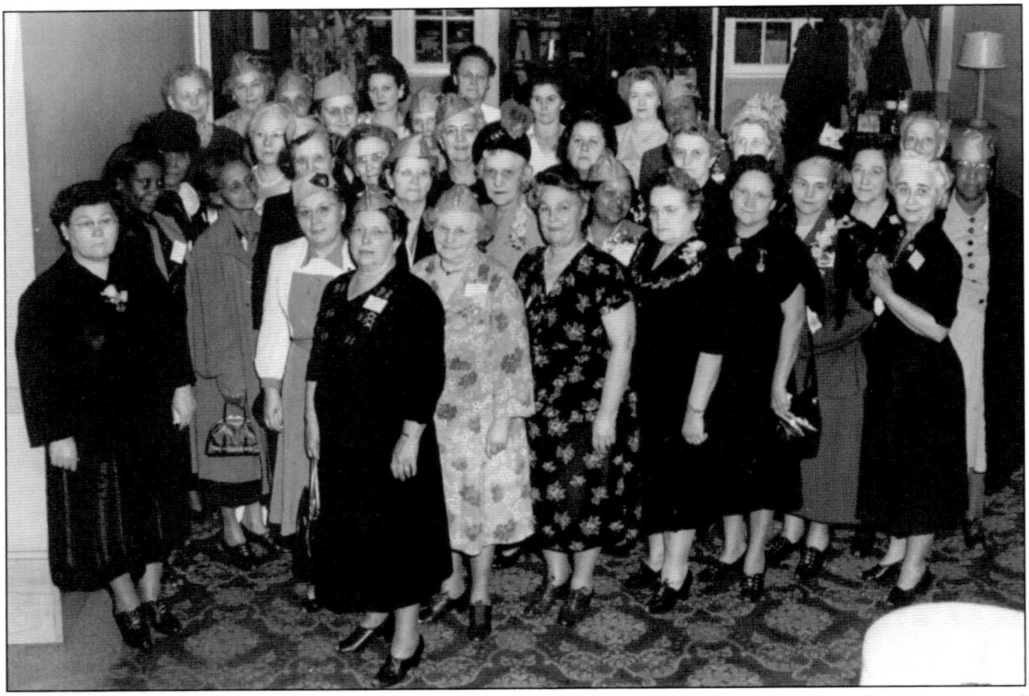

World War II broke out in 1939, and military contracts with Boeing, Beechcraft, Cessna, and Culver resulted in a growing need for workers that only increased once the United States entered the war. New housing communities such as Planeview emerged to house these workers. African Americans, however, faced segregated facilities, including those for nursery care and recreation. By 1945, a migration of white and black workers had nearly doubled the city's population. (Below, courtesy Kansas Aviation Museum.)

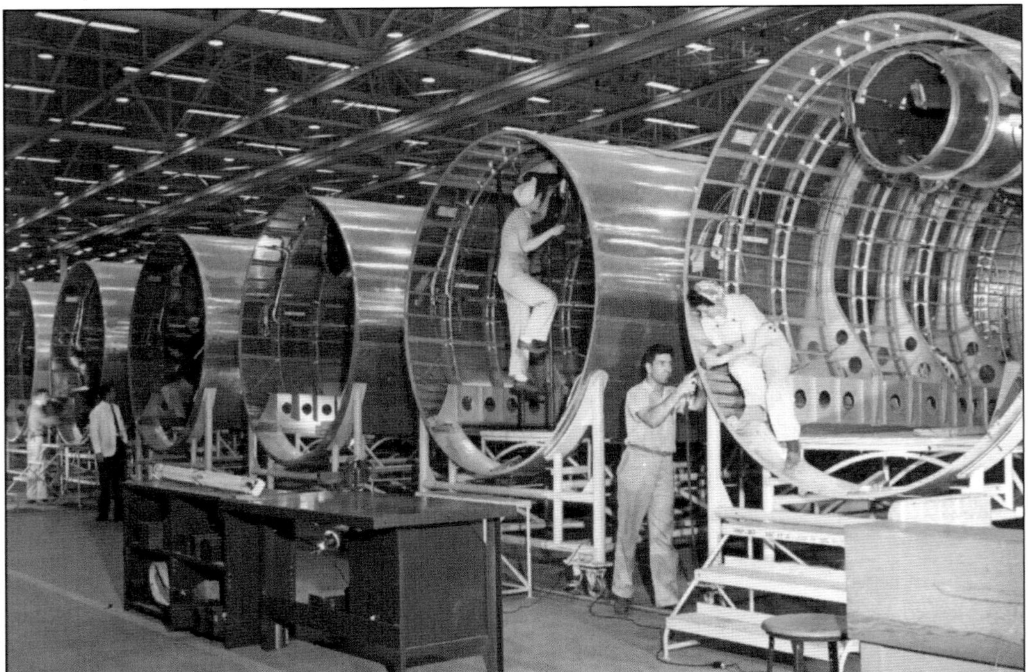

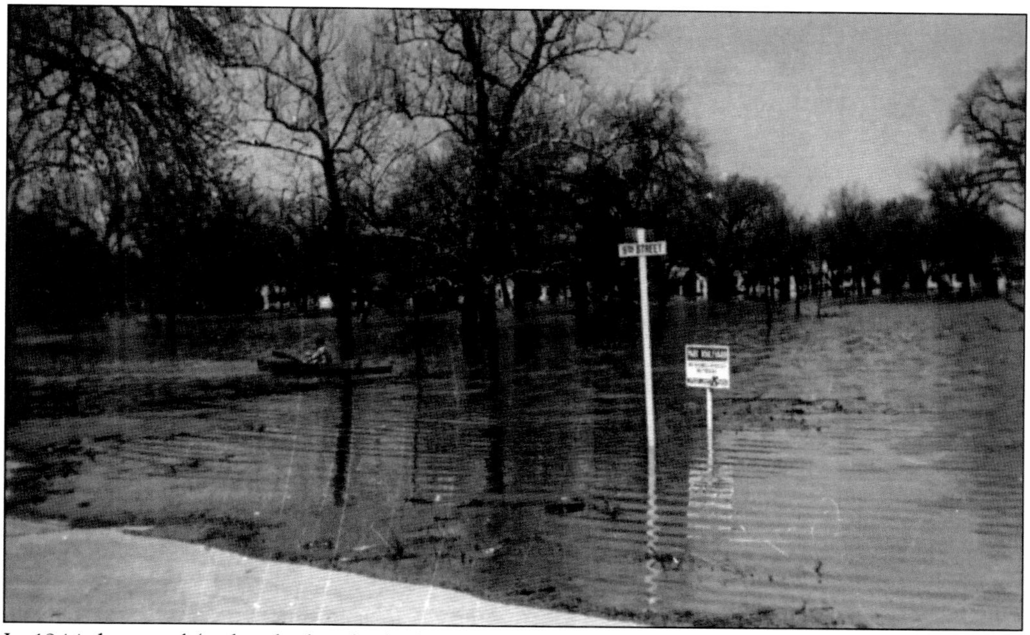

In 1944 the canal (today the big ditch along I-135) flooded, devastating black homes as far west as Mosley Street and from Murdock Avenue north to Thirteenth Street. Some African Americans bought homes in adjacent white residential areas, assisted by GI Bill loans. Real estate agents encouraged whites to flee newly integrated neighborhoods, producing more home sales and profits. Neighborhoods transitioned from white, to mixed, to black. (Courtesy Wichita–Sedgwick County Historical Museum.)

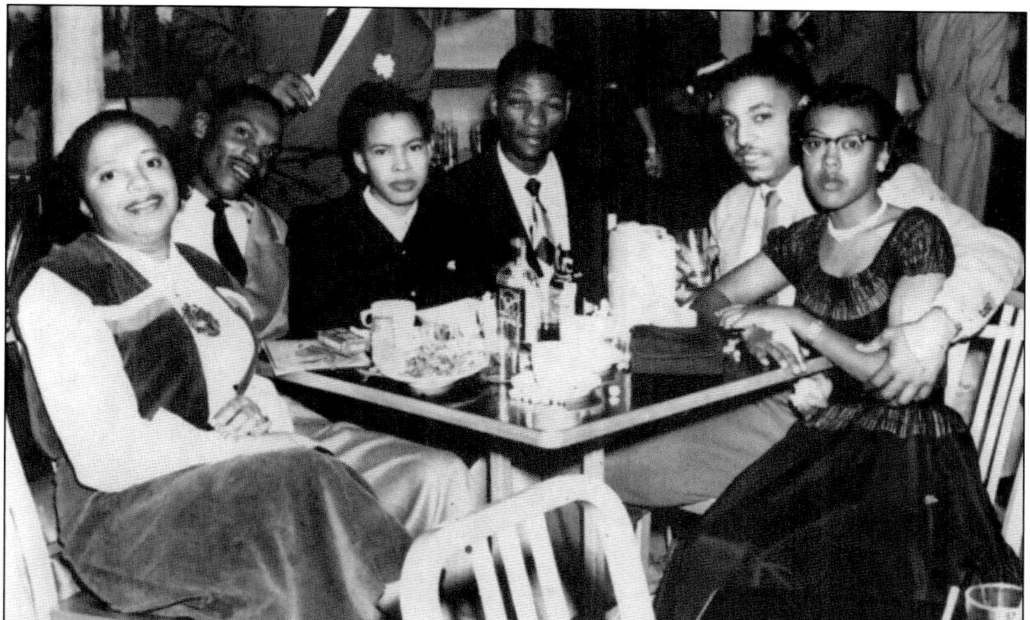

Aviation jobs before, during, and after World War II drew whites and blacks to Wichita. By the early 1950s, black students could get permits to get out of school early to work at Boeing and the other aircraft companies. Opportunities in aviation and other industries made Wichita a center for migration from Oklahoma and the Ozarks, part of what is now called "The Southern Diaspora."

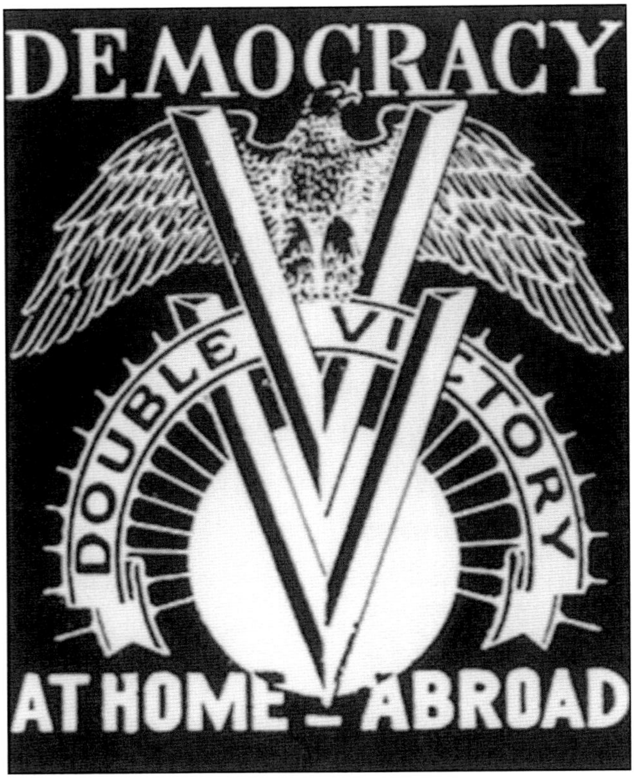

In 1941, James G. Thompson—a 26-year-old cafeteria worker in a Wichita aircraft plant—wrote to *The Pittsburgh Courier*, "Let we colored Americans adopt the double V for a double victory. The first V for victory over our enemies from without, the second V for victory over our enemies from within." His letter started the national Double V campaign, spread by black newspapers and the NAACP—victory against Hitler and Japan *and* victory against racism at home. (Courtesy *The Pittsburgh Courier.*)

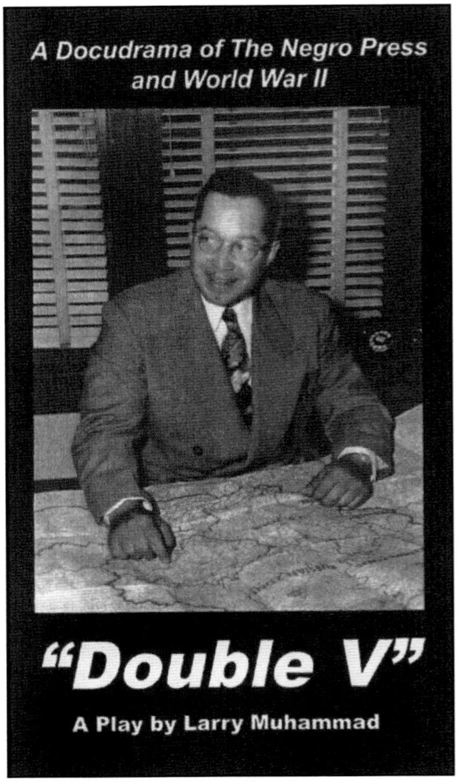

In 2001, Louisville, Kentucky, journalist and author Larry Muhammad wrote a docudrama inspired by the Double V campaign.

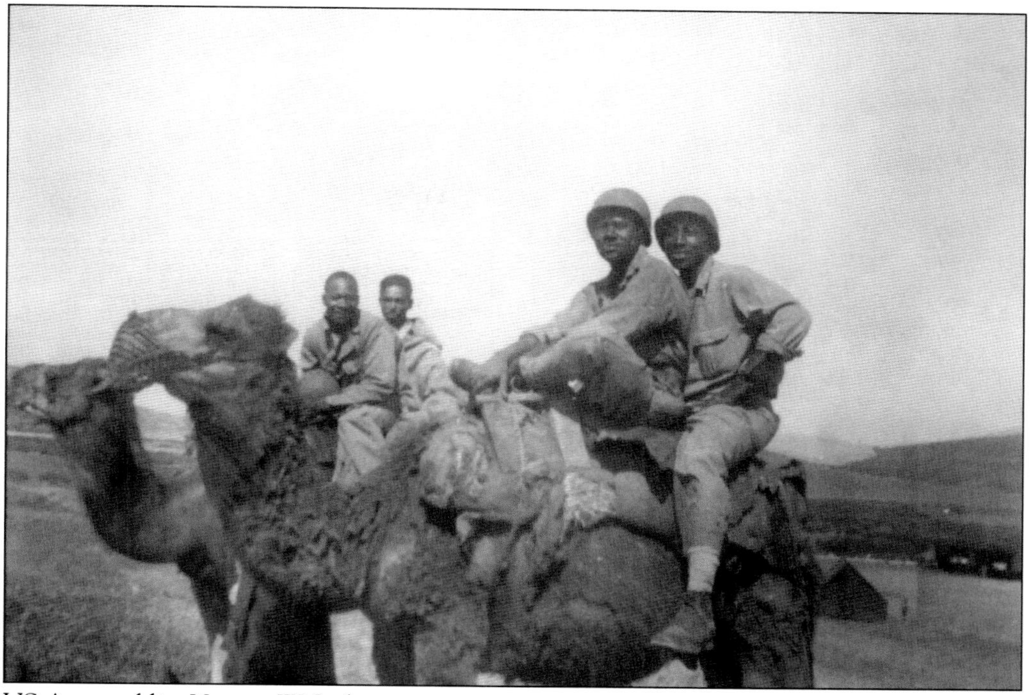

US Army soldier Vernon W. Jackson inscribed the above picture to his aunt Xavia Hightower. A member of the 549th Quartermaster Laundry Company during World War II, he is seen here with his buddies riding camels in North Africa. Donald Jackson is shown at right in his pilot's uniform. In August 1945, Jackson graduated from Tuskegee's Air Corps Pilot Training Program too late to see active service in the war. He attended college on the GI Bill, earning a degree in veterinary medicine from Kansas State University, and settled in Wichita. (Above, courtesy Kansas State Historical Society; right, courtesy Dr. Donald Jackson.)

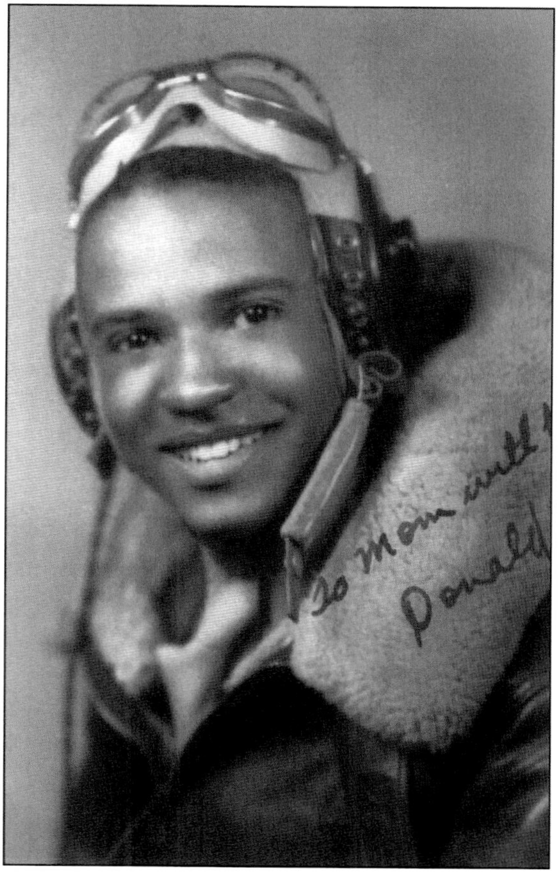

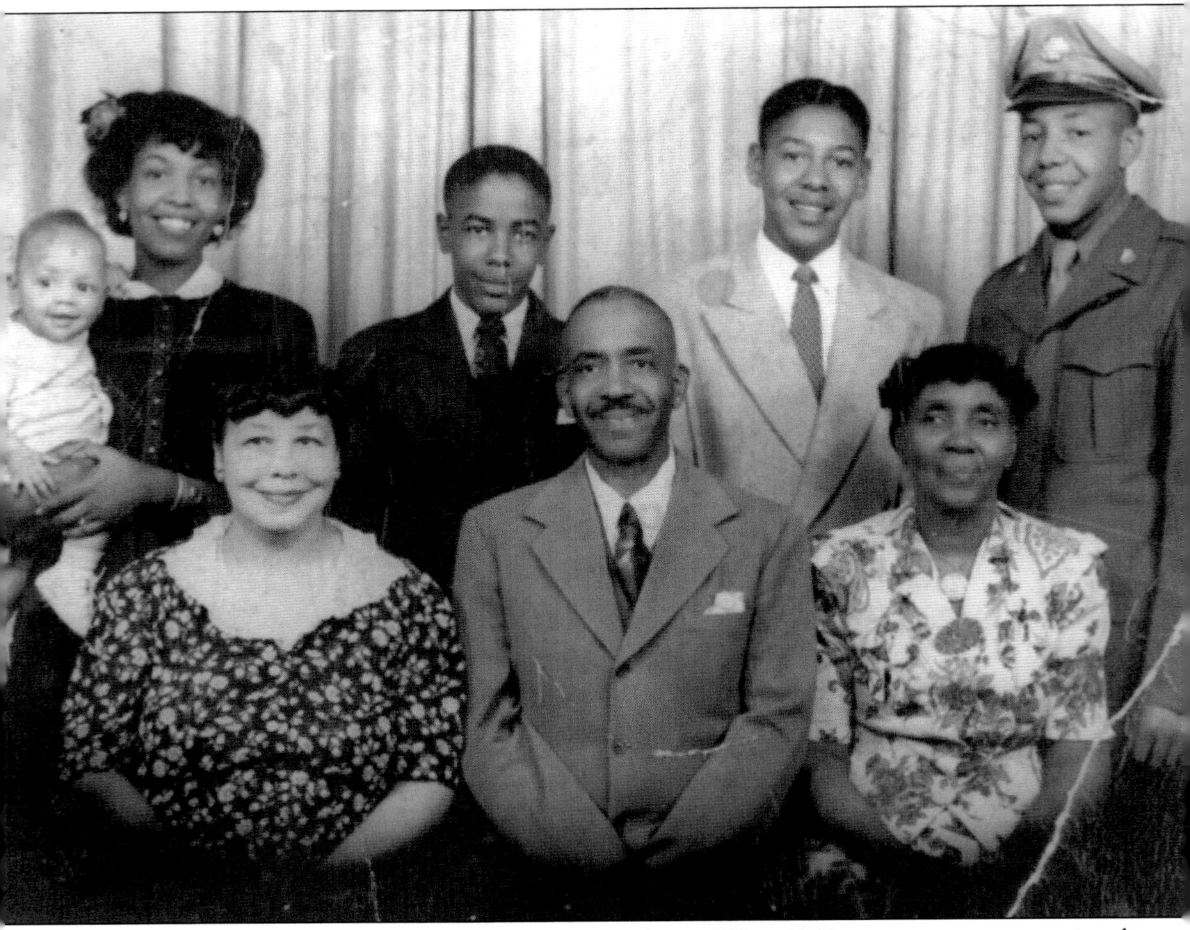

Chester Lewis Jr., who led the Wichita NAACP from 1957 to 1968, was a prominent national civil rights leader. He is at far right in this family photograph, wearing his uniform after returning from Okinawa. In 1953, he brought the first civil rights suit against the city and achieved the desegregation of both city swimming pools and Wesley Hospital. A national vice president of the NAACP, he successfully challenged discrimination, trained Wichita police in race relations, and successfully confronted the city's largest employer, Boeing, for hiring its black employees—400 out of a workforce of 30,000—only for unskilled jobs.

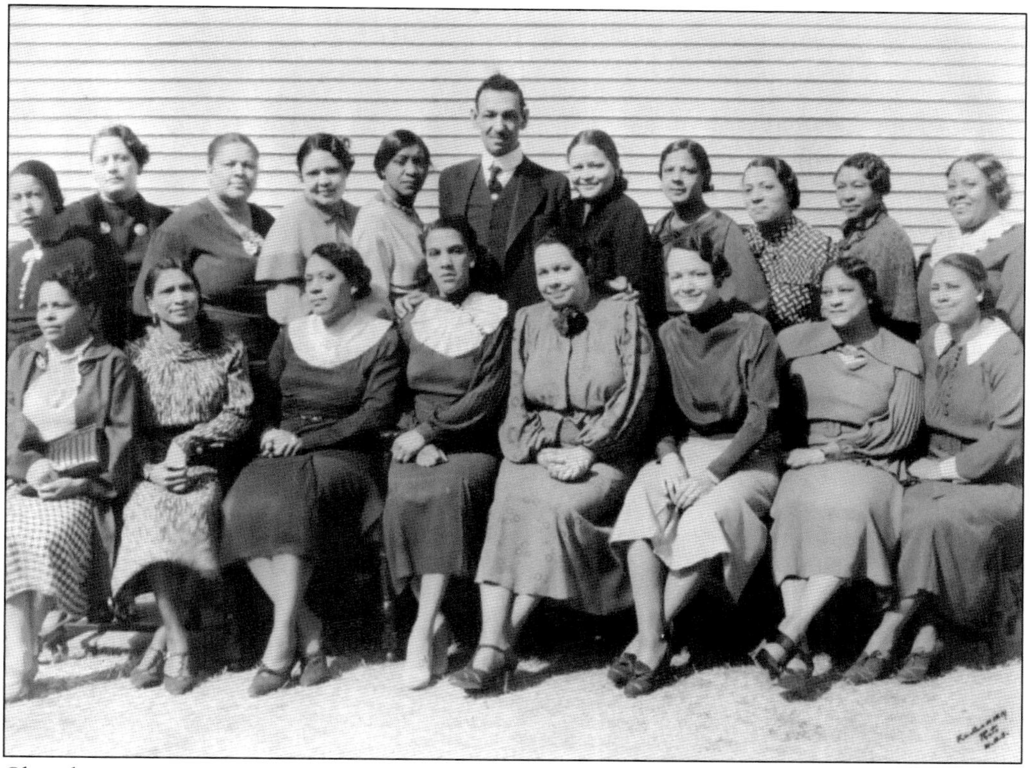

Churches were community and cultural centers as well as religious ones. Serving as a deacon or church official connoted status—regardless of whether that person was a doctor or a janitor during the week. It also helped educate the next generation of leaders, such as these Junior Matrons.

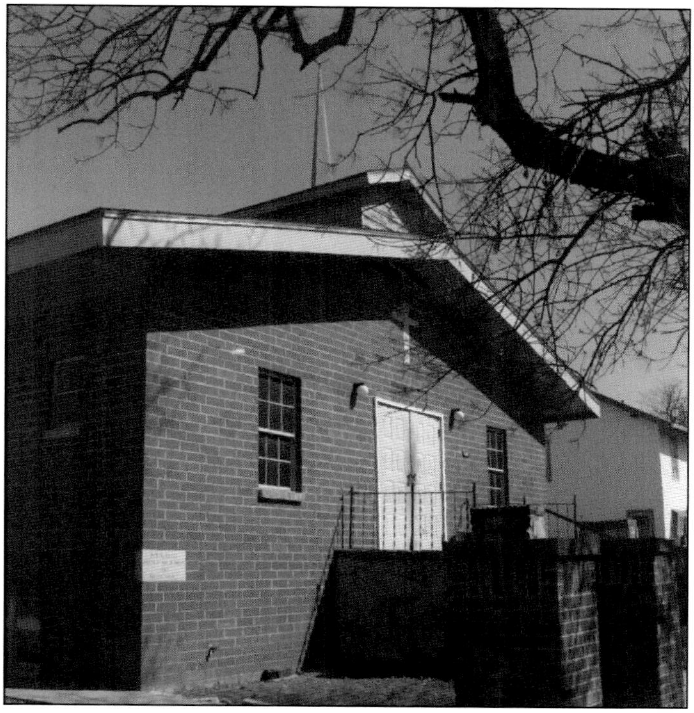

C.J. Taylor came to Wichita to work at Beechcraft. In 1948, he became a member of the Murdock Church of God in Christ and, later, a minister in the Pentecostal denomination. In 1956, Taylor became pastor of his own congregation, which later moved out of its small storefront and into this new building at 730 North Cleveland Avenue. It is now the Greater Pentecostal Church of God in Christ.

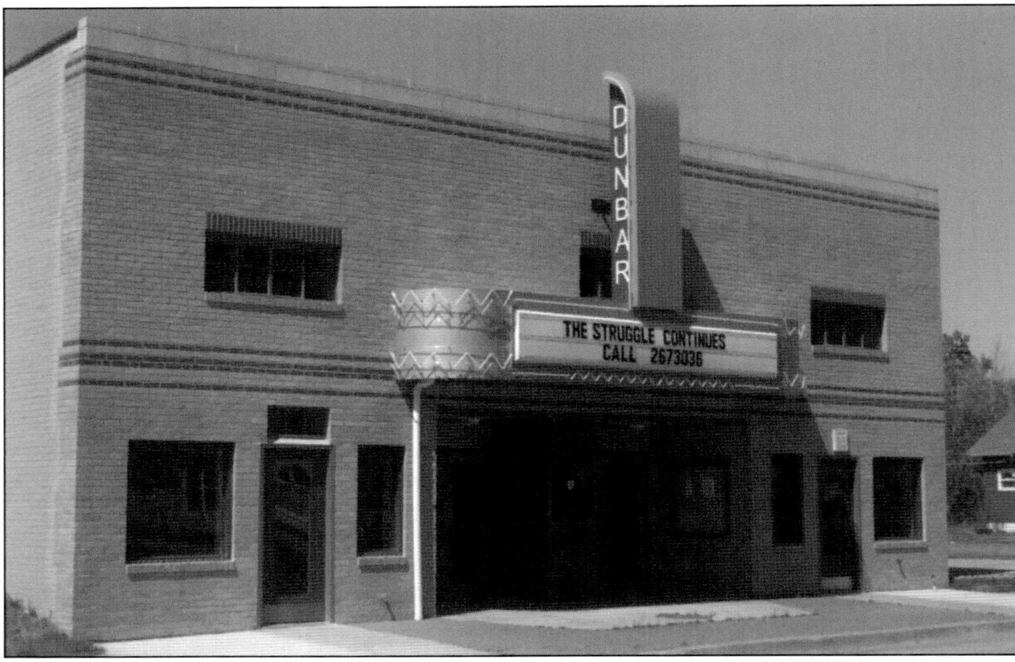

In the 1930s and 1940s, persons of color had to sit in the balconies of the local theaters unless the event was for a black audience. The Dunbar Theater, which opened in 1941, gave African Americans the opportunity to view movies in a non-discriminatory setting. It was the hub of a business district at Ninth Street and Cleveland Avenue, which was eclipsing Water Street as the city's main black neighborhood. On the southwest corner sat Dunbar School, and on the northwest corner, the Dunbar Theater and Turner Drug. The Austin Book Shoppe was across the street. The Phyllis Wheatley Home lay just to the east. The image below shows an NAACP gathering outside of the Dunbar in 1947.

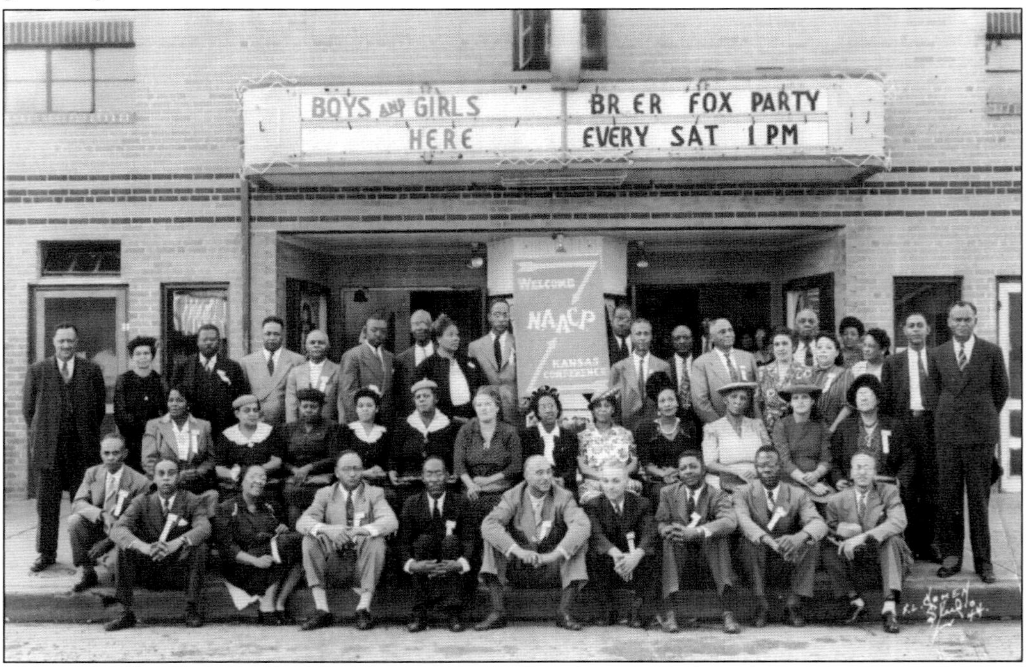

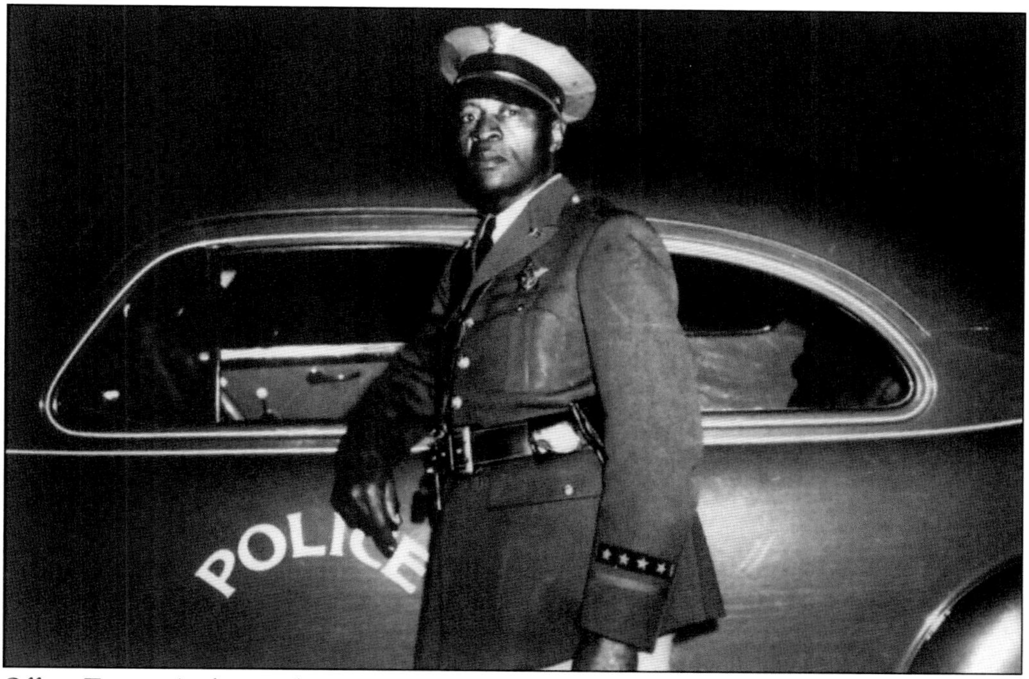

Officer Tommy Anderson, shown in 1940, joined the Wichita Police Department in 1922. During his 20 years of service, he garnered the respect of black business leaders, educators, parents, clergymen, and others in law enforcement. His home at Murdock and Cleveland Avenues was a regular gathering place for the community to reflect on the problems or news of the day.

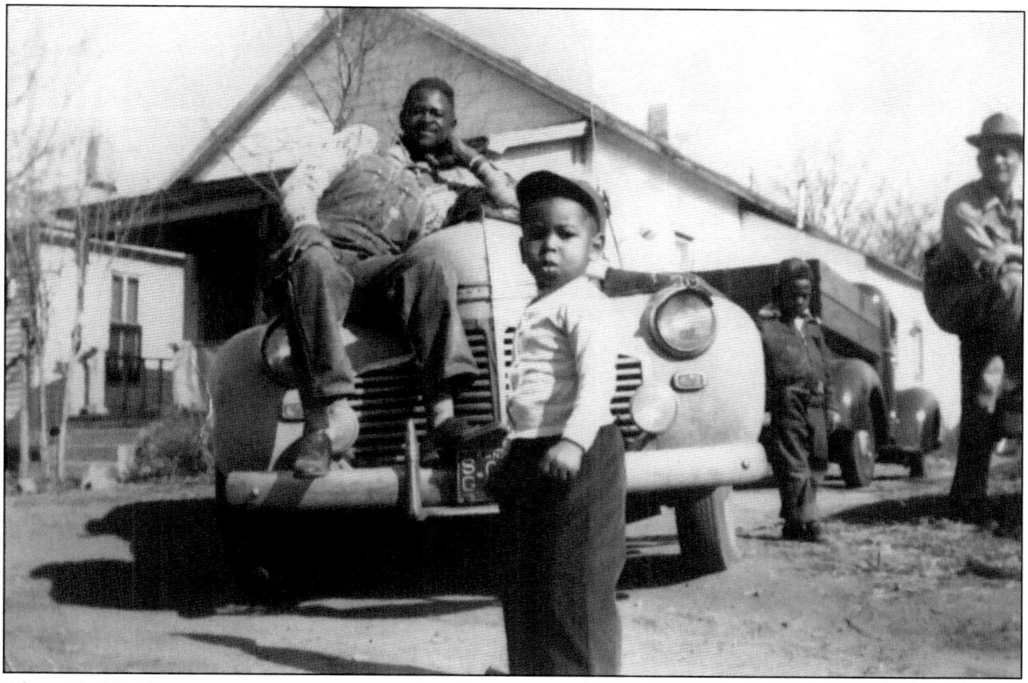

Theo Cribbs Sr., a state representative for 19 years, is seen here with a tiny Tommie Cribbs, who years later retired as a lieutenant of the Sedgwick County sheriff's office. The picture was taken in the early 1950s. (Courtesy Karmina Hill.)

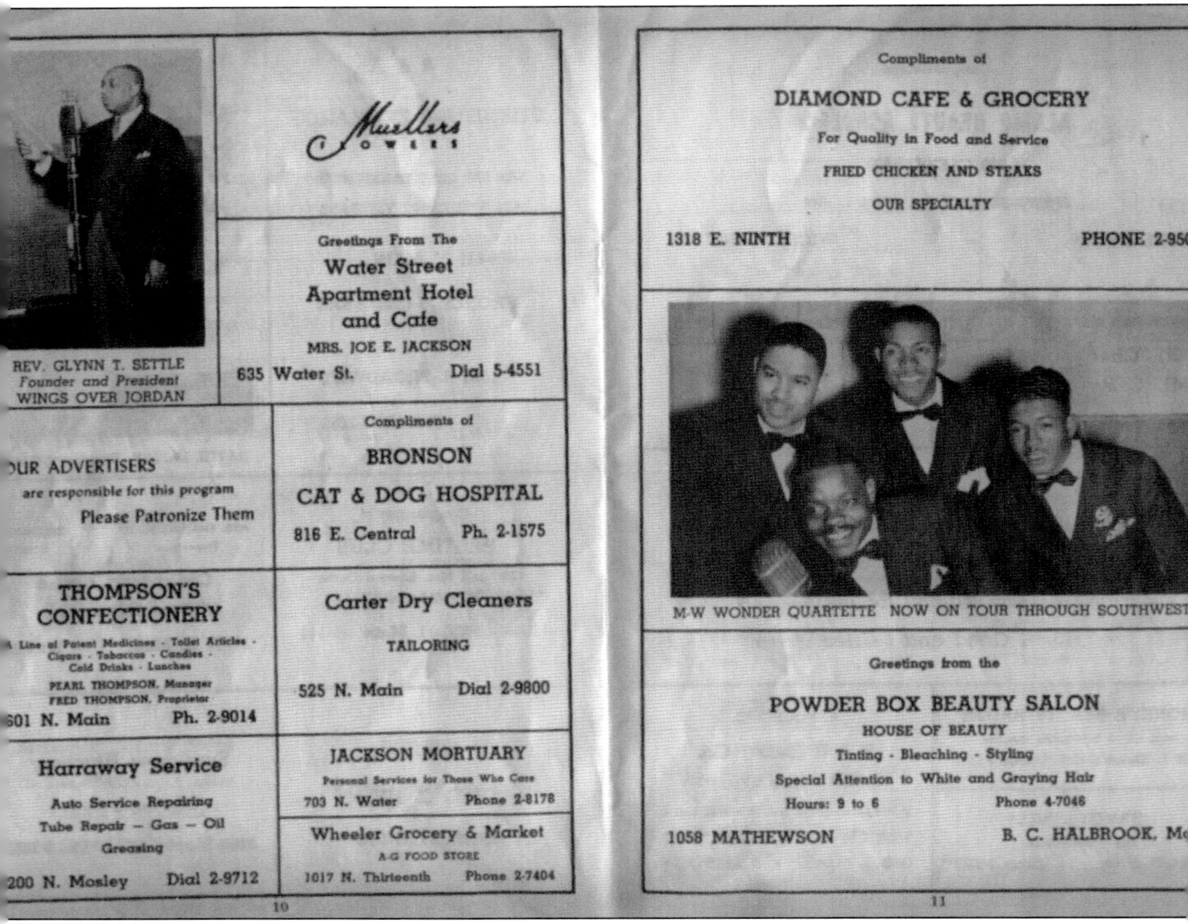
REV. GLYNN T. SETTLE
Founder and President
WINGS OVER JORDAN

Muellers
Flowers

Greetings From The
Water Street
Apartment Hotel
and Cafe
MRS. JOE E. JACKSON
635 Water St. Dial 5-4551

OUR ADVERTISERS
are responsible for this program
Please Patronize Them

Compliments of
BRONSON
CAT & DOG HOSPITAL
816 E. Central Ph. 2-1575

THOMPSON'S
CONFECTIONERY
A Line of Patent Medicines - Toilet Articles - Cigars - Tobaccos - Candies - Cold Drinks - Lunches
PEARL THOMPSON, Manager
FRED THOMPSON, Proprietor
601 N. Main Ph. 2-9014

Carter Dry Cleaners
TAILORING
525 N. Main Dial 2-9800

Harraway Service
Auto Service Repairing
Tube Repair — Gas — Oil
Greasing
200 N. Mosley Dial 2-9712

JACKSON MORTUARY
Personal Services for Those Who Care
703 N. Water Phone 2-8178

Wheeler Grocery & Market
A-G FOOD STORE
1017 N. Thirteenth Phone 2-7404

10

Compliments of
DIAMOND CAFE & GROCERY
For Quality in Food and Service
FRIED CHICKEN AND STEAKS
OUR SPECIALTY
1318 E. NINTH PHONE 2-950

M-W WONDER QUARTETTE NOW ON TOUR THROUGH SOUTHWEST

Greetings from the
POWDER BOX BEAUTY SALON
HOUSE OF BEAUTY
Tinting - Bleaching - Styling
Special Attention to White and Graying Hair
Hours: 9 to 6 Phone 4-7046
1058 MATHEWSON B. C. HALBROOK, M

11

The Rev. Glen T. Settles of Cleveland, Ohio, organized the Wings Over Jordan traveling African American chorus. This program is from a performance in Wichita, which took place at the close of World War II. The advertisements in the booklet provide insight into the businesses that served the African American community.

Among the activities of the NAACP was its "Don't Shop" campaign, which encouraged African Americans not to patronize stores that had discriminatory practices. (Courtesy Melody McCray Miller.)

STOP! Before You Shop!

The NAACP general membership adopted a resolution Sunday, Nov. 26, that had been previously passed by the executive committee, urging Negroes and other concerned citizens to be selective in their buying and that downtown retail stores (possessing a sizeable workforce) should not be patronized if Negroes are not employed in sales and as cashiers.

A survey taken December 1, 1962 showed the following:

Stores that do not hire Negro clerks or cashiers

Thurston's
220 E. Douglas
Buck's
300 E. Douglas
The Model
121 E. Douglas
Askin Credit Clt.
402 E. Douglas
Kress
224 E. Douglas
Woolworth
205 E. Douglas
S. G. Holmes
120 E. Douglas
The Model
Parklane
Henry's
Suburban
Thurston's
Parklane
Factory Outlet
SHOE STORE
118 E. Douglas
Croney's
Ladies Ready-To-Wear
123 E. Douglas
Wolf Bros.
127 E. Douglas
W. T. Grant—5c-10c
STORE
201 E. Douglas
Lerner's
Ladies & Girls' Ready-to-Wear
212 E. Douglas
Helzberg's Jewelry
219 E. Douglas
Lewin's
Downtown—223 E. Douglas
Twin Corners—Eastgate
Martin's Ladies
Wearing Apparel
309 E. Douglas
Gay Clothing
319 E. Douglas
Hall's
Credit Clothing—320 E. Douglas
Davis Clothing
418 E. Douglas
Fair Shoe
Store Downtown—135 N. Broadway
Long's Shoe Store
110 S. Broadway
Walker Bros.
123 N. Main
Baker's Shoe Store
217 E. Douglas

Stores that hire Negro clerks or cashiers

Innes
121 S. Broadway
Henry's (Downtown)
J. C. Penney
132 N. Broadway
Harvey Bros.
(Richman)
122 E. Douglas
Sears Roebuck
901 Geo. Washington Blvd.
Montgomery Ward
401 E. Douglas
Zales
318 E. Douglas
Levitts Jewelers
222 E. Douglas
Gateway
Sporting Goods
323 E. Douglas

Don't put your money in cash registers, that your hands cannot ring.

"WE WANT EQUAL JOB OPPORTUNITIES"

Buy Selectively — They Hire Selectively

The Wichita Branch N.A.A.C.P.

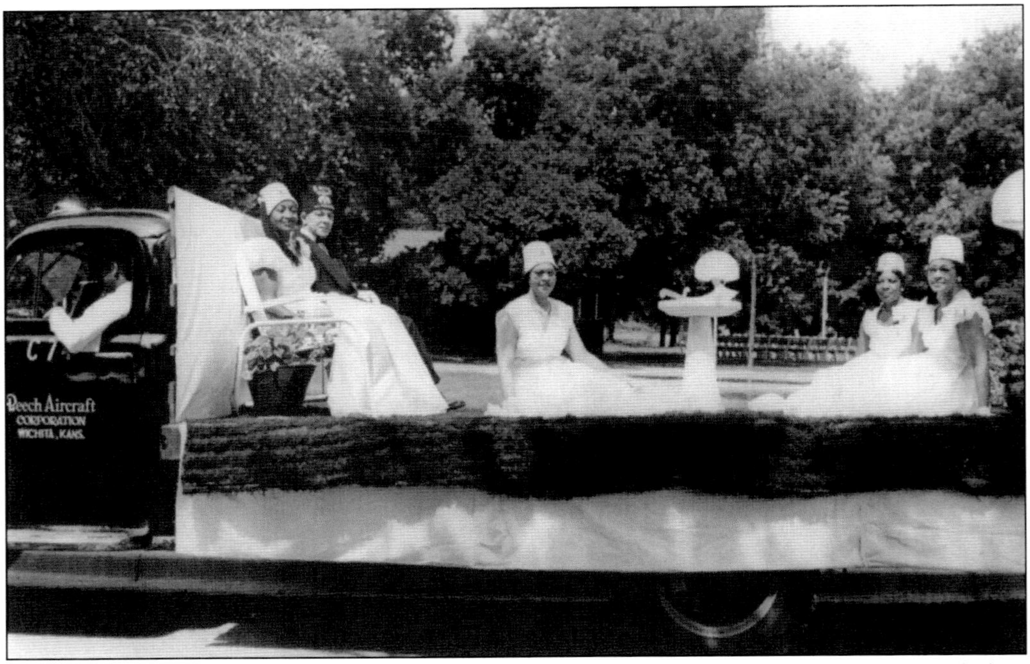

In the postwar years, America was known as a "nation of joiners." National organizations, including the Masons, were usually segregated—resulting in the formation of African American parallel groups, such as the Ancient Egyptian Arabic Order Nobles Mystic Shrine. Seen here is the float of the AEAONMS Emith Temple 30 in 1944. Loretta Buckner is in the chair.

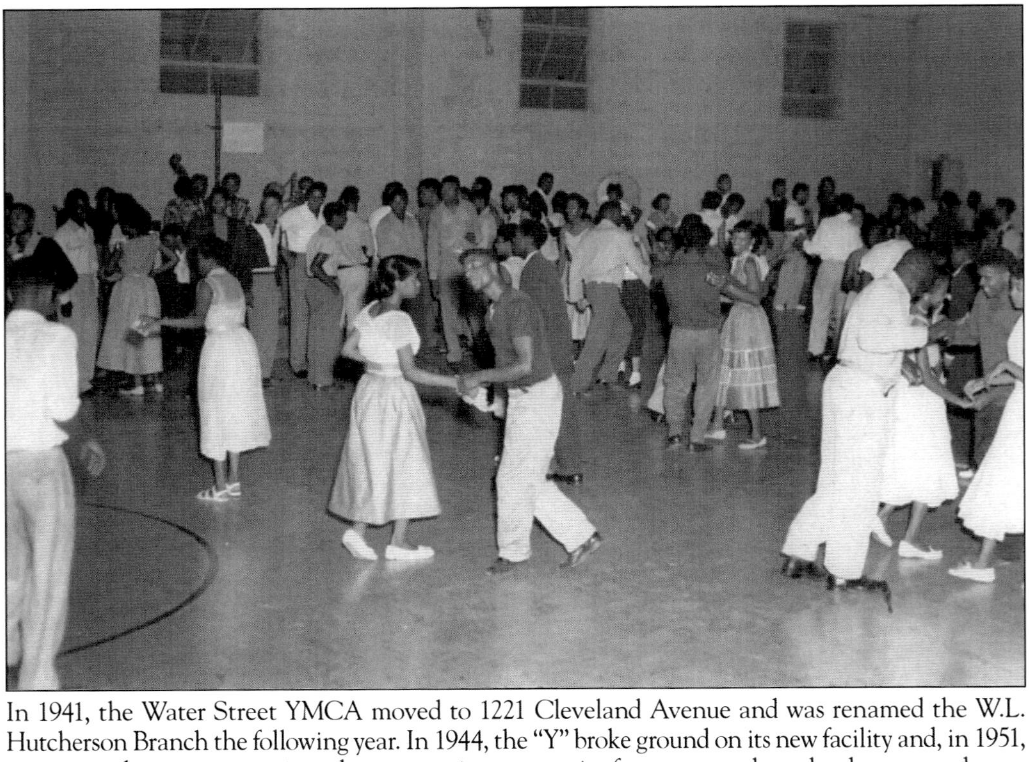

In 1941, the Water Street YMCA moved to 1221 Cleveland Avenue and was renamed the W.L. Hutcherson Branch the following year. In 1944, the "Y" broke ground on its new facility and, in 1951, constructed a new gymnasium that was an important site for events such as the dance seen here.

Vivian Curtis, née Parks, was a college-educated stay-at-home mom and a leader in the Girl Scouts and the YWCA. She became the first female president of the Wichita NAACP in 1956 and organized a citywide conference to examine institutional racism. She met with the police chief to protest discriminatory practices and was a founder of the women's interracial Community Committee on Social Action (CCSA), which visited restaurants seeking equal treatment. (Courtesy Carol Parks Hahn.)

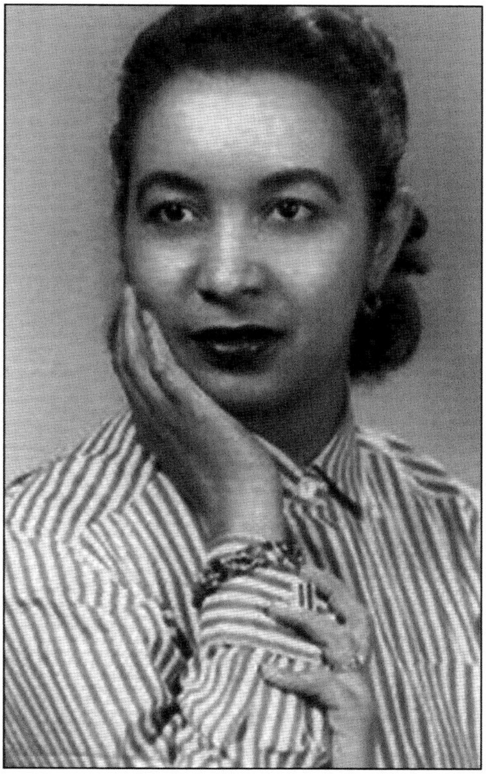

In 1956, Wichita had nine African American attorneys. Seven of them appear here. From left to right are Fred Helm, John Pyles, Theo Gardiner, Judge Howard Kline, Ambrose P. Woodard Sr., Robert Watson, Ben Brown, and Roscoe Austin. (Courtesy St. Martin's Press, New York.)

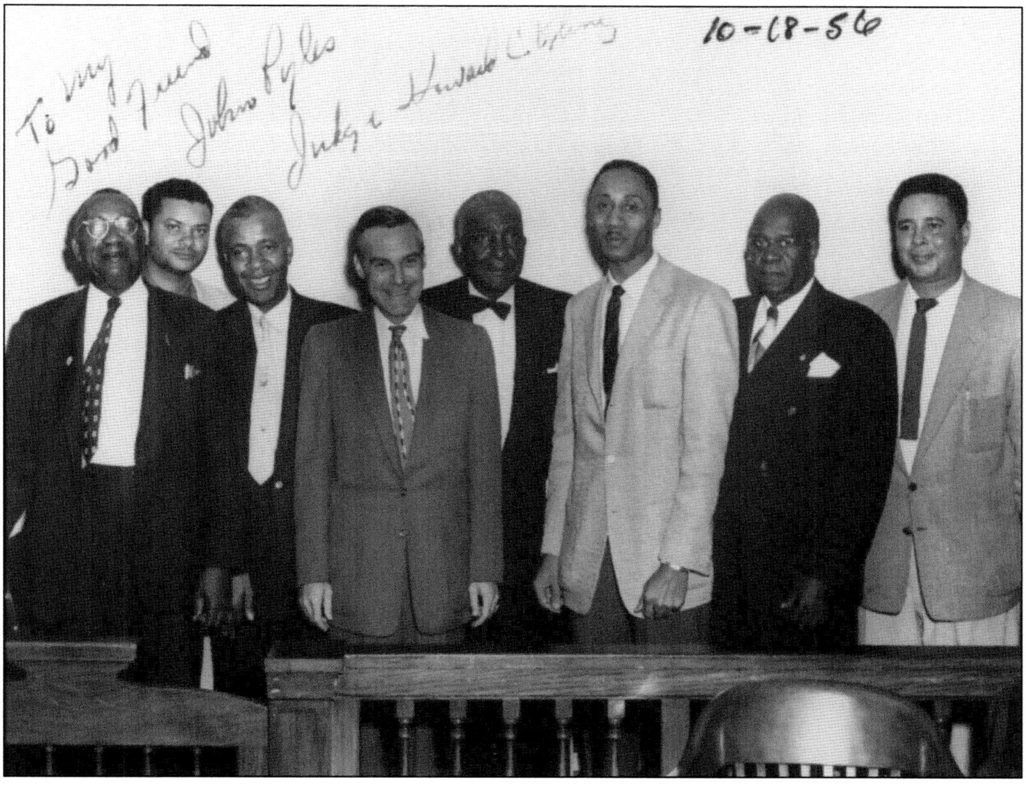

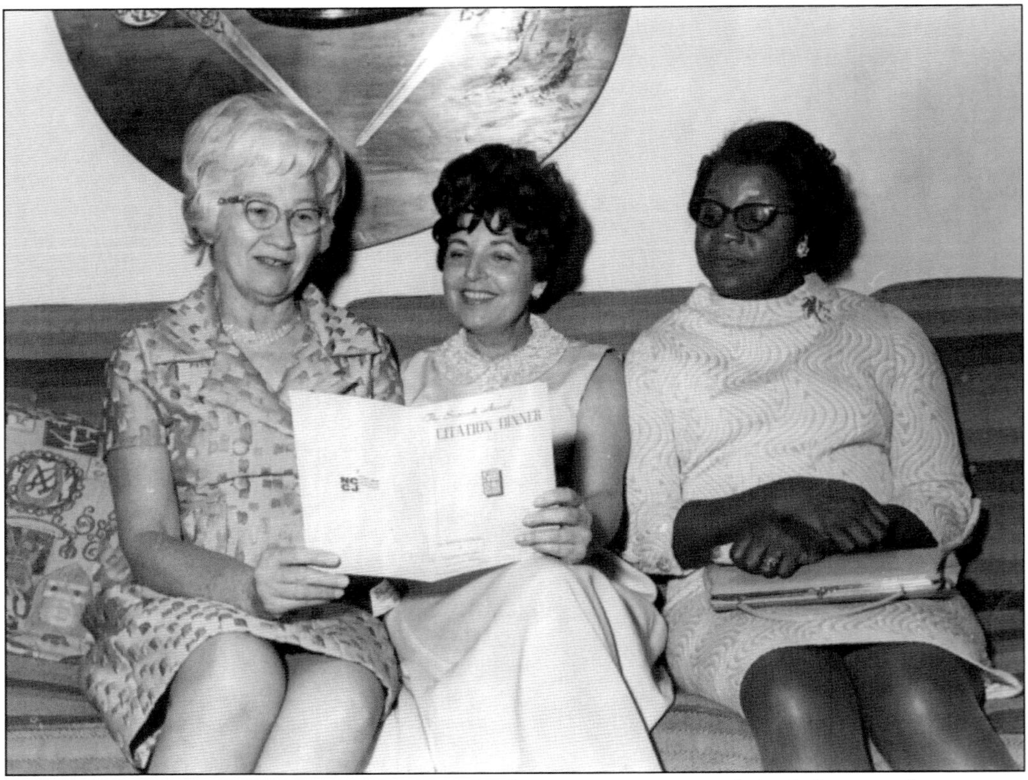

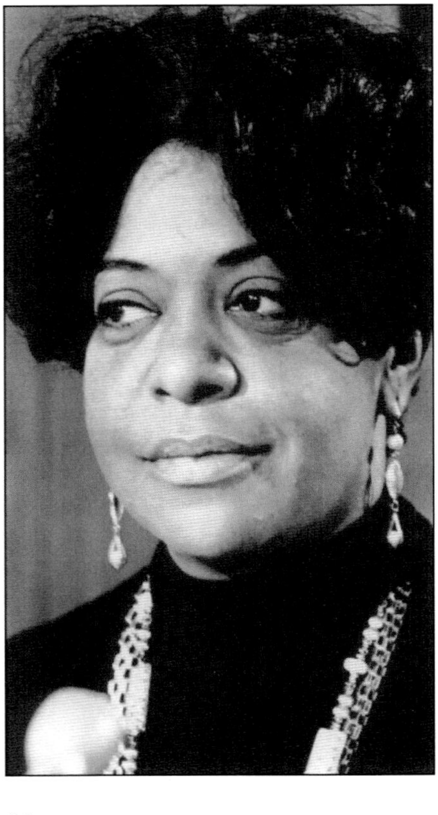

CCSA women monitored the behavior of restaurant wait staff toward persons of color from 1956 to 1963—meeting with management to politely insist on equal treatment. The Council of Churches distributed CCSA labels to attach to bill payments, which told businesses not to discriminate. From left to right, Annabelle Haupt, Esther Brown (of Kansas City), and Anita Burney plan a presentation they took to towns across Kansas, combating racism through their Panel of American Women. (Courtesy Annabelle Haupt.)

Many black women with college degrees were denied access to teaching jobs, including the mother of Chester I. Lewis Jr. Hired in 1957, Jeanne Ponds was the area's first black high school teacher and taught at East High. (Courtesy Calotta Ponds.)

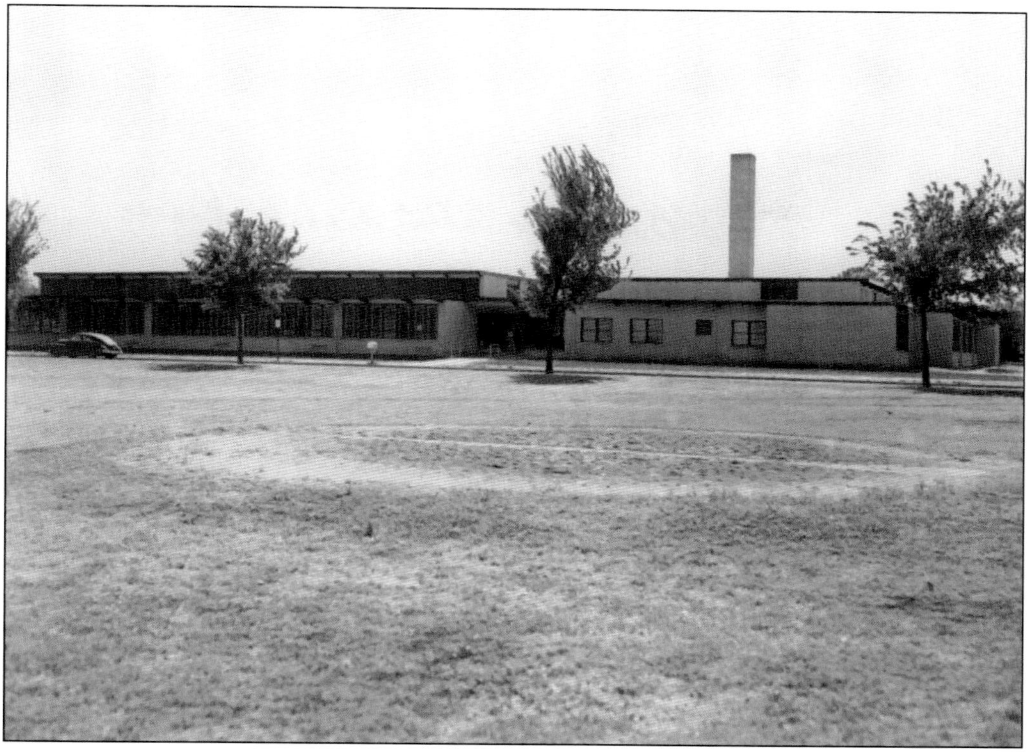

L'Ouverture School still serves Wichita today, but not in its original building. The original school at Thirteenth and Mosley Streets was demolished after the new school, at 1539 North Ohio, was built in 1951. It was named for the great Haitian general Toussaint L'Ouverture, whose slave rebellion ousted French colonialists in the first decade of the 1800s.

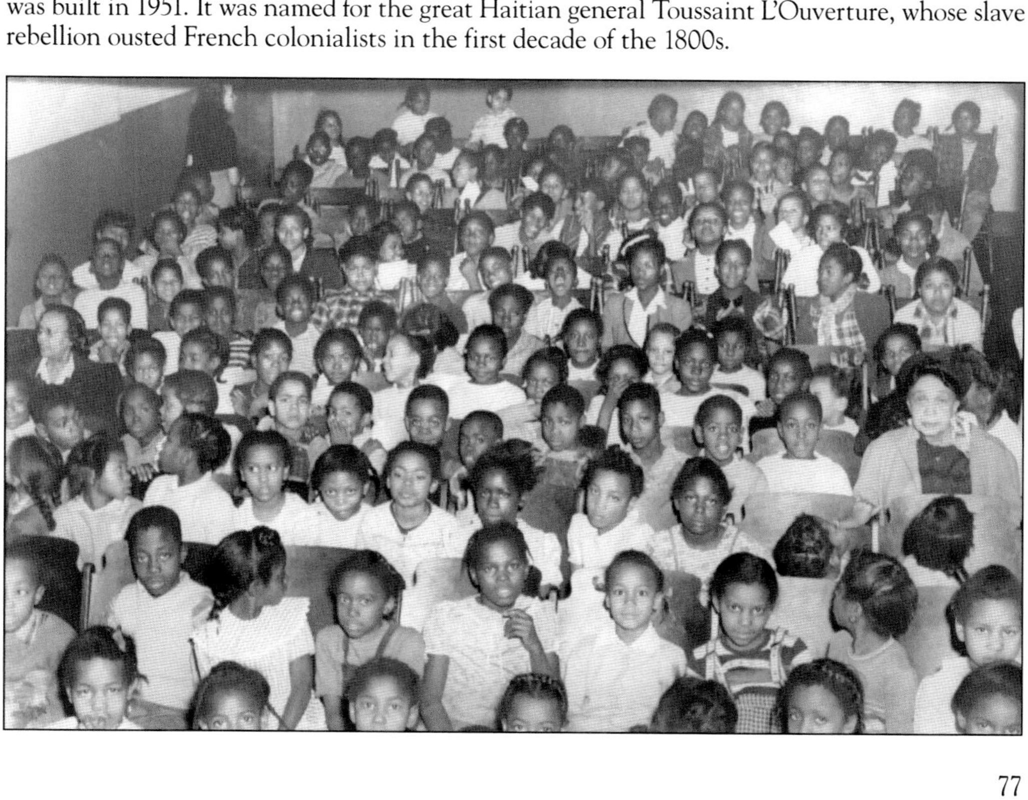

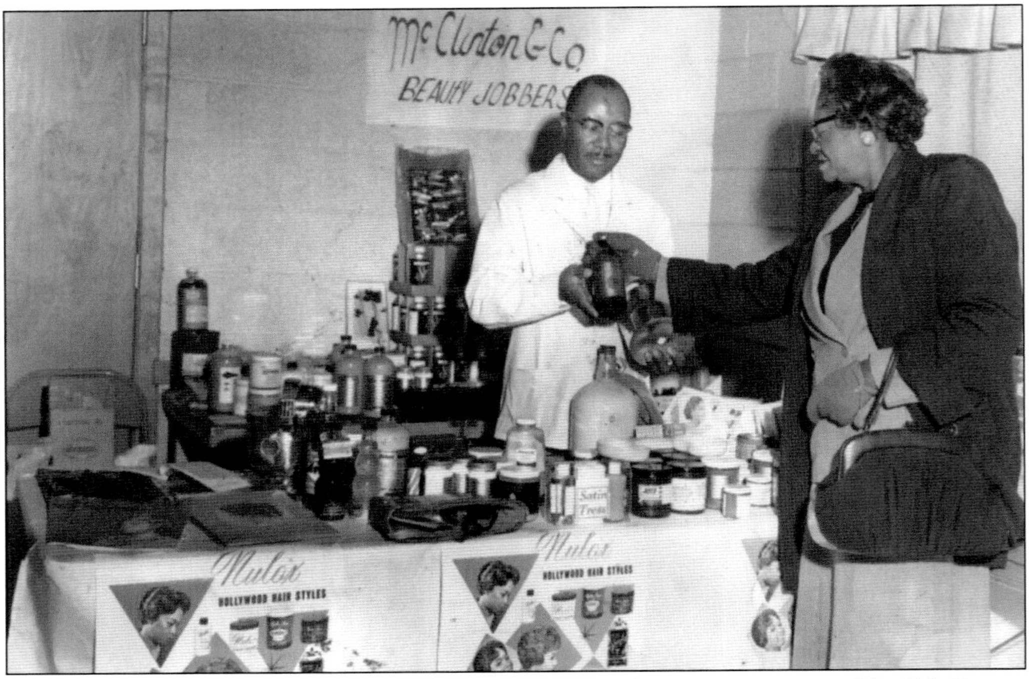

From 1943 through 1973, Curtis McClinton Sr. operated a grocery store on Twelfth Street. McClinton was elected to the Kansas House in 1956—the first African American from outside the Kansas City area to serve—and, after two terms, to the Senate. He was later defeated in his 1968 reelection bid. He lectured his colleagues as he tried to win their support for his amendment outlawing discrimination in hotels, motels, camps, and restaurants, saying, "the Pursuit of Happiness does not mean whites getting their happiness by pursuing blacks." The Dew Drop Inn, seen below, was another popular local hangout.

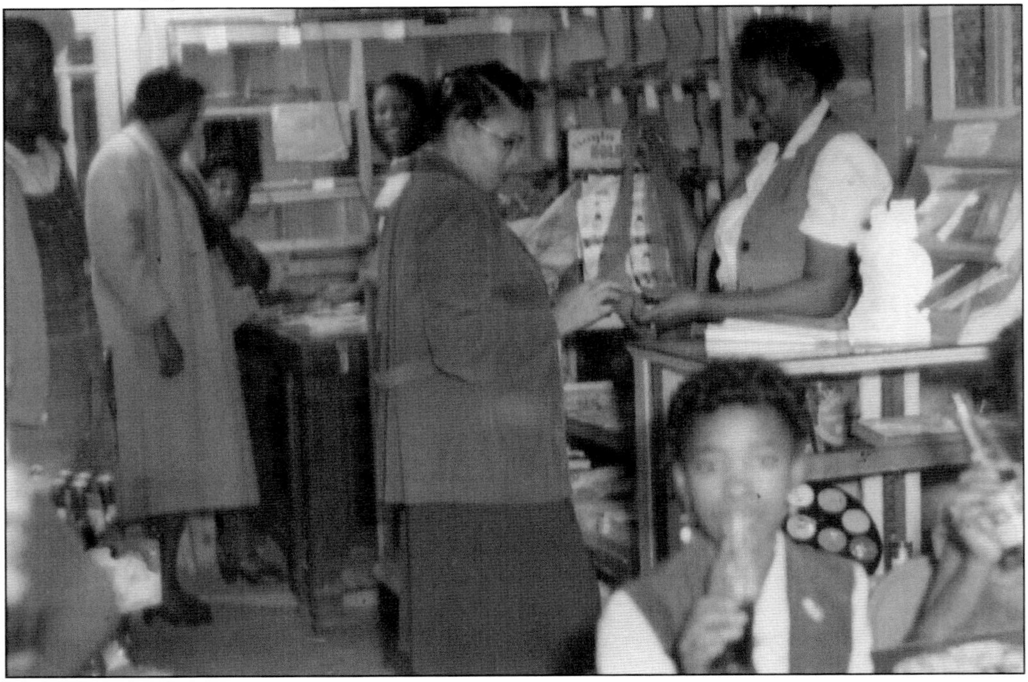

Henry Wofford was one of the few African Americans to be active in the oil industry. Wofford serviced oil wells in the surrounding counties of Reno, Rice, and Butler. His Wichita-based company operated Africo Explorations, which sought new oil fields to drill. Heavy financial losses, resulting from oil production that did not meet projections, caused the company to declare bankruptcy in 1986 after nearly 30 years in business.

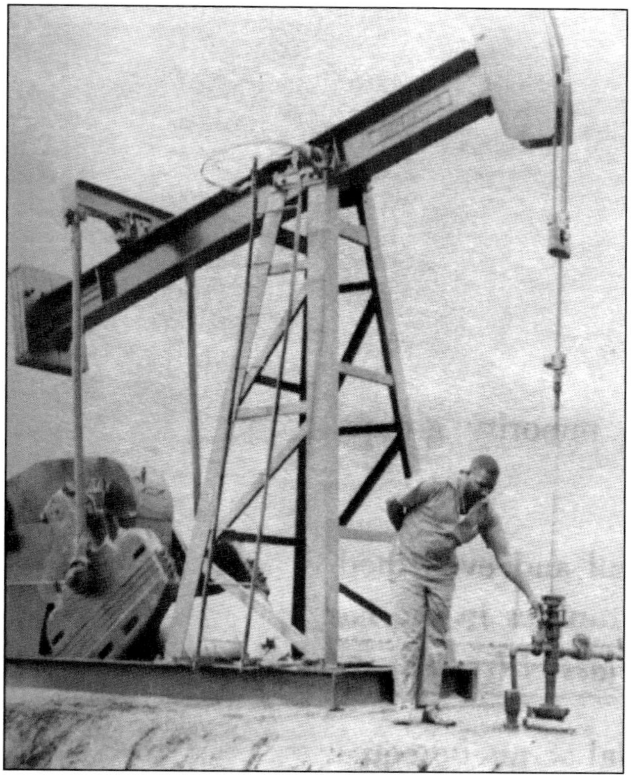

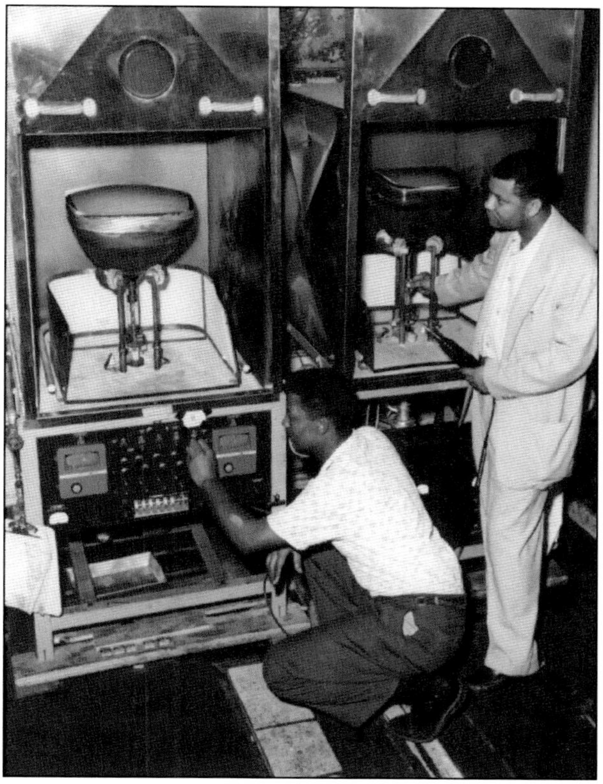

The arrival of television resulted in businesses that sold and repaired television sets. Talmadge Walters operated one of these radio and television repair shops. Here, two young men identified as Mr. Estes and Mr. Pyle are at work in the store. In addition to being a successful businessman, Walters was also an influential supporter of the Hutcherson Branch of the YMCA.

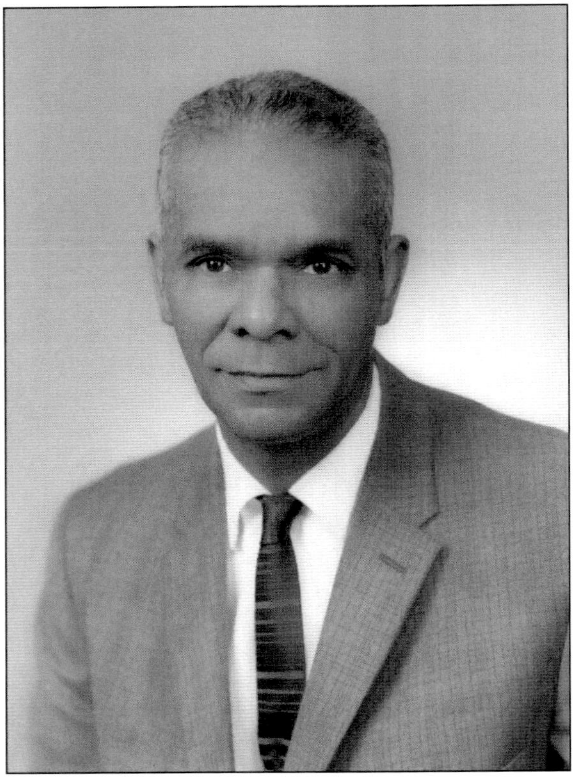

Dentist Hugh N. Sims ran for an open seat on the school board in 1947, and again in 1949. He became the first African American to serve on the board. He and Edwana Collins, a white woman, persuaded the board to allow some black families to choose whether to attend a predominantly white or predominantly black school. Sims was the uncle of Gloria McAfee, who later became a teacher and principal. (Courtesy Charles McAfee.)

Rosie Hughes and her husband, Leon, were photographers as well as aircraft industry workers. In 1958, she advised the NAACP youth council that held the first successful, student-led sit-in of the civil rights movement. The Hughes collection of photographs is available online through the University of Kansas's Spencer Research Library. (Courtesy Rosie Hughes.)

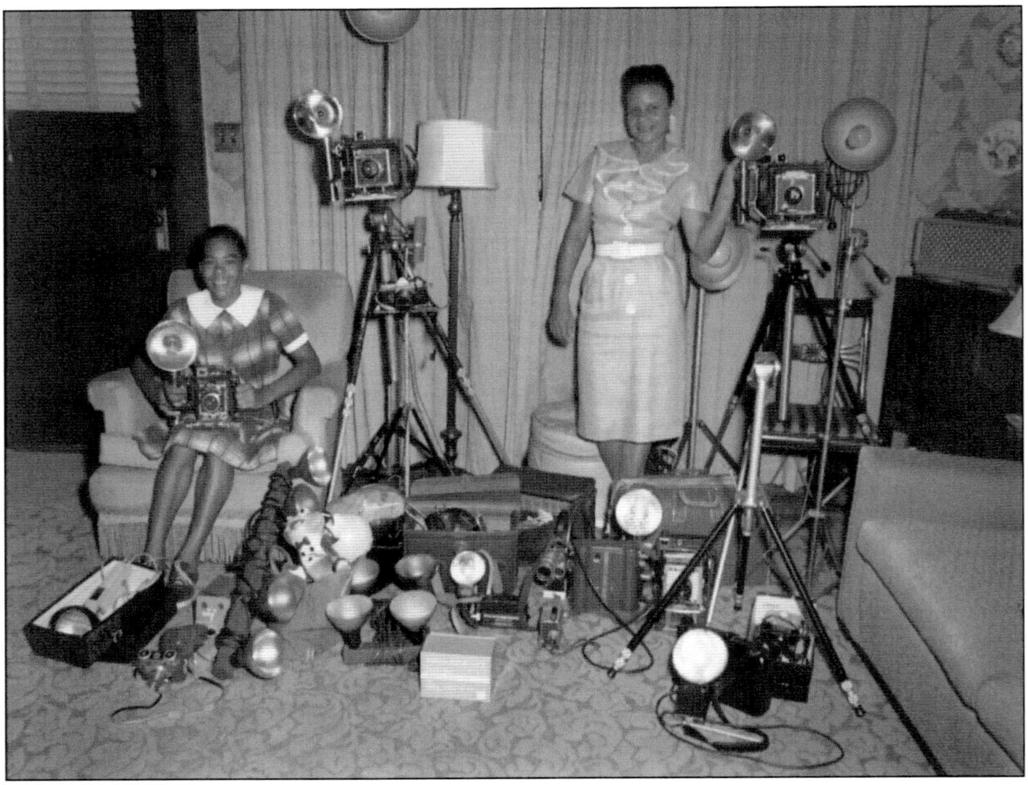

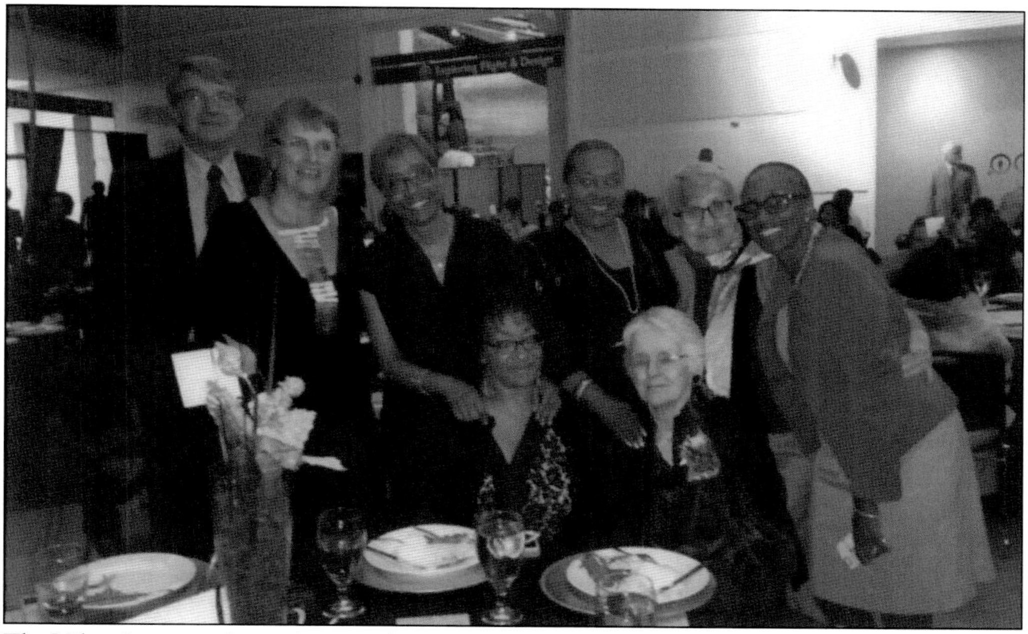

The Urban League, a biracial national organization, encouraged white-owned businesses to practice equal employment and combat discrimination. In 1954, Floyd Watson Jr., Steven Worth, and Fern Van Gieson formed an Urban League chapter in Wichita and got the Community Chest to fund it. Here, Fern (front right) and Floyd Watson's daughters (center) celebrate at a November 2014 event where she was honored as a Trailblazer.

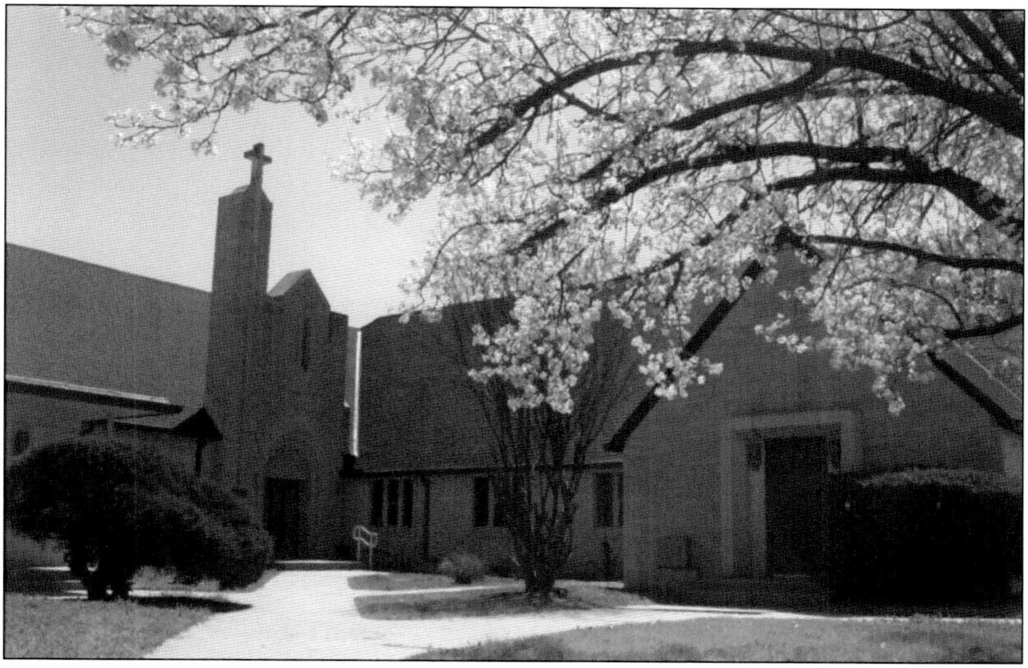

The city's decision to build a new county courthouse in the middle of what had been the black community forced the oldest black churches—St. Paul AME, Tabernacle Baptist, and Calvary Baptist—to relocate from the West End. St. Paul and Tabernacle moved to then-white neighborhoods near Grove Street.

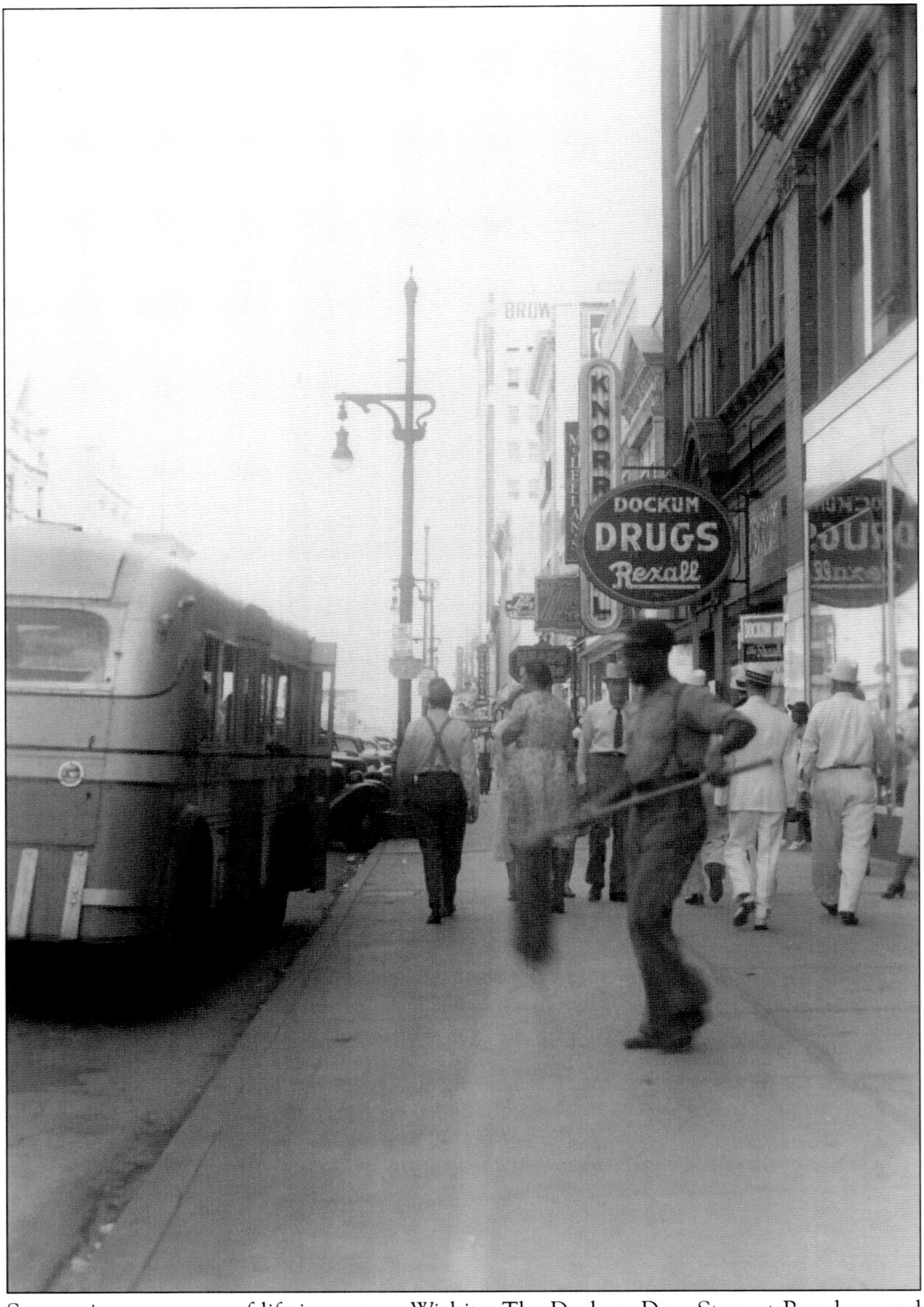

Segregation was a way of life in postwar Wichita. The Dockum Drug Store at Broadway and Douglas Avenue refused service to African Americans except at a take-out window. (Courtesy Wichita–Sedgwick County Historical Museum and Rosie Hughes.)

Four

Challenging the System

Wichita's NAACP youth led the nation's first successful student-led sit-in in 1958. Over the next decade, protests accelerated, and by 1964, discrimination in employment, education, and public accommodations because of race, color, religion, national origin, or gender was a federal crime. By 1965, interference with the rights to vote or register to vote was a federal crime. These laws were passed in part due to Wichita churches, unions, and the NAACP, and the murder of white, Wichita-born Universalist Unitarian minister Rev. James Reeb in Selma, Alabama.

In 1964, the federal War on Poverty began funneling dollars and jobs into the city. Enforcement of these laws required vigilant monitoring. As housing segregation continued, most African Americans lived in Northeast Wichita—assigned to all-black elementary schools and Mathewson Junior High. In 1967, Chester Lewis's documentation of this school segregation resulted in the first federal investigation of school segregation in the Midwest.

In 1967, frustrated over rising expectations and overly aggressive policing in Northeast Wichita, youths acted out by throwing rocks and bottles. African American city commissioner A. Price Woodard, who was the acting mayor, mediated an end to the conflict. It resumed a few days later after returning mayor Clarence Vollmer re-imposed a curfew and deployed 100 police officers against a group of black youths, arresting 26. Bonds were set for $1,500, and those found guilty received 30-day jail sentences. A year later, three white men shot a young black man in Northeast Wichita and violence resumed. The mayor called in 400 national guardsmen to patrol Northeast Wichita with tanks, and 95 people were arrested for curfew violations for which they were charged $2,500 in bail or were sent to the prison farm. Meanwhile, black consciousness emerged at Wichita State University, thanks to a new Black Studies program, new black faculty, African American book and clothing stores, and the annual Black Arts Festival—launched in 1968. The Kansas African American Museum soon followed.

All this change was not easy. Social access was coming to the black community through sports, music, politics, and civic service. However, access's twin, alienation, continued to rear its head as the FBI planted paid informers among Black Nationalists, angry black youths were frequently incarcerated, and the school board proved resistant to desegregating.

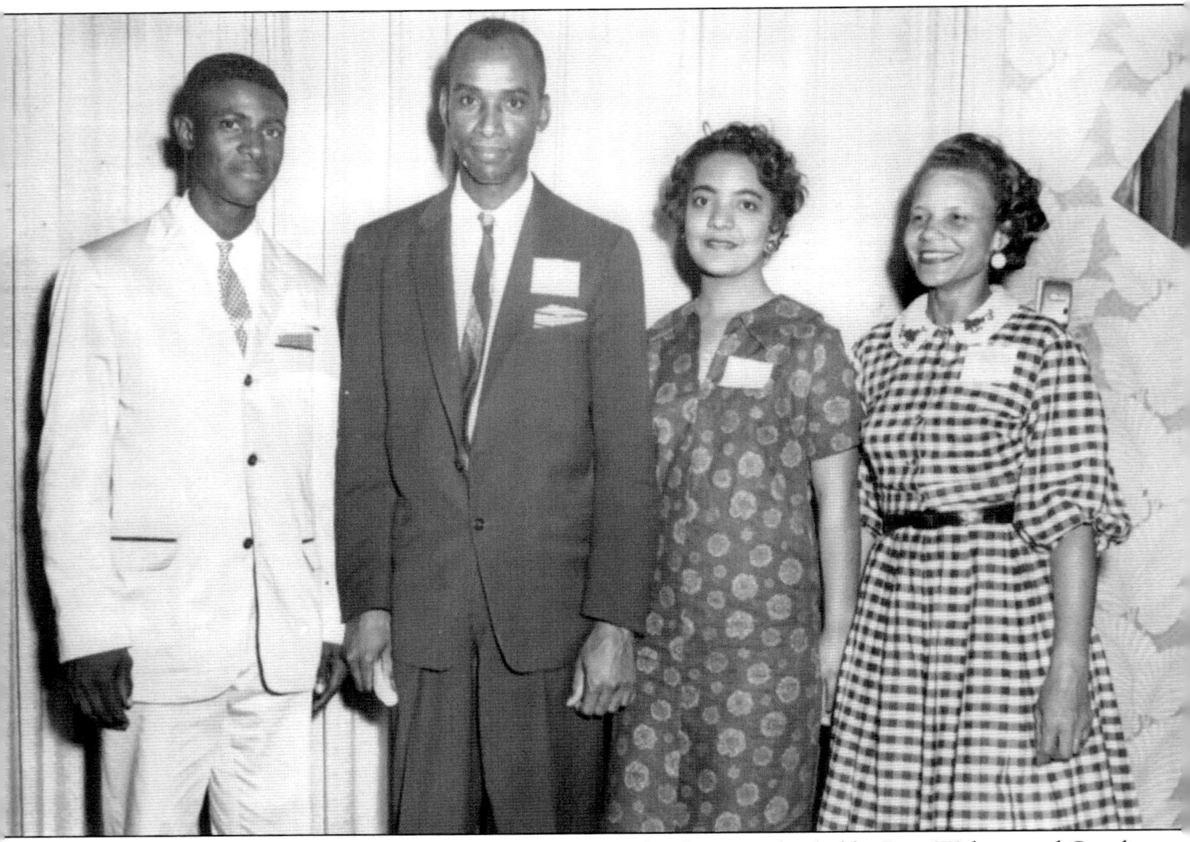

NAACP youths sat in at the Dockum Drug Store for three weeks, led by Ron Walters and Carol Hahn, née Parks. The national NAACP opposed the effort, but the local chapter supported the youths. Three weeks after the protest began, on August 11, 1958, that store agreed to desegregate. The Rexall chain—the nation's largest and to which Dockum's belonged—then agreed to desegregate all of its stores nationwide. It was the first successful student-led sit-in of the civil rights movement. Pictured here are, from left to right, Ron Walters, Hervie Wright of the national NAACP, Carol Parks, and their advisor Rosie Hughes. (Courtesy Carol Parks Hahn.)

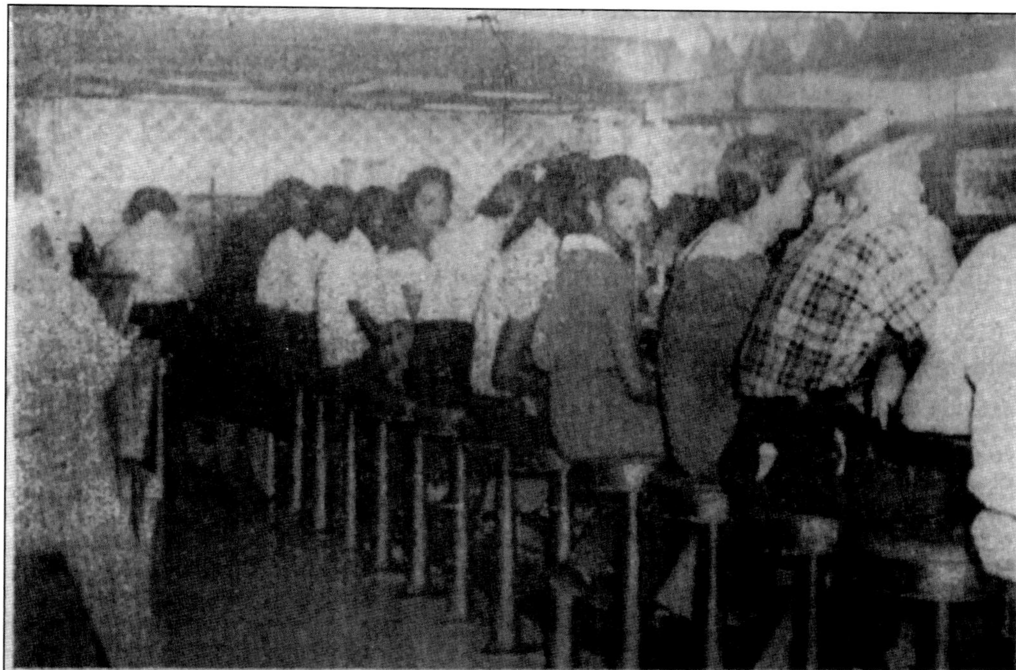

SEATED AT DOCKUM'S lunch counter in an attempt to break down the store's policy against Negroes eating at the lunch counter in the seating area are young members of the NAACP Youth Council. The above picture was taken before the entire group occupied the entire counter at Dockum's store on Douglas at Broadway. The occupation lasted till the store closed.

Youth Group Attempts Break In Discriminatoy Practices At Dockum Drug Store

Edwin Sexton's *The Enlightener* newspaper, which served the African American community, carried this photograph of the sit-in and publicized the protests that followed at stores that would not hire African Americans. It remains the only known image capturing the historic protest. Jo Gardenhire coordinated the campaign, which was supported by churches, fraternities and sororities, the NAACP, and Federated Colored Women's Clubs. When Sexton left to work for the Republican National Committee, Leonard Garrett's *News-Hawk* covered news not included in *The Wichita Eagle/Beacon*. Save for a single passing reference, neither of the city's two main papers covered the event for fear of alienating their large downtown advertisers. (Courtesy Arlene Harris Ruffin.)

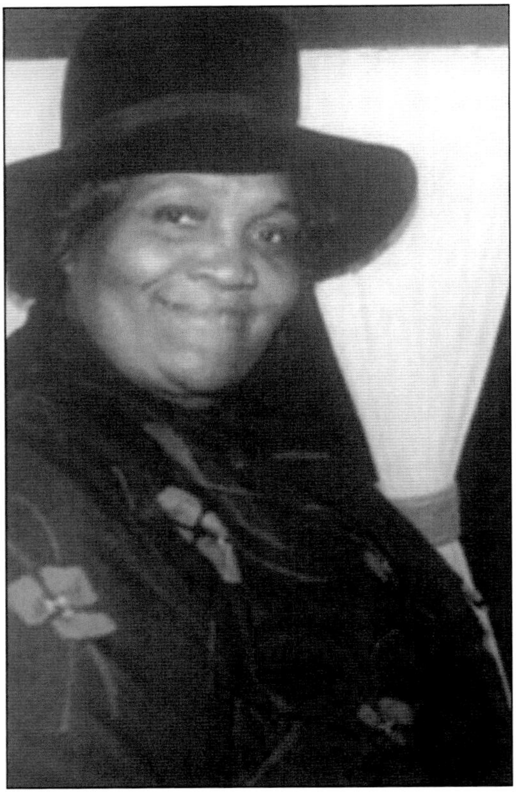

In 1964, Oretha Faust—the first person to receive the Martin Luther King Award in Wichita, for her activism—led a group to the National Welfare Rights Association March on Washington to lobby for anti-poverty legislation. Chester Lewis personally flew Wichitans to Washington, DC, to lobby for the Civil Rights Act of 1964. The Urban League's Hugh Jackson and Rev. Kelsey Jones, of the St. Matthew Christian Methodist Episcopal Church, joined Lewis in challenging discrimination in hiring and promotion at a state and city level.

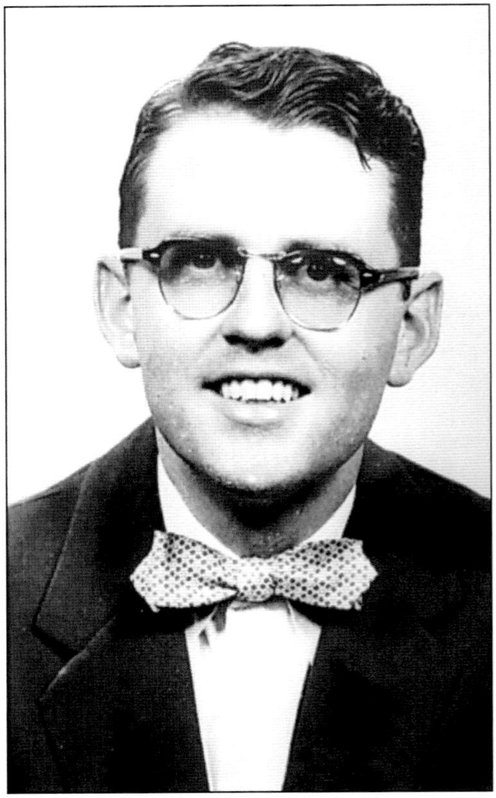

The Rev. James Reeb was a Wichita native who went on to become one of the most important and symbolic martyrs of the American civil rights movement. Reeb was a Universalist Unitarian minister who after watching the "Bloody Sunday" voting rights march in Selma, Alabama, went to Selma and marched. Segregationists beat Reeb not long after he arrived and he died days later from his injuries. Dr. Martin Luther King Jr. gave his eulogy.

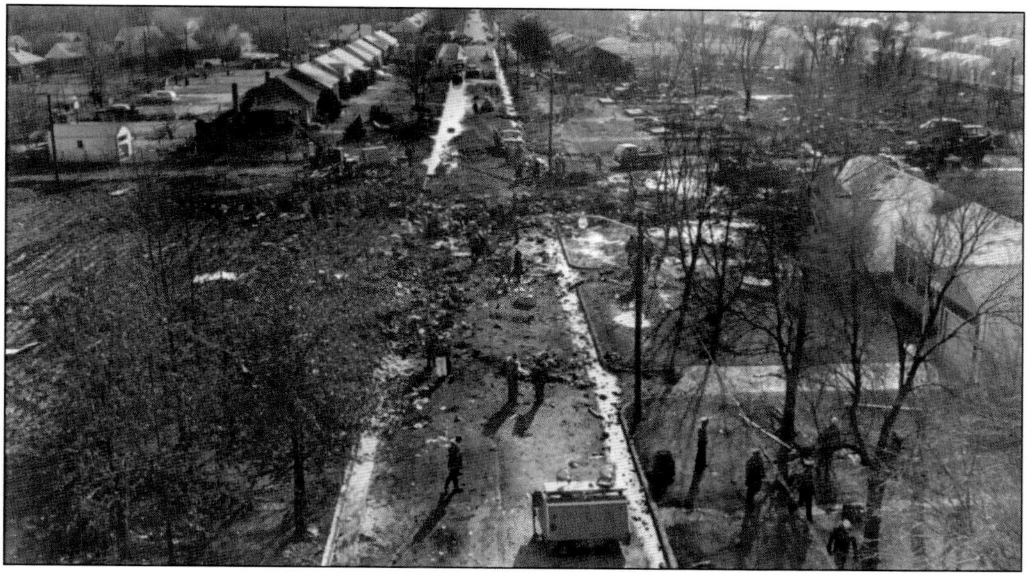

Families in Northeast Wichita woke on Saturday, January 16, 1965, to a scene from hell. A KC-135 tanker aircraft from McConnell Air Force Base—loaded with fuel—crashed into the neighborhood of Twentieth and Piatt Streets. The crash killed 23 residents and 7 crewmen, and the burning fuel consumed whole blocks of the community. It was the most devastating plane crash in Kansas's history. (Courtesy *The Wichita Eagle*.)

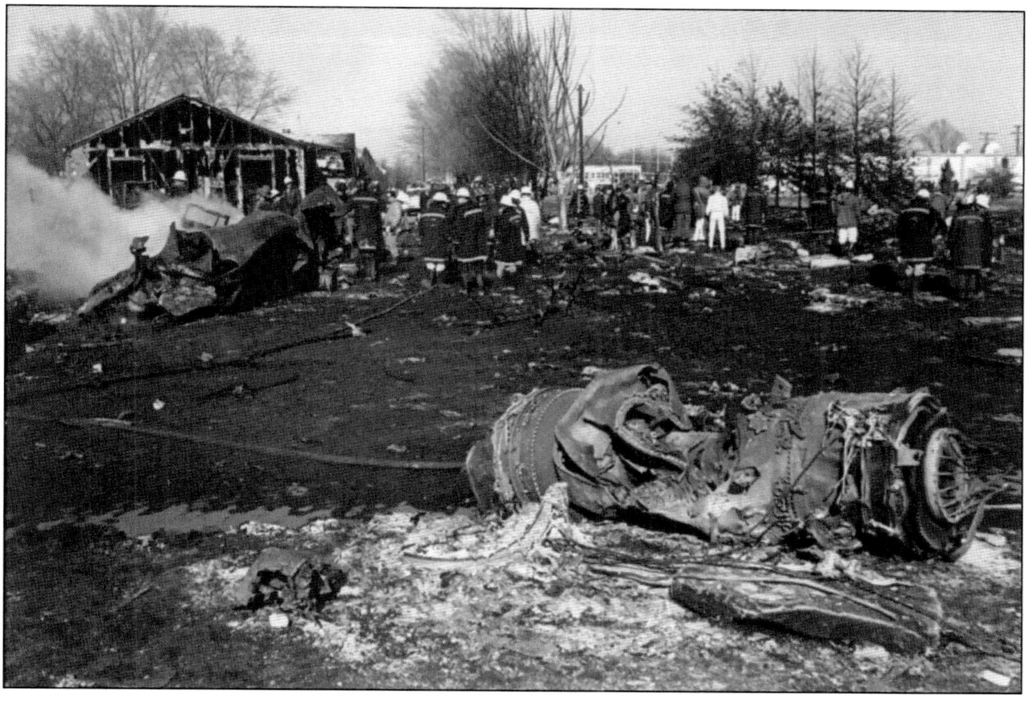

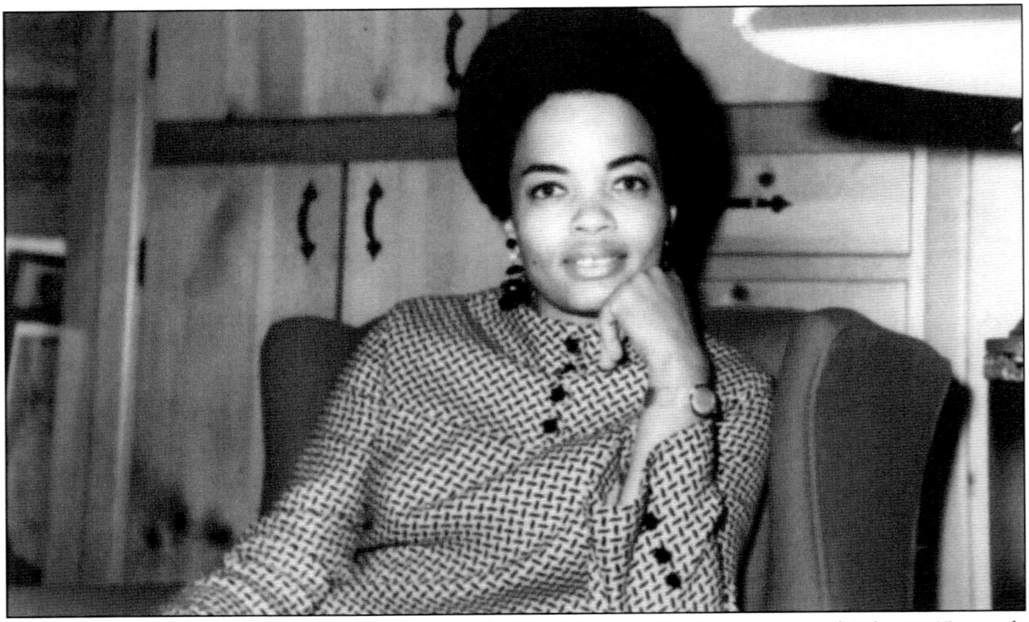

Vashti Lewis (above) chaired the effort to get the Fair Housing Ordinance passed. The 1965 march supporting an enforceable Fair Housing Ordinance was the largest demonstration in Wichita up to that time. Black families met resistance when they moved into previously white areas, as people burned crosses on their lawns, fired bullets into their homes, and denied them mortgages. After eight years of protest, an ordinance passed, leaving it up to the city attorney to decide whether or not to prosecute housing discrimination. It was replaced two years later by a weaker state law. (Both, courtesy Gretchen Eick and Spencer Research Library.)

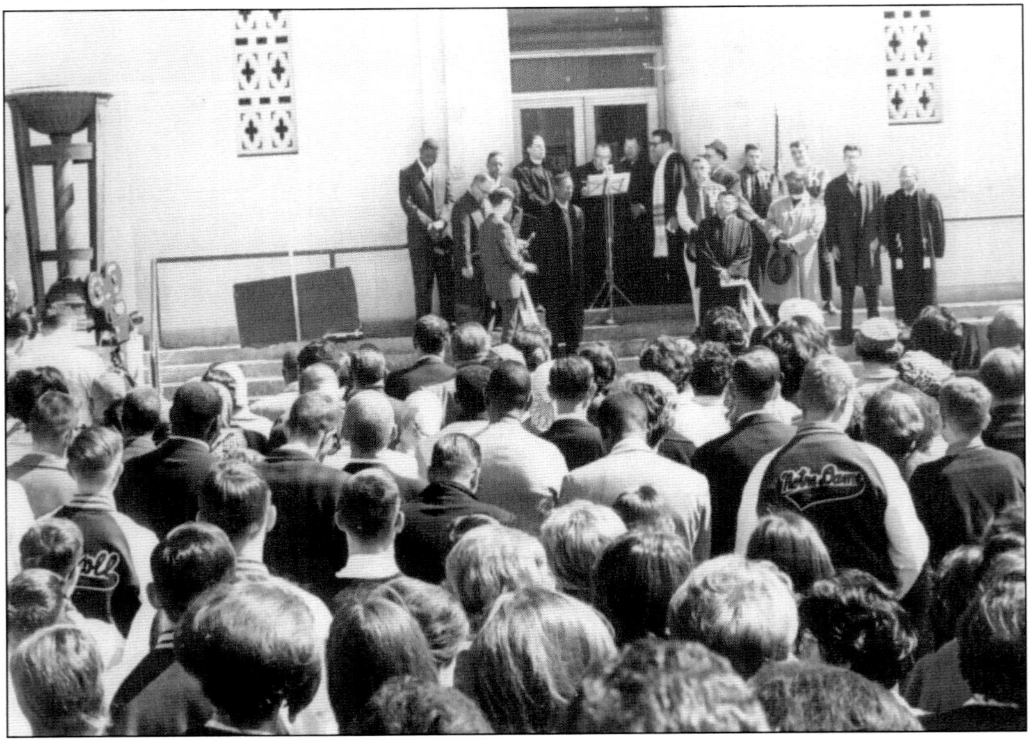

In 1965, East High enlarged its cheerleader squad from six to eight, including a black cheerleader—Anita Guidry, née Williams (far right). In 1966 and 1967, however, the school decided to reduce the squad to six again, all of whom were white. This precipitated a fight in the spring of 1967 at Sandy's Drive-In (below)—across from East High at Douglas Avenue and Grove Street. That month, an African American, Oscar Jones, was elected homecoming king at East and kissed the white queen, despite administrators telling him not to. (Both, courtesy *The Community Voice* and *The Wichita Eagle*.)

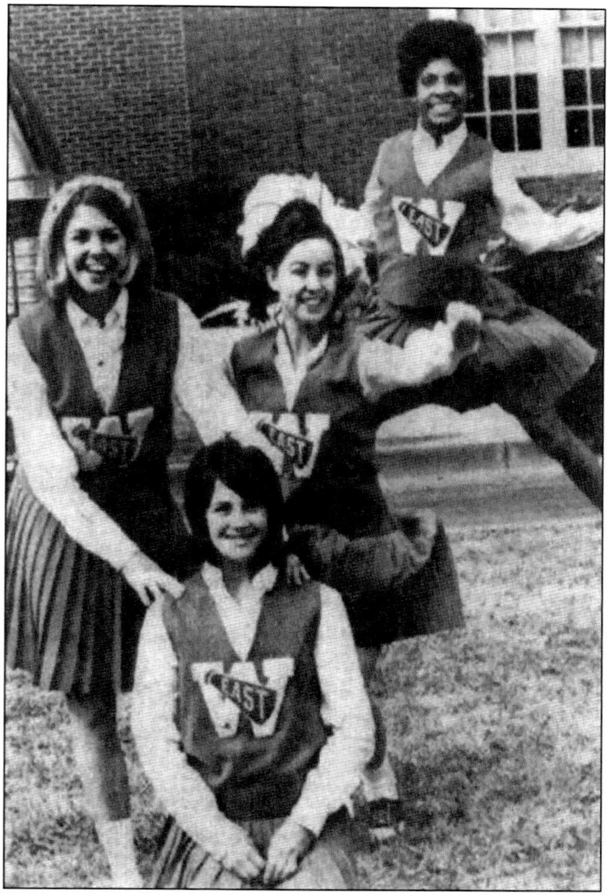

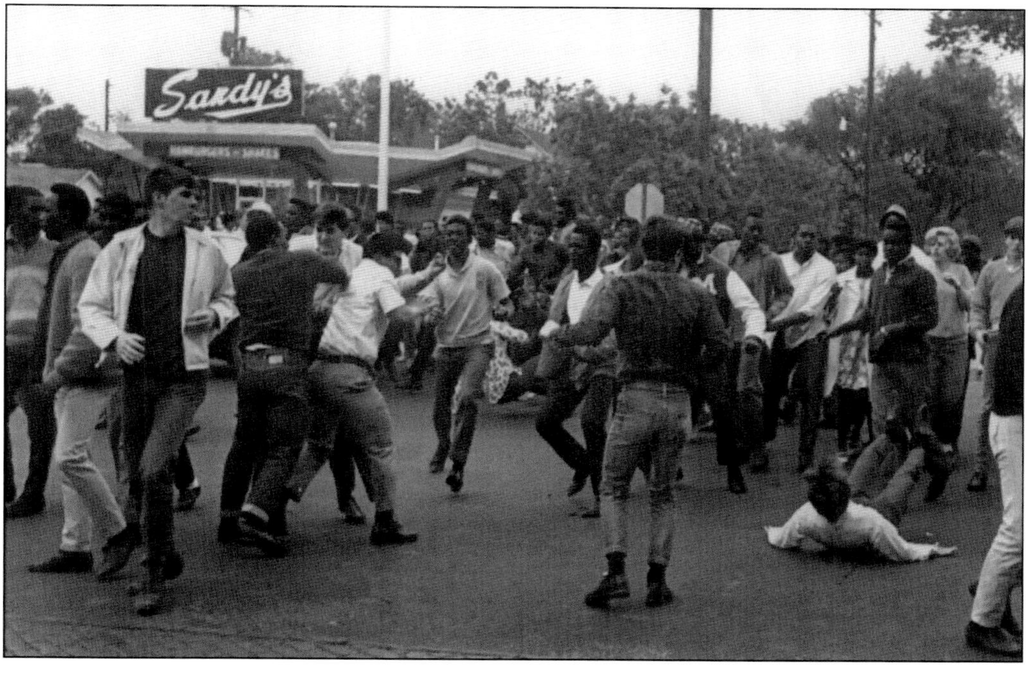

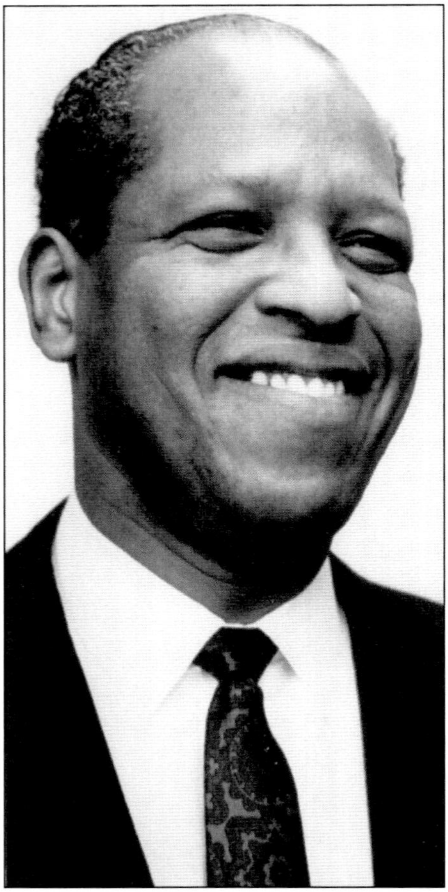

A. Price Woodard, a World War II veteran and attorney, had served on the school board and, in 1967, became the first African American elected to the city commission. Police confrontations with black youths on July 31 of that year resulted in Woodard, then the acting mayor, meeting with black youths (below) and calming the storm. After a second tense summer in 1968, the commission made Woodard mayor in 1970. He died a year later, at age 52.

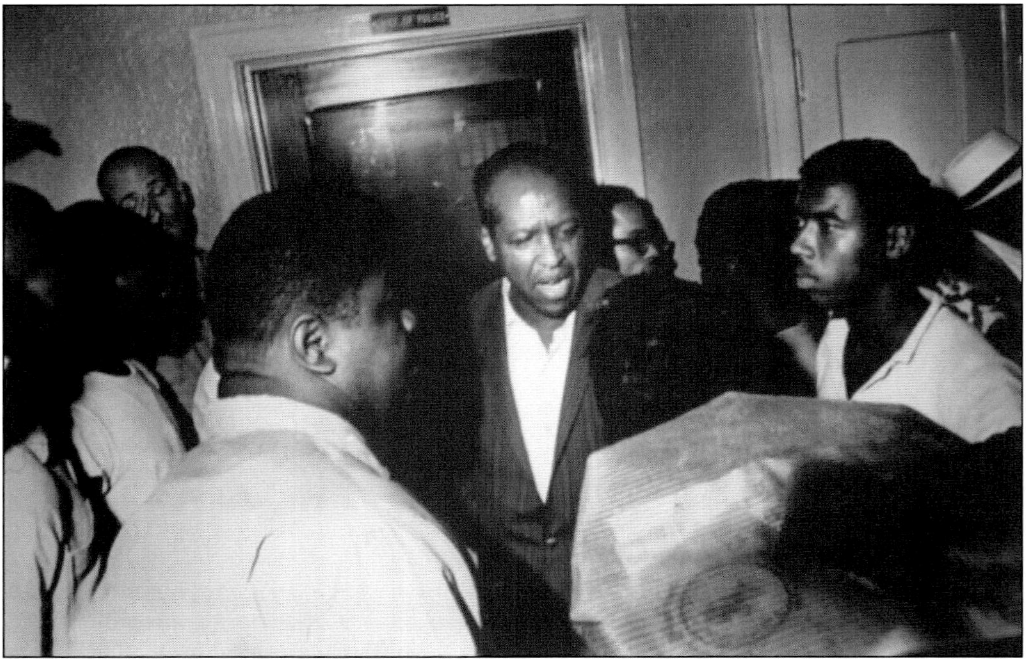

After the tensions of 1967, Police Chief Eugene Pond and Chester Lewis raised funds for a Northeast Patrol of black youths (pictured at right, with Lewis) to keep Northeast Wichita safe. St. Paul AME and New Hope Missionary Baptist built low-income housing, Calvary Baptist built a senior center, and St. Mark United Methodist built the MEFSEC community center. Lewis (below) raised funds for two Brothers' Supermarkets. (Both, courtesy *The Community Voice*.)

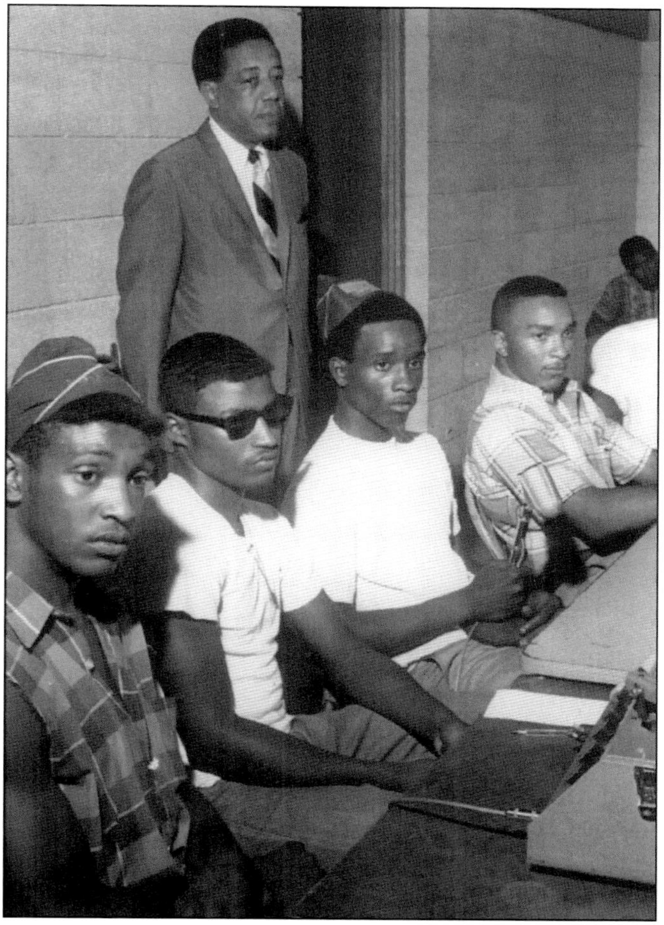

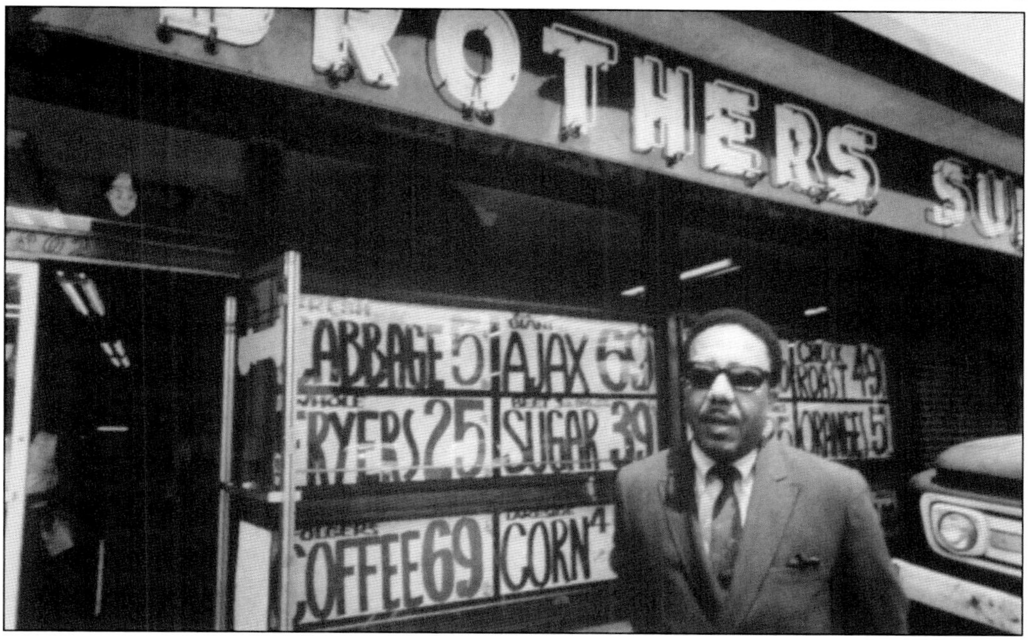

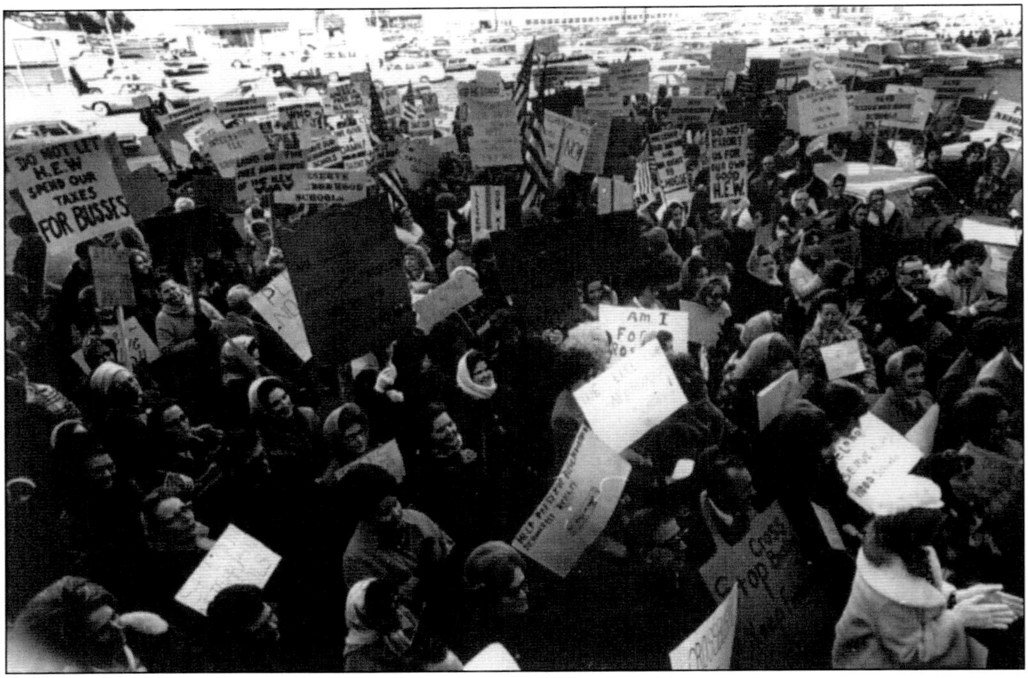

When the Supreme Court ruled school segregation unconstitutional in 1954, black children in Northeast Wichita attended schools with a student population that was 90 percent black (or higher), unless parents petitioned the superintendent on a case by case basis and provided transportation. In 1967, Chester Lewis's 300-page document on the issue triggered the first federal investigation of school segregation in the Midwest. In 1971, when Wichita was found to be in violation of the 14th Amendment and the Civil Rights Act of 1964, the school board agreed to bus black students out of Northeast Wichita. (Above, courtesy *The Wichita Eagle*.)

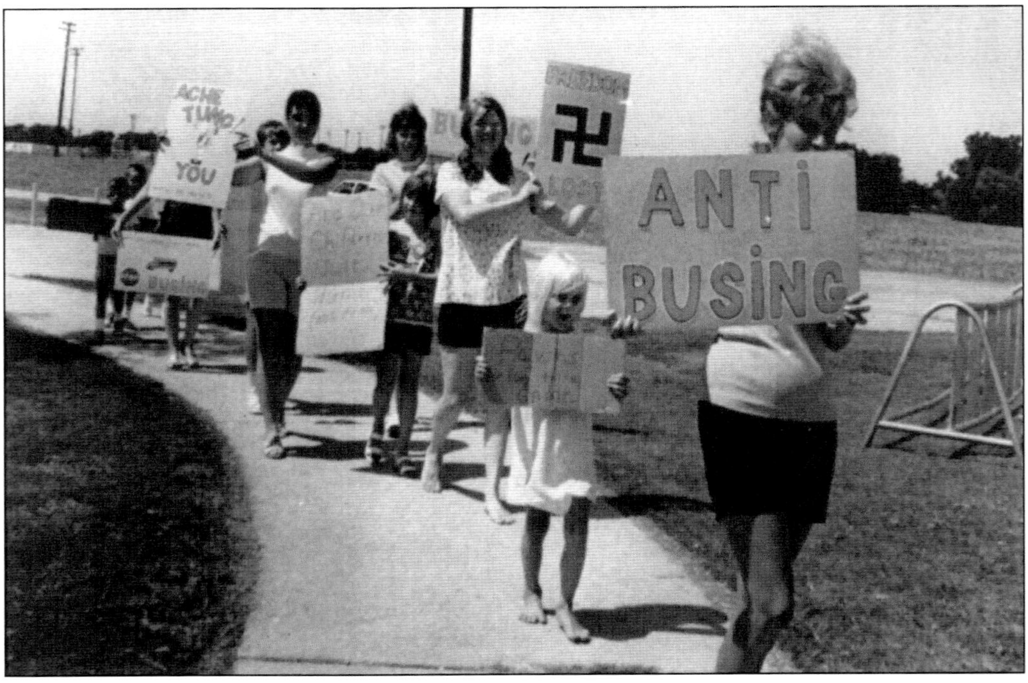

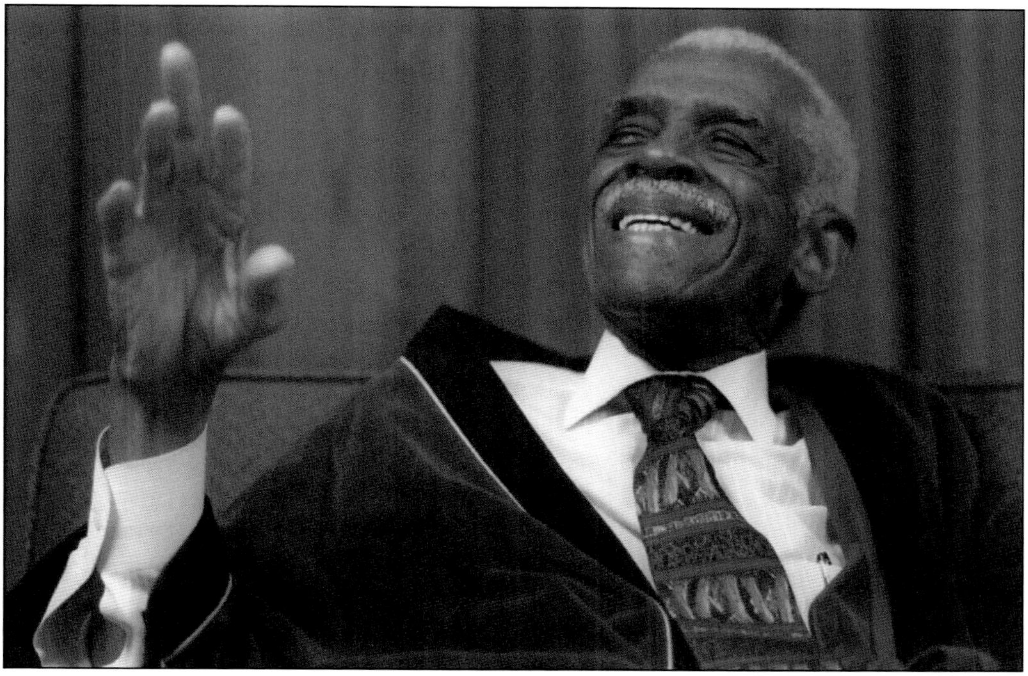

Donald Hollowell, born on Indiana Street, served as the Rev. Martin Luther King Jr.'s lawyer and helped free him from Reidsville Prison. His lawsuit got Charlayne Hunter Gault (later an award-winning journalist) into the University of Georgia, and he defended black defendants before all-white juries in rural Georgia. In King's hometown of Atlanta—Hollowell's adopted home—Hollowell was known as "Mr. Civil Rights." (Courtesy *The Wichita Eagle*.)

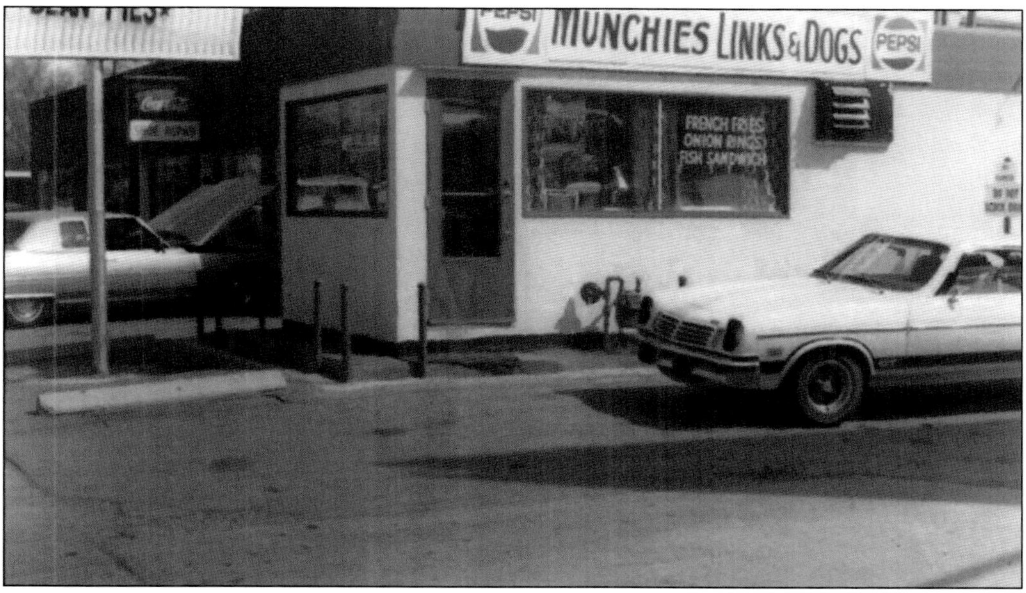

The 1960s and 1970s saw the rise of Black Power groups that advocated challenging the racism in American institutions by building African American networks, organizations, and businesses. One was the Nation of Islam, which operated a number of businesses—including this cafe on Thirteenth and Grove Streets. The Movement for Afro-American Unity and the Black Immediate Action Committee were among the other groups.

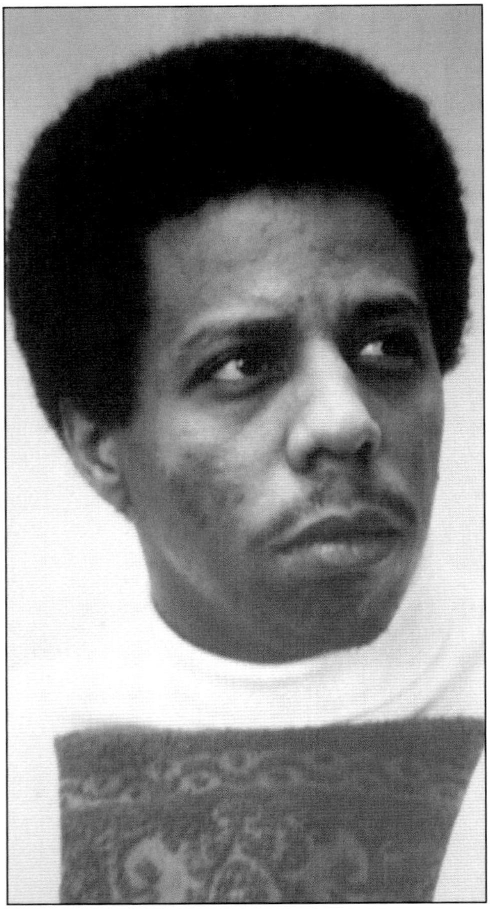

Anti-poverty organizations included people from poor communities in decision-making, and three of Wichita's six neighborhood centers were in black areas. Matt Greene, the director of the Grove Neighborhood Center from 1967 to 1973, recalled, "The Office of Economic Opportunity graduated tens of thousands of people from the street to universities and social service work." When Greene discovered elderly people living on cat food, he enlisted Sen. Bob Dole to sponsor the Food Stamp Program and piloted Meals on Wheels.

The founders of the community center at the corner of Eighteenth and Volutsia Streets called it "MEFSEC," or "Moving Effectively for Social and Economic Change." It was intended to offer not only wholesome recreation for youths, but also job training for the community's adults. It was renamed to honor basketball hall of famer Lynette Woodard in 1993.

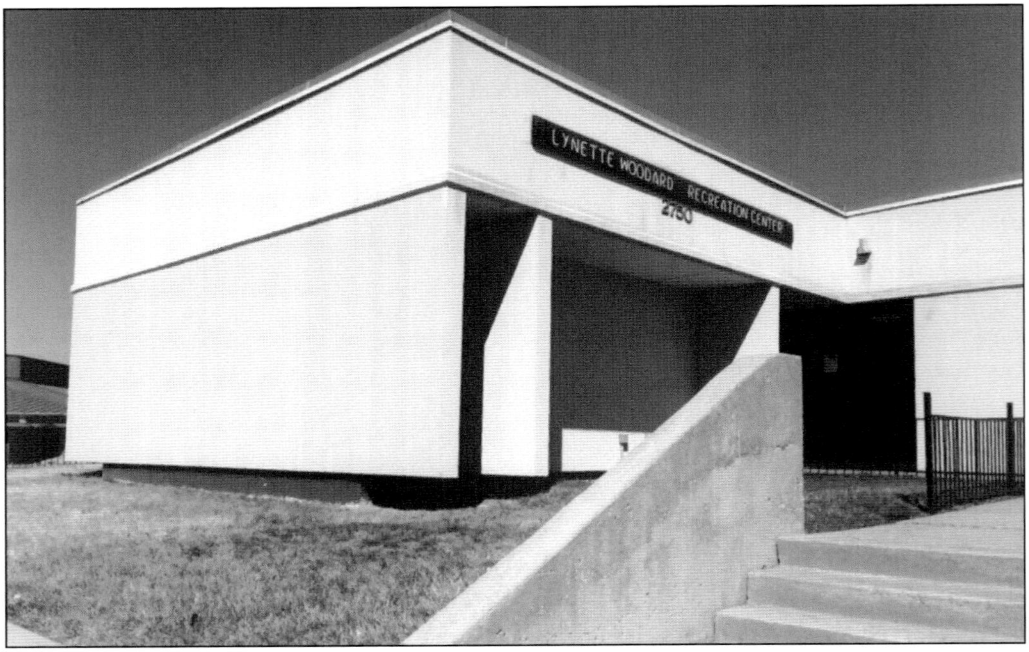

Cultural changes were visible by the late 1960s and 1970s: dashikis and Afros, identifying as "Black," African American bookstores, Afro-American Studies at Wichita State, and a black faculty that included Jo Gardenhire, Bobbye Humphrey, Vashti Lewis, Lavonna Spencer, and George Rogers. For a short time, Maya Angelou was a guest professor. Organizations also proliferated, including Black Concerned Parents, Black United Front, Mothers Organized Movement, Citizens' Committee for Neighborhood Schools, and Wichita Minority Contractors Association. Black activists also demanded reparations from the First Methodist Church during Easter 1969.

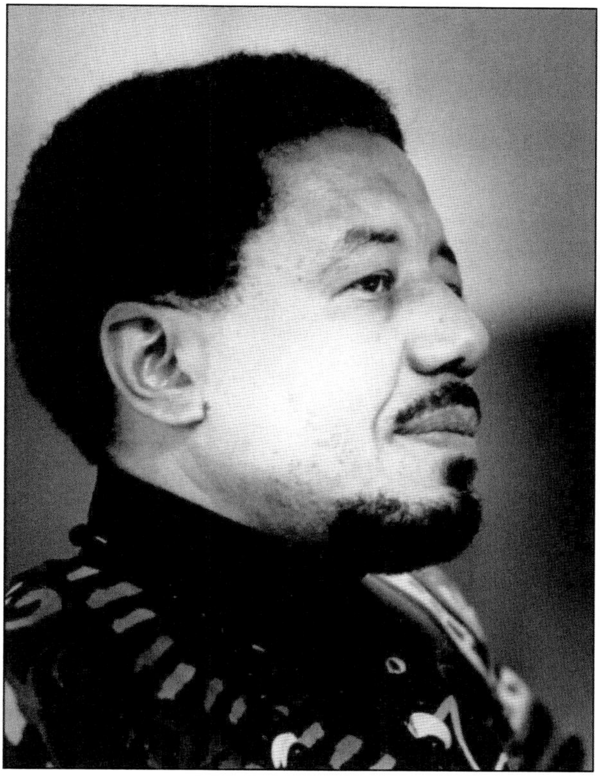

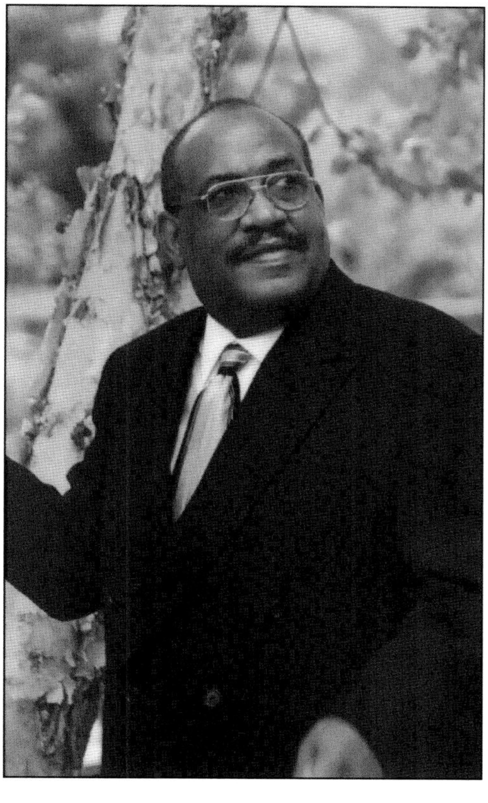

In 1965, George T. Johnson earned the Distinguished Flying Cross for bravery when he rescued a downed helicopter crew in Vietnam. The grandson of Reverend Van Leu, Johnson was among the first black pilots to graduate from US Army Aviation School's Helicopter Pilot Course at Fort Rucker, Alabama. Johnson was inducted into the National Black Aviator's Hall of Fame and was a charter member of Black Pilots of America.

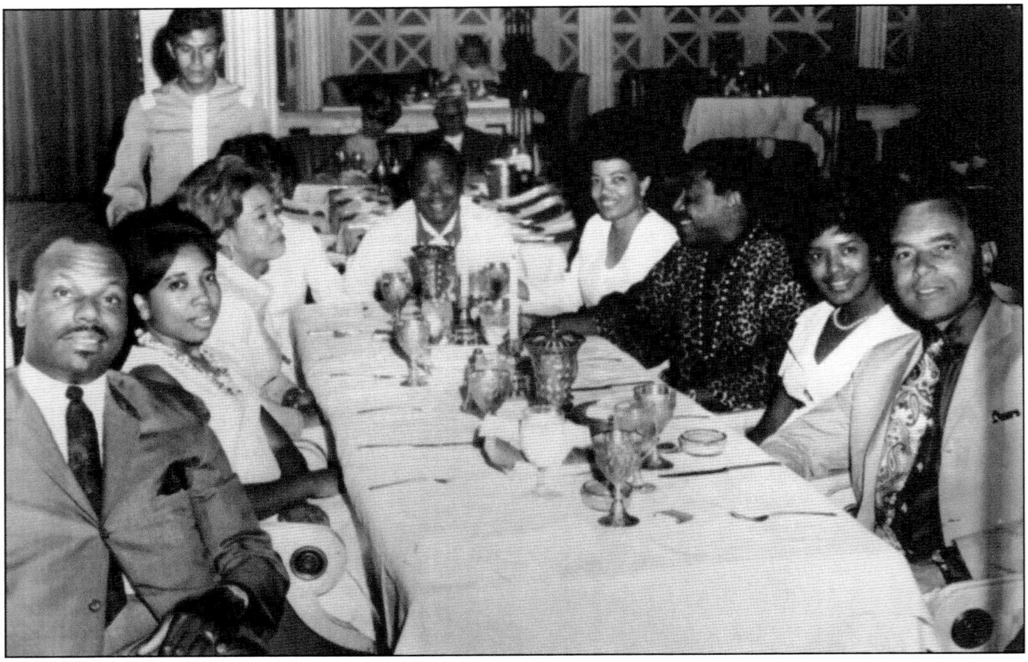

Chester Lewis led younger members of the national NAACP in a five-year campaign to oust Roy Wilkins from the executive director position and replace him with someone willing to tackle the problem of persistent poverty. Here, the Young Turks gather at a national NAACP convention. Lewis is seated third from the right, with Vashti to his right. When Wilkins defeated the Young Turks in 1968, Lewis resigned from all levels of the NAACP.

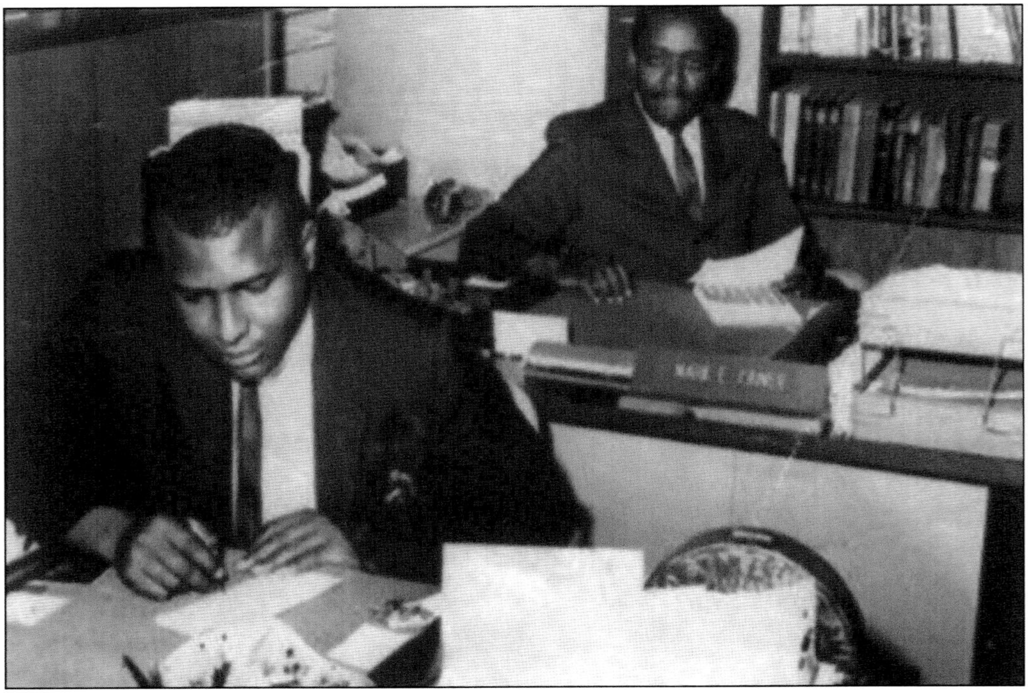

Insurance agents Billy Alexander (left) and Mark Criner ran an African American bookstore and sold encyclopedias of black history during this era. (Courtesy Mark Criner.)

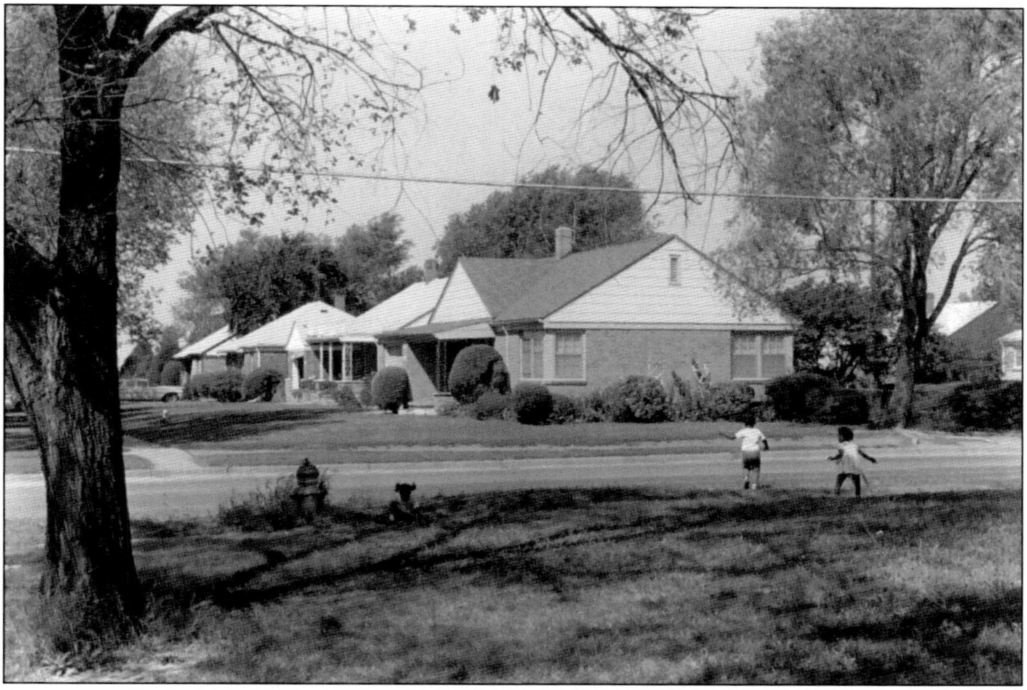

African Americans moved east to Grove Street (above), and by the 1960s, Hillside Avenue. In 1965, the new Interstate 135 bisected the community, and the North Industrial Park Urban Renewal Project removed 94 black and 14 white families. Below, an aerial view from 1974 shows construction of I-135 on-ramps at Ninth Street, and the black business district at Ninth Street and Cleveland Avenue at center left. (Above, courtesy Gretchen Eick; below, courtesy Wichita City Planning.)

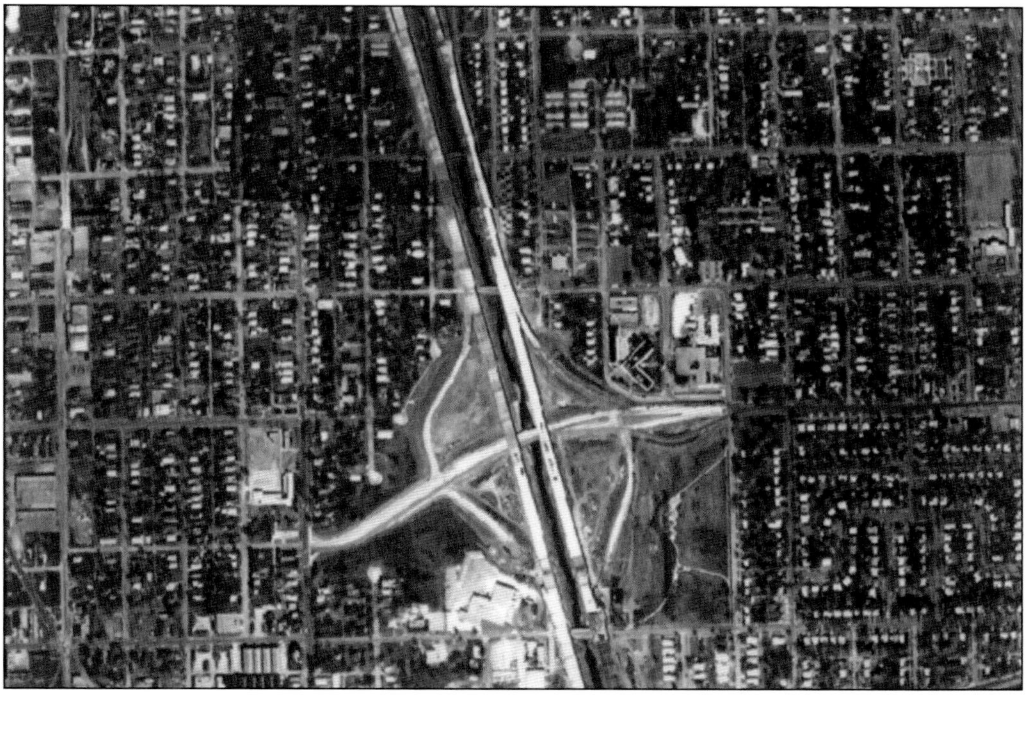

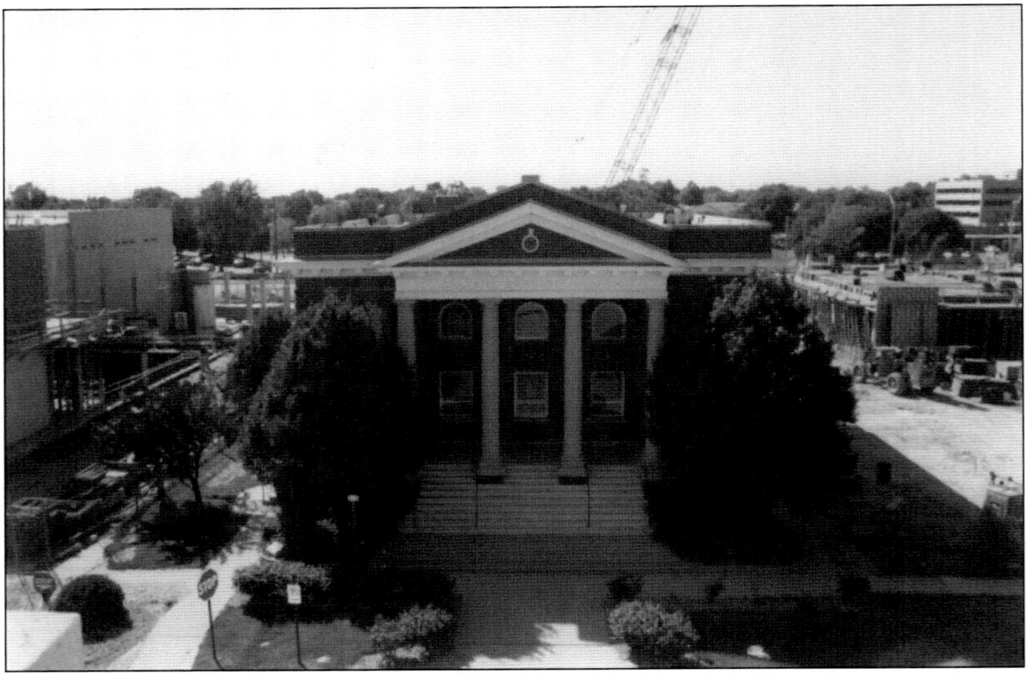

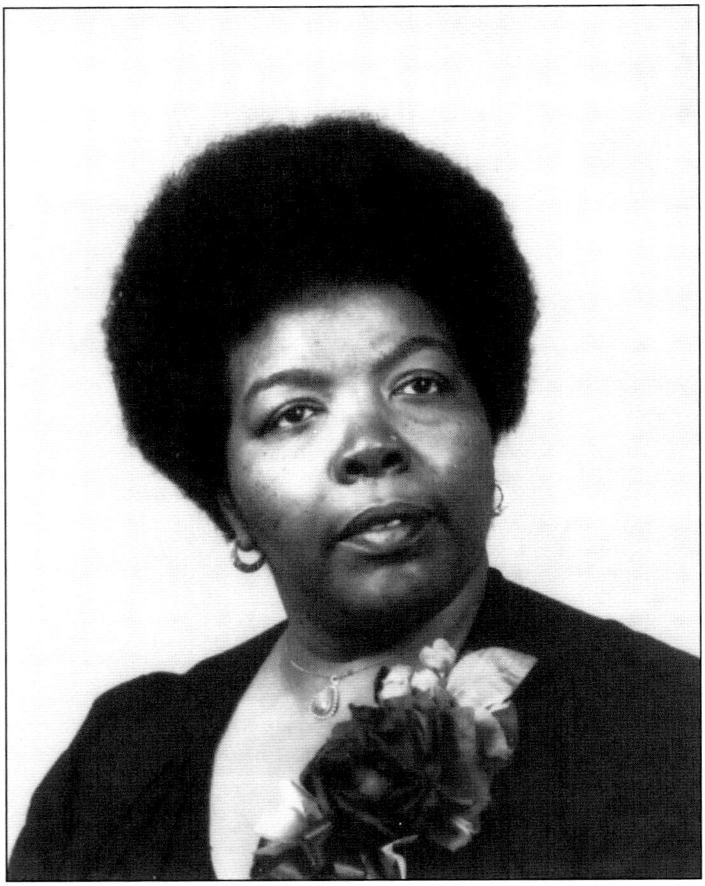

When urban renewal projects threatened to demolish the old Calvary Baptist building on Water Street, Doris Kerr Larkins (left) organized the community to preserve it. In 1972, it became the first Black Historical Society Museum, and today it is The Kansas African American Museum. Despite African American opposition, the city expanded the Sedgwick County Jail around the museum—demolishing Douglass Elementary and St. Paul AME to make room. (Above, courtesy *The Community Voice*.)

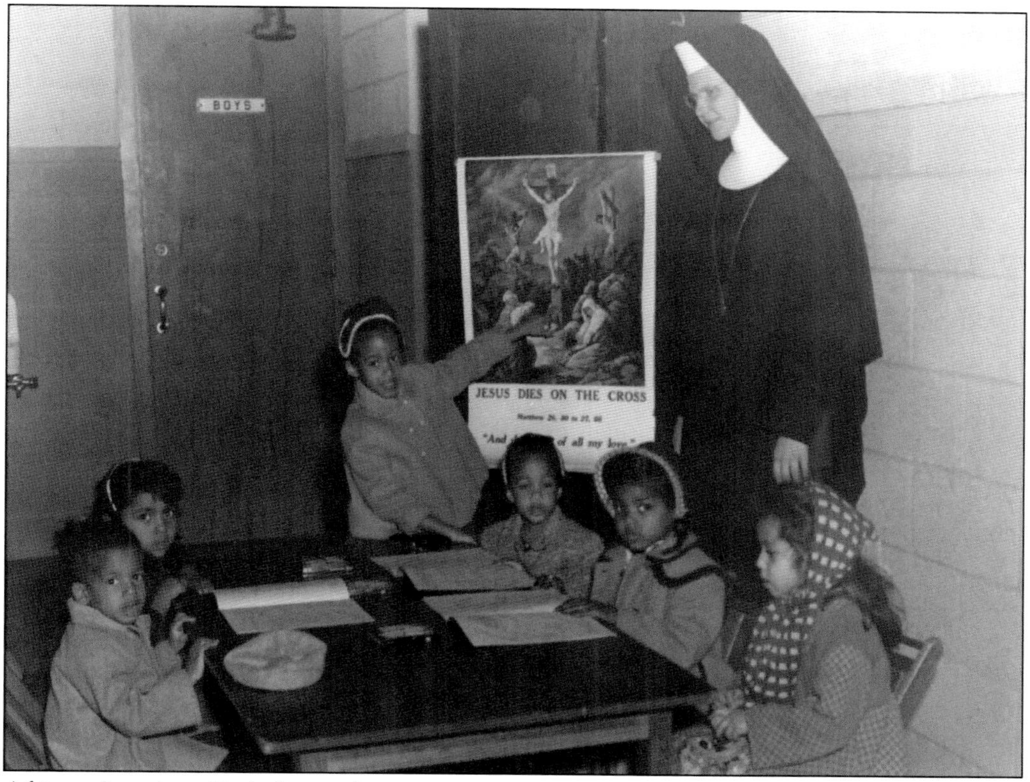

African American Catholics and Episcopalians had their own parishes. For Catholics, that parish was initially St. Peter Claver. In 1966, that parish closed and African American Catholics in Northeast Wichita began attending Holy Savior. Seen here on the right, Bishop Mark Carroll's support for civil rights is remembered by black Catholics. (Above, courtesy Adorers of the Blood of Christ; right, courtesy *The Wichita Eagle*.)

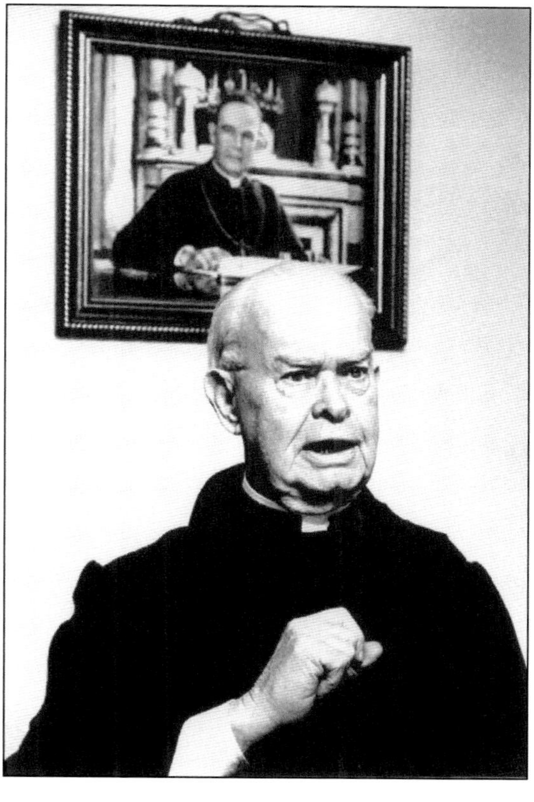

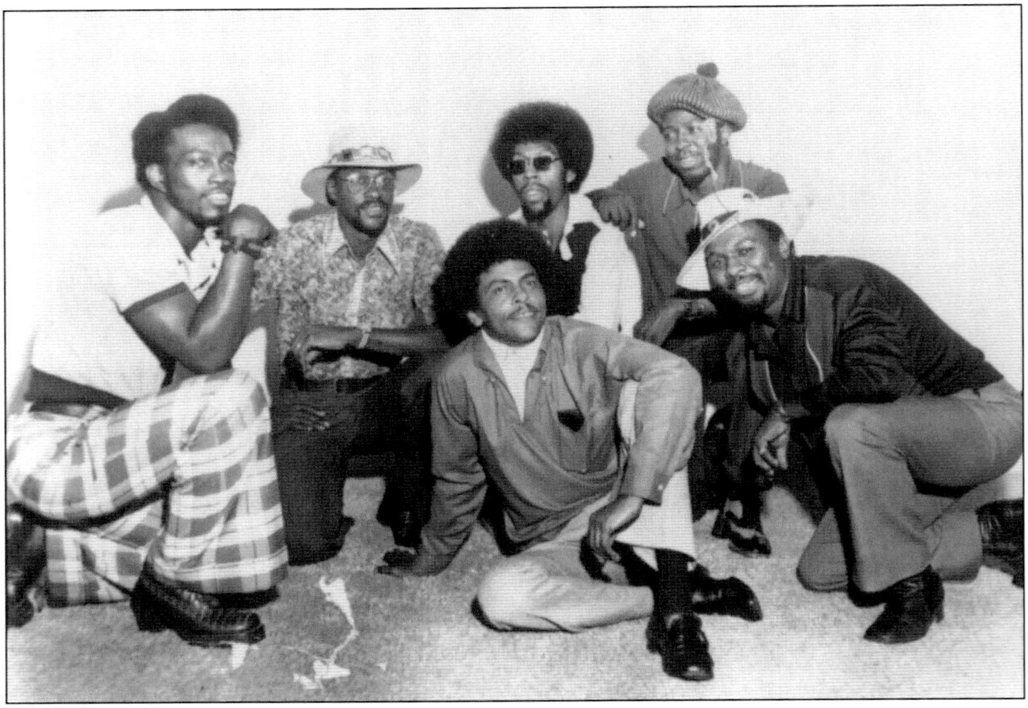

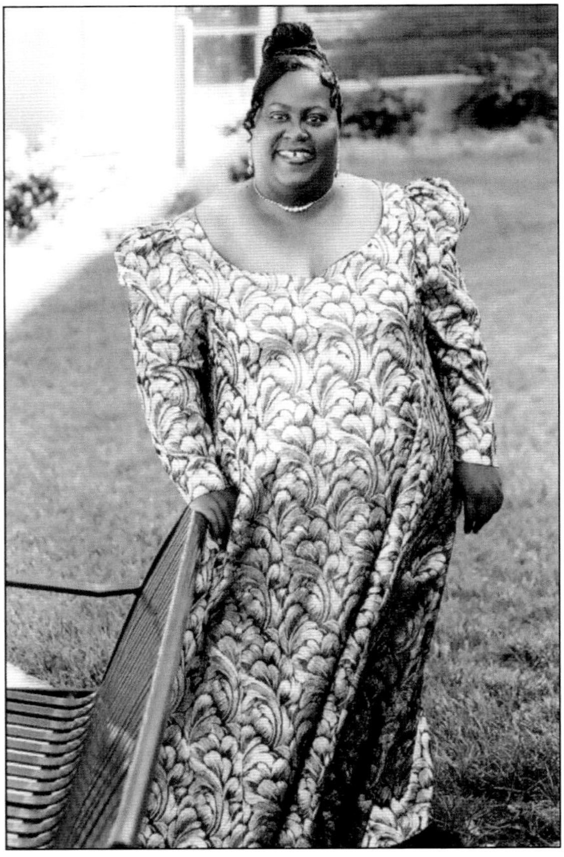

Nationally and locally, popular culture was being Africanized in the 1960s and 1970s. Among the local music groups was The Jive Five—not to be confused with a Brooklyn-based group of the same name—Rudy Love, and others. Pictured above around 1975, are (from left to right) Jive Five members Stanley House, Eddie Gains, Berry Harris, Woodrow Cooper, Lee Williams, and Herbie Welch. (Courtesy Yvette Harris.)

Karla Burns is a Tony nominated singer and actress perhaps best known for her role as Queenie in the Broadway musical *Showboat*. Burns has been featured in *Time*, *People*, *The New Yorker*, *Vanity Fair*, and *Newsweek*, and has met Queen Elizabeth, Princess Diana, and Sarah Ferguson, the Duchess of York. "It's hard to believe that a kid from Kansas has had these experiences," she once recalled.

Lynette Woodard's house survived the Piatt plane crash, and she often played basketball in Piatt Park across the street. Basketball brought her to the University of Kansas and made her the first female member of the Harlem Globetrotters. She earned an Olympic gold medal playing basketball for the United States in 1984. Woodard played for the WNBA's Cleveland Rockers and the Detroit Shock. (Courtesy Kansas Sports Hall of Fame and *Topeka Capital-Journal.*)

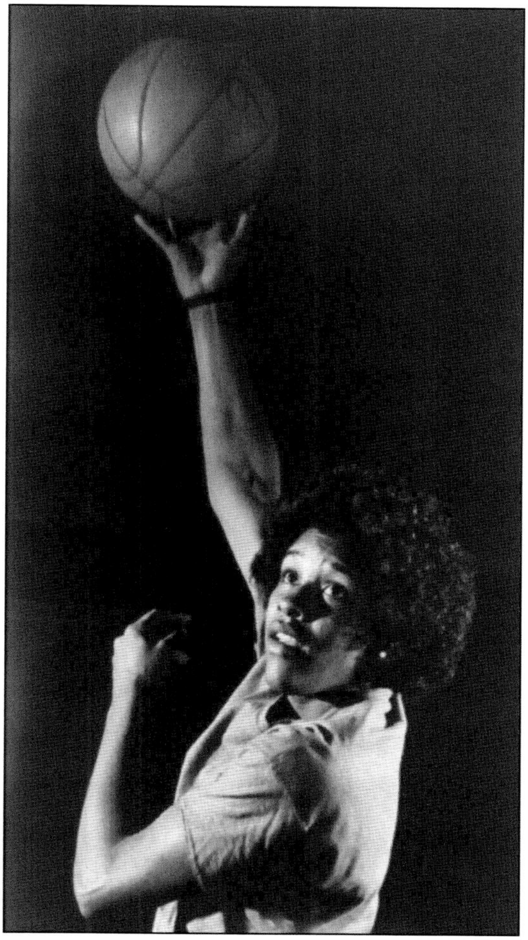

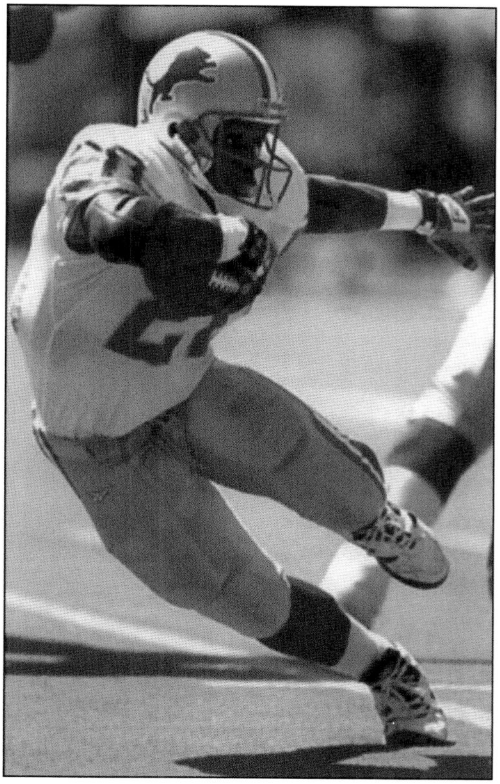

As a boy, Barry Sanders's coaches feared he might be too small to play football, but as a senior at North High School, it was opposing defensive coordinators who were fearful whenever Sanders touched the ball. He finished his senior year averaging more than 10 yards per carry, played for Oklahoma State University, won the Heisman Trophy, and finished his NFL career with the Detroit Lions as a Hall of Famer.

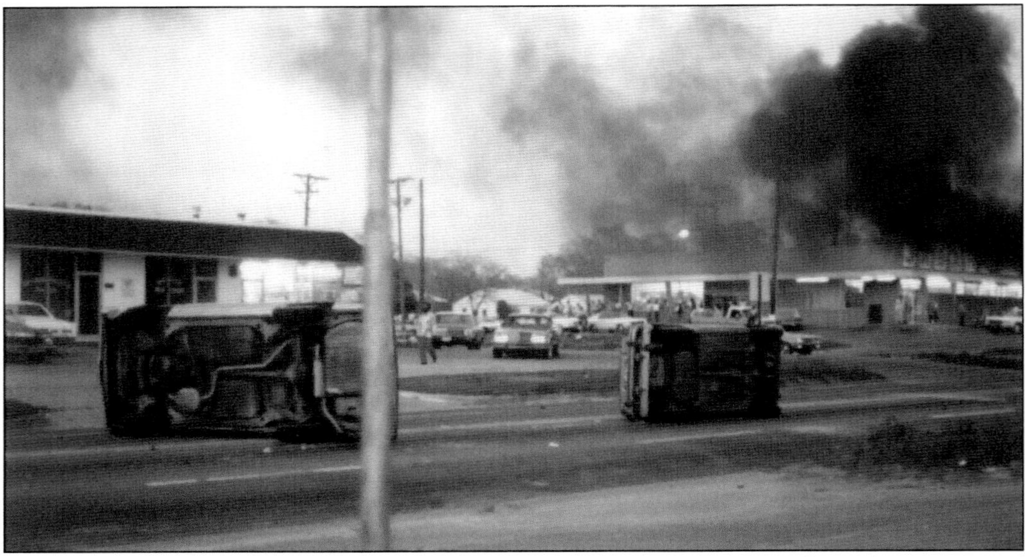

Once an important business district for African Americans in Northeast Wichita, the area around Twenty-first and Grove Streets was shattered in April 1980, when according to KAKE news, "more than 30 people were treated for injuries, including 21 police officers. Most of them were hit by flying rocks or bottles." The event began when police tried to arrest a man and resulted in a period of unrest rooted in the economic and social challenges of that community—including poor relations with the police. (Courtesy MyPictureman.)

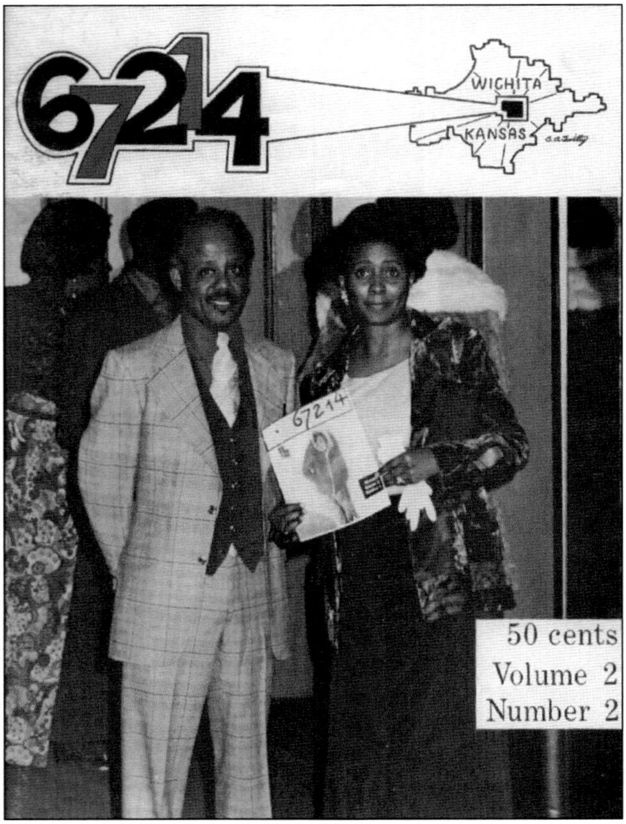

By the 1970s, a significant number of African Americans in Wichita lived in the zip code 67214—an area that covered the center of the city. While the white population could view the area with suspicion, residents saw it as a place of challenge, pride, and identity. In 1973, Donald "Laubuo" Williamson created this journal to celebrate "positive Black directions in Wichita." (Courtesy Charles McAfee.)

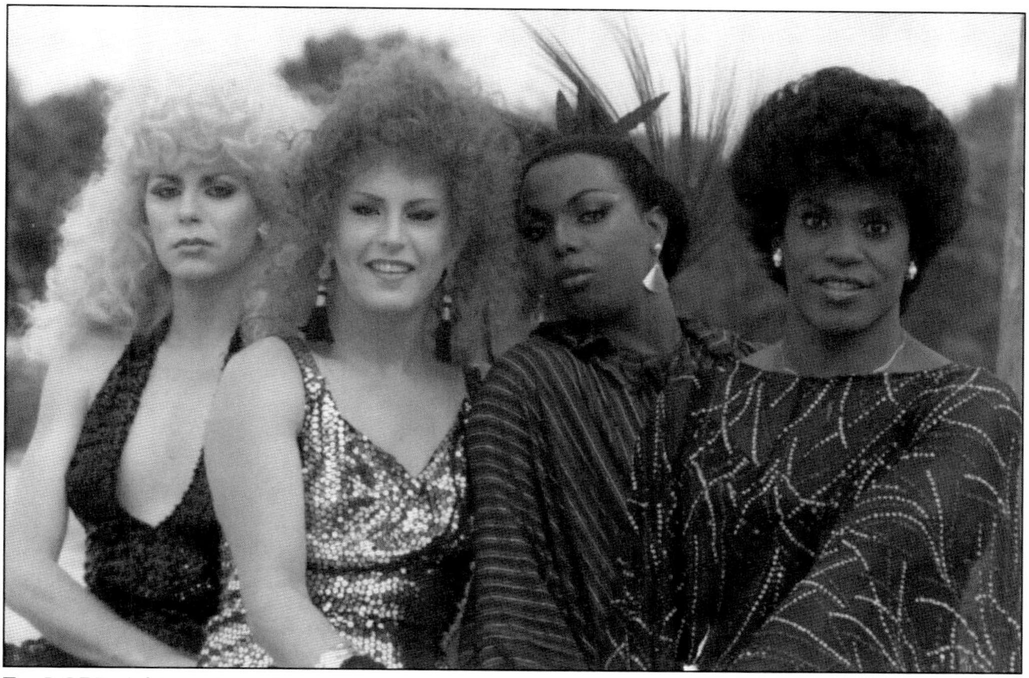

For LGBT African Americans, navigating both race and sexual orientation takes great courage. In 1978, for example, the city passed a non-discrimination ordinance protecting lesbian and gay persons, only to have the community vote 5 to 1 to repeal it just weeks later. A number of the best known drag queens in the community were African American. Here (from left to right), Rusty Franklin, Fritz Capone, Sahdji, and Tish De Williams perform around 1980. (Courtesy *Liberty Press.*)

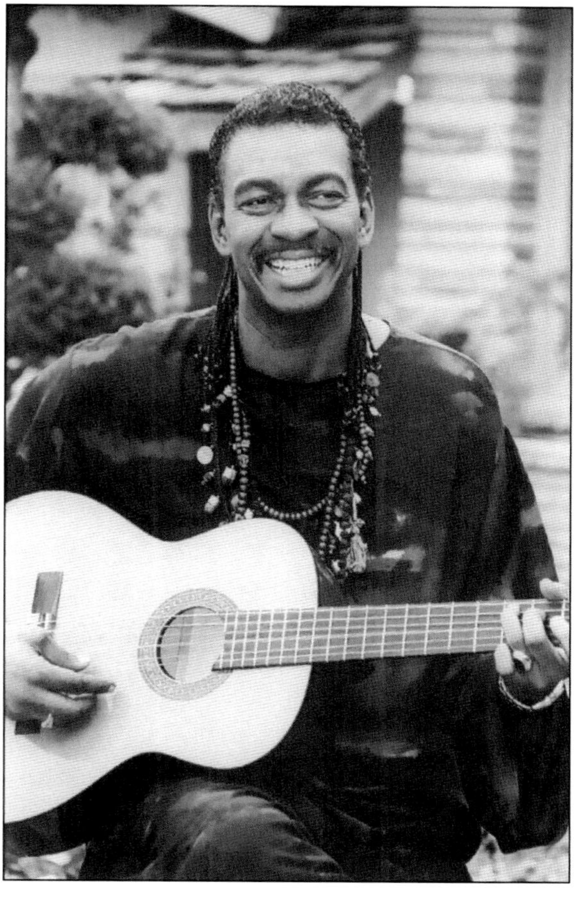

Since the 1960s, Rudy Love has worked with Marvin Gaye, Sly and the Family Stone, and other major stars in the music industry. Rudy knew by the time he was a teenager that he wanted to make music his career and was given that chance when he was discovered by Little Richard's bandleader. A graduate of North High School, Love toured Europe and Asia and worked for Motown Records during his career.

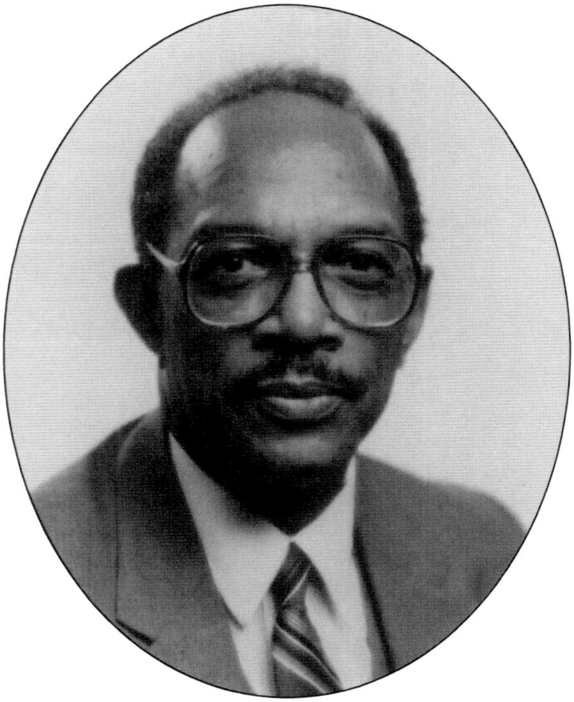

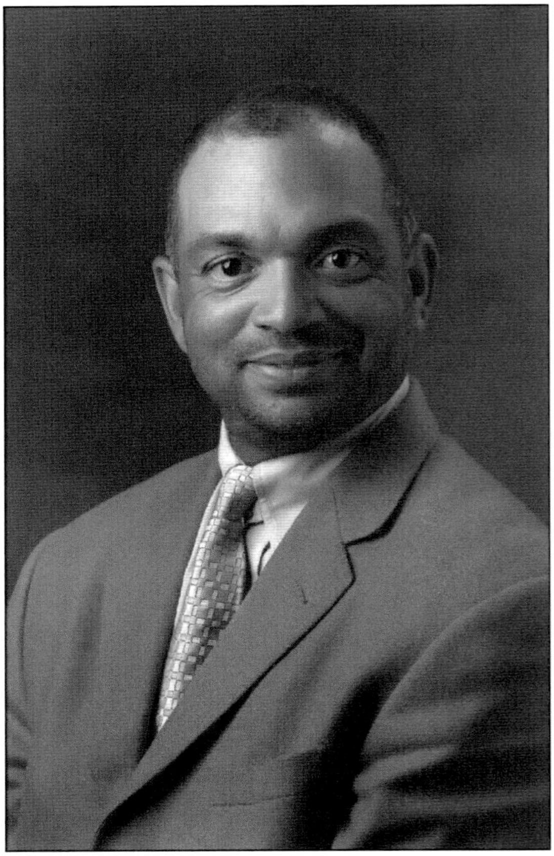

Linwood Sexton (above) is a legendary figure in Wichita. One of the first black athletes to compete in the Missouri Valley Conference, Sexton was named to the A-Missouri Valley First Team as a running back three times during his football career at Wichita University (later renamed Wichita State University). His number, 66, was retired before he graduated in 1948. In 1979, Sexton was a charter inductee into the Wichita State University Sports Hall of Fame. Besides his athletic accomplishments, Sexton became involved in a multitude of service-related activities—including membership on the Kansas Board of Regents—later in life. His son, Dr. Eric Sexton (right), became the athletic director of Wichita State University as well as vice president of student affairs. The younger Sexton was instrumental in Congress's decision to build the Smithsonian's National Museum of African American History and Culture. (Right, courtesy Wichita State University.)

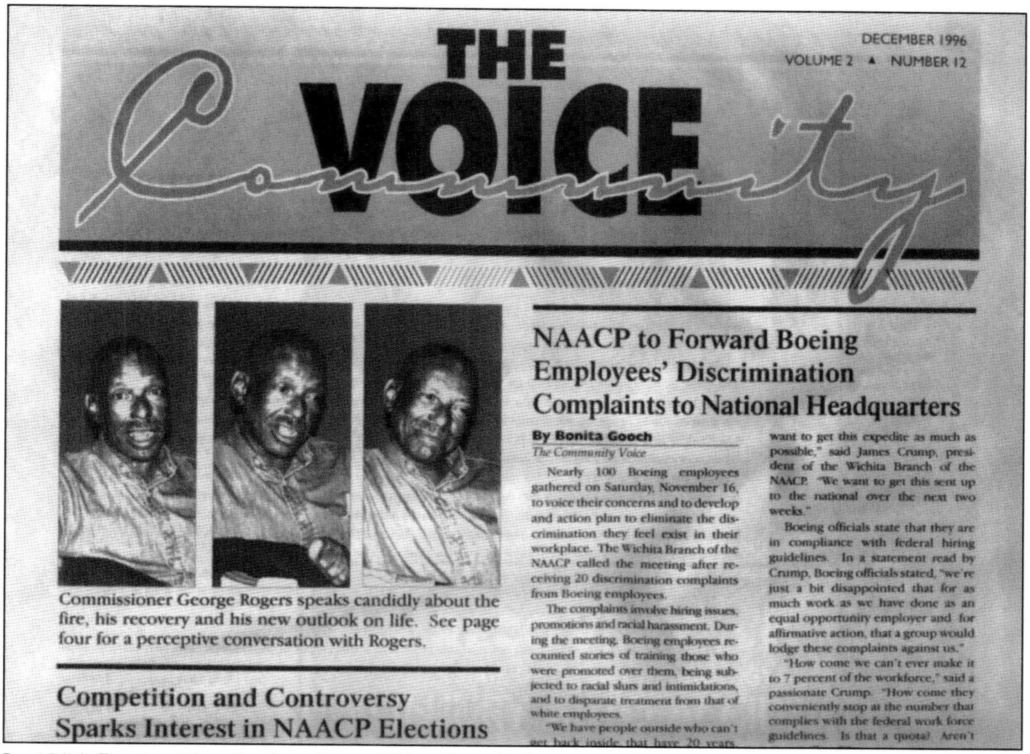

THE Community VOICE

DECEMBER 1996
VOLUME 2 ▲ NUMBER 12

Commissioner George Rogers speaks candidly about the fire, his recovery and his new outlook on life. See page four for a perceptive conversation with Rogers.

NAACP to Forward Boeing Employees' Discrimination Complaints to National Headquarters

By Bonita Gooch
The Community Voice

Nearly 100 Boeing employees gathered on Saturday, November 16, to voice their concerns and to develop and action plan to eliminate the discrimination they feel exist in their workplace. The Wichita Branch of the NAACP called the meeting after receiving 20 discrimination complaints from Boeing employees.

The complaints involve hiring issues, promotions and racial harassment. During the meeting, Boeing employees recounted stories of training those who were promoted over them, being subjected to racial slurs and intimidations, and to disparate treatment from that of white employees.

"We have people outside who can't

want to get this expedite as much as possible," said James Crump, president of the Wichita Branch of the NAACP. "We want to get this sent up to the national over the next two weeks."

Boeing officials state that they are in compliance with federal hiring guidelines. In a statement read by Crump, Boeing officials stated, "we're just a bit disappointed that for as much work as we have done as an equal opportunity employer and for affirmative action, that a group would lodge these complaints against us."

"How come we can't ever make it to 7 percent of the workforce," said a passionate Crump. "How come they conveniently stop at the number that complies with the federal work force guidelines. Is that a quota? Aren't

Competition and Controversy Sparks Interest in NAACP Elections

In 1996, Bonita Gooch, daughter of Rip Gooch, became editor of *The Community Voice*, which today serves as the main source of news within the African American community. (Courtesy *The Community Voice*.)

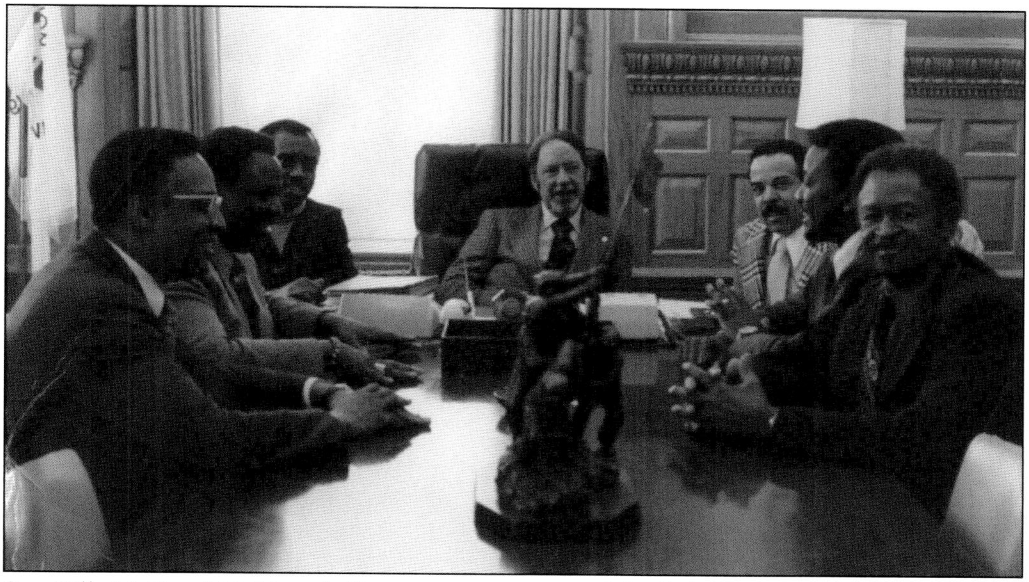

Sen. Billy McCray (third from left), a veteran, represented the 77th District—which was virtually all black—in the state legislature for 18 years. Elected to the senate in 1972 from a 60 percent white district, McCray helped end the death penalty, secured funding for sickle cell research, and organized several hundred minorities across Kansas for Days on the Hill, which began in 1975. His 2000 book is *Between These Walls: Working for the People*.

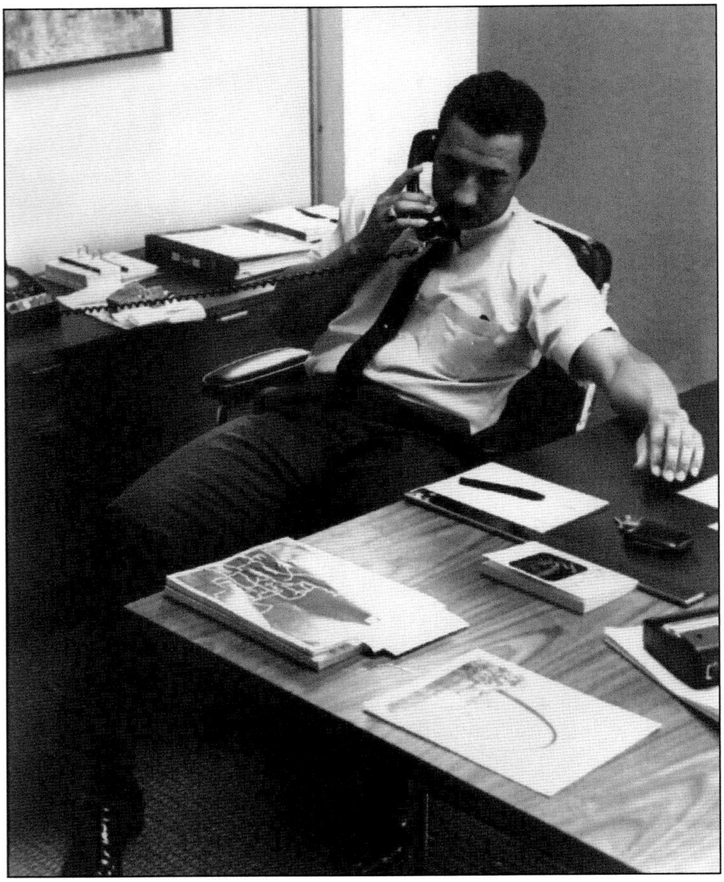

Facing limited opportunities in Wichita, architect Charles McAfee designed projects around the world, from homes and public transportation facilities to the 1996 Atlanta Olympics. In Wichita, McAfee designed the McKnight Art Center at Wichita State University (below), and the new home of Calvary Baptist Church. (Both, courtesy Charles McAfee.)

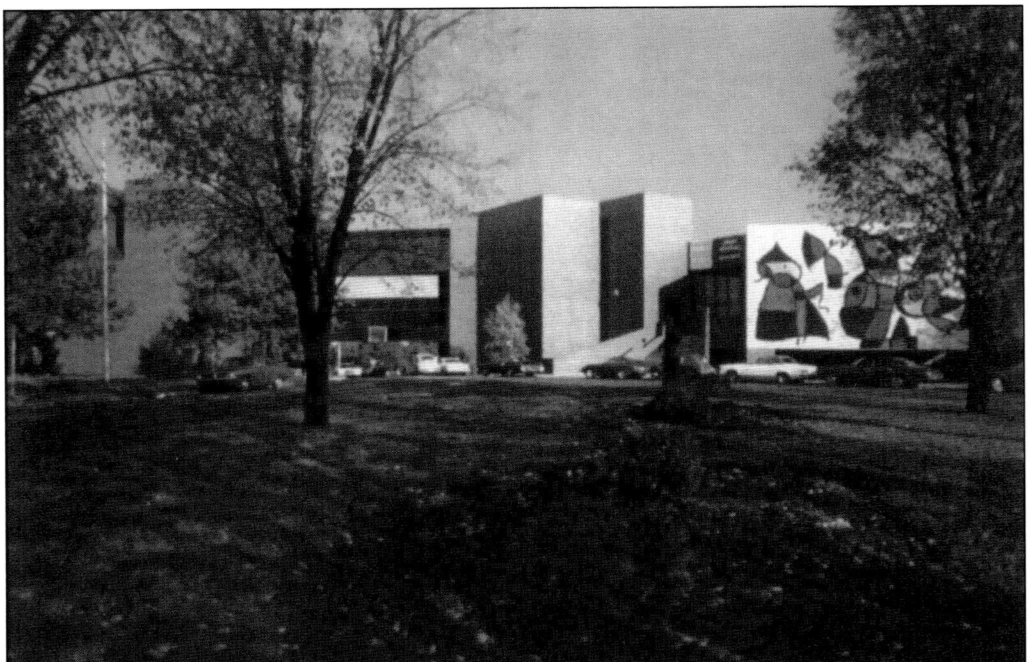

During the 1990s, Charles McAfee, Val and Gene Jackson of Jackson Mortuary, and Dale Diggs of Diggs Construction Company formed The McAfee Manufacturing Company to produce, market, and install affordable modular homes in Wichita's predominantly black Northeast area. Assisted by the AFL-CIO's carpenters' union, McAfee Manufacturing hired and trained former drug addicts, ex-convicts, and welfare recipients. (Courtesy Charles McAfee.)

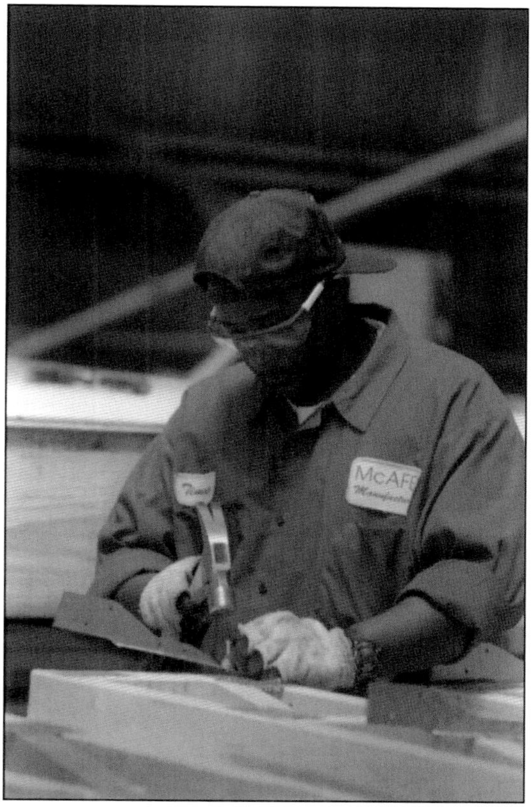

By the 1980s, Abner Jackson's sons, Anderson E. Jackson and Val Jean Jackson, had become the face of Jackson Mortuary. They engaged the services of Charles McAfee to design their facility on Thirteenth Street. Constructing the building was a challenge given that, in spite of Jackson Mortuary's long reputation in the city, local financial institutions would not loan to them. (Courtesy Charles McAfee.)

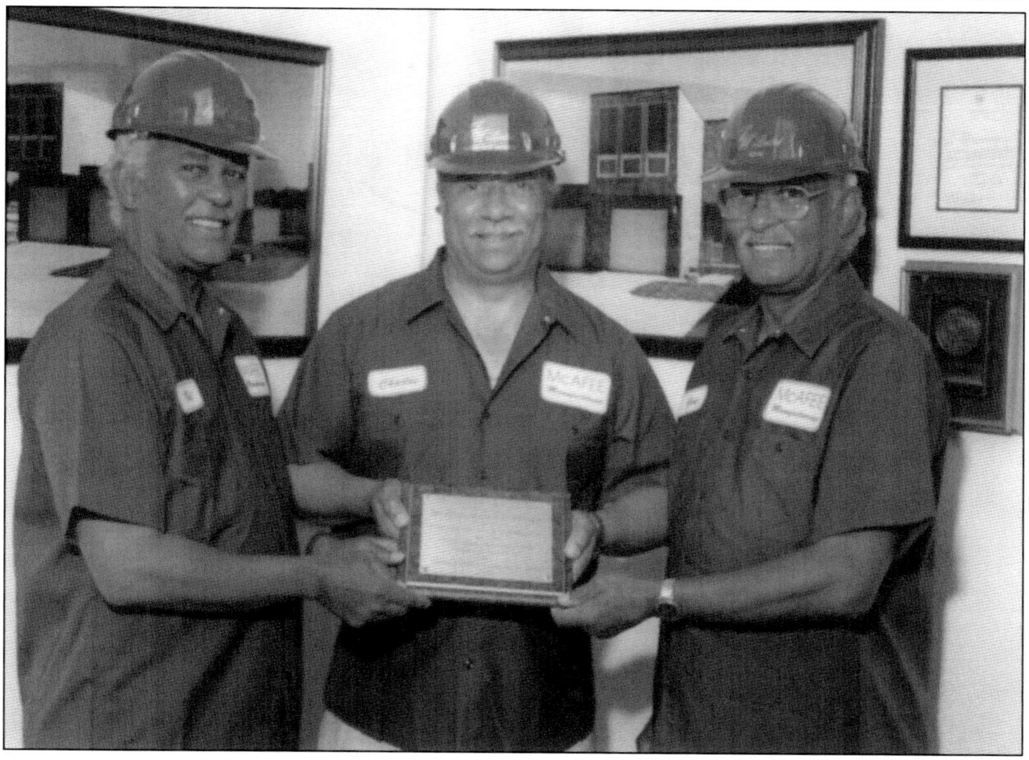

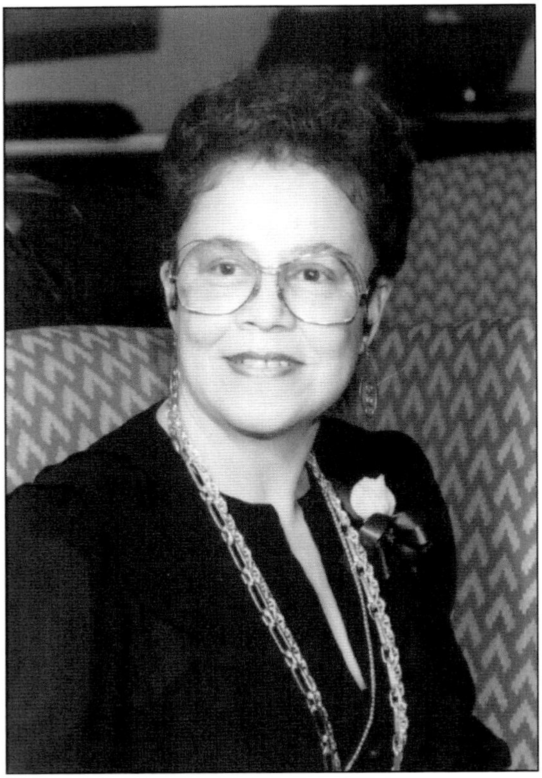

Active in the NAACP and her sorority, and a leader among Wichita's black middle class, Jo Brown was elected to the Wichita School Board in 1970—the first African American woman to serve. She made her independence clear by opposing the desegregation plan that the board adopted in order to keep federal dollars flowing, stating that it was unfair for black students to shoulder the bulk of the busing burden while most white students remained in their neighborhood schools. She also commissioned a book about the history of the school district, which mentioned, among other things, how high schools drained and cleaned swimming pools after black students swam. In 1989, she formed Wichita's version of the Jubilee Singers—ARISE—who continue to perform and interpret spirituals across the state. Jo is the wife of Dr. Val Brown—the middle of three generations of Dr. Browns in Wichita. (Both, courtesy Sheila Kinnard.)

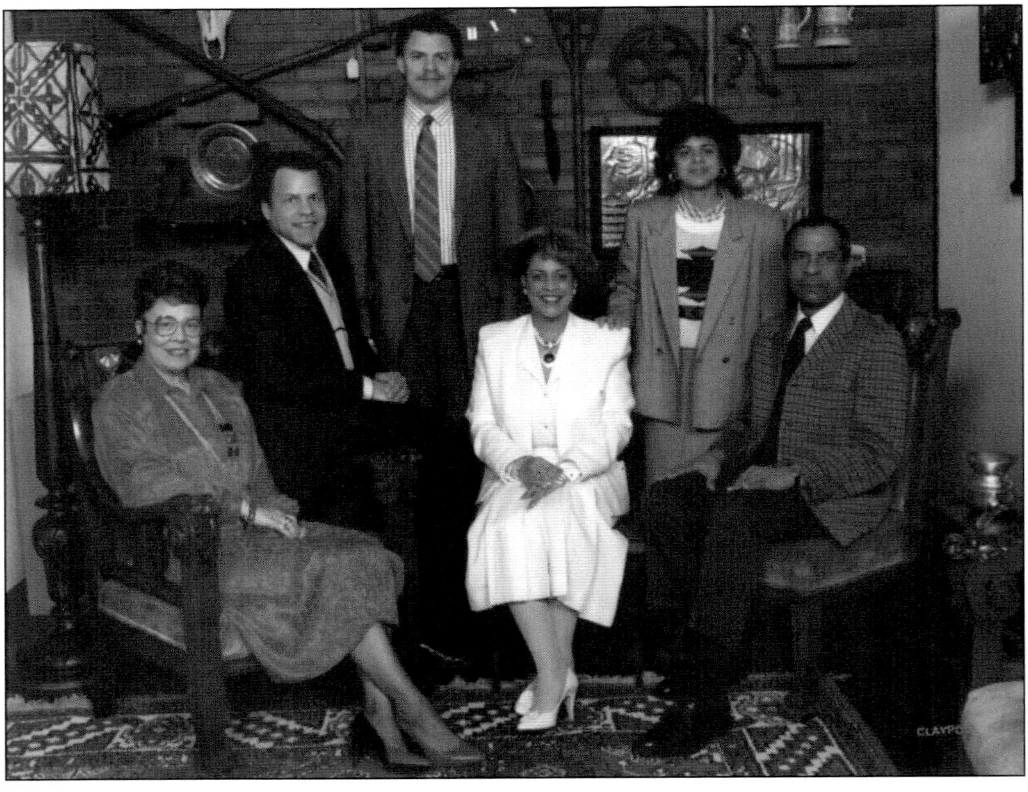

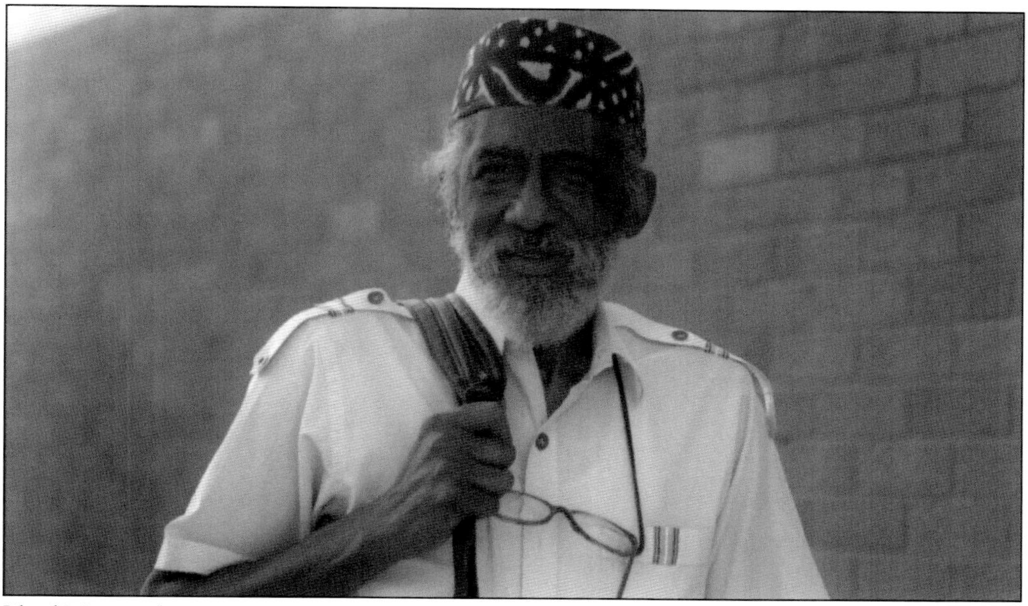

Jihad Muqtasid was a prominent community activist and entrepreneur who possessed a profound interest in education and young people. Muqtasid was a charter member of the Wichita/Sedgwick County African American Council of Elders, established in 2001. Until his death in 2006, Muqtasid personified the Council of Elders' primary purpose by providing advice to the community, and to organizations serving the community, for the betterment of black Wichita. (Courtesy *The Community Voice*.)

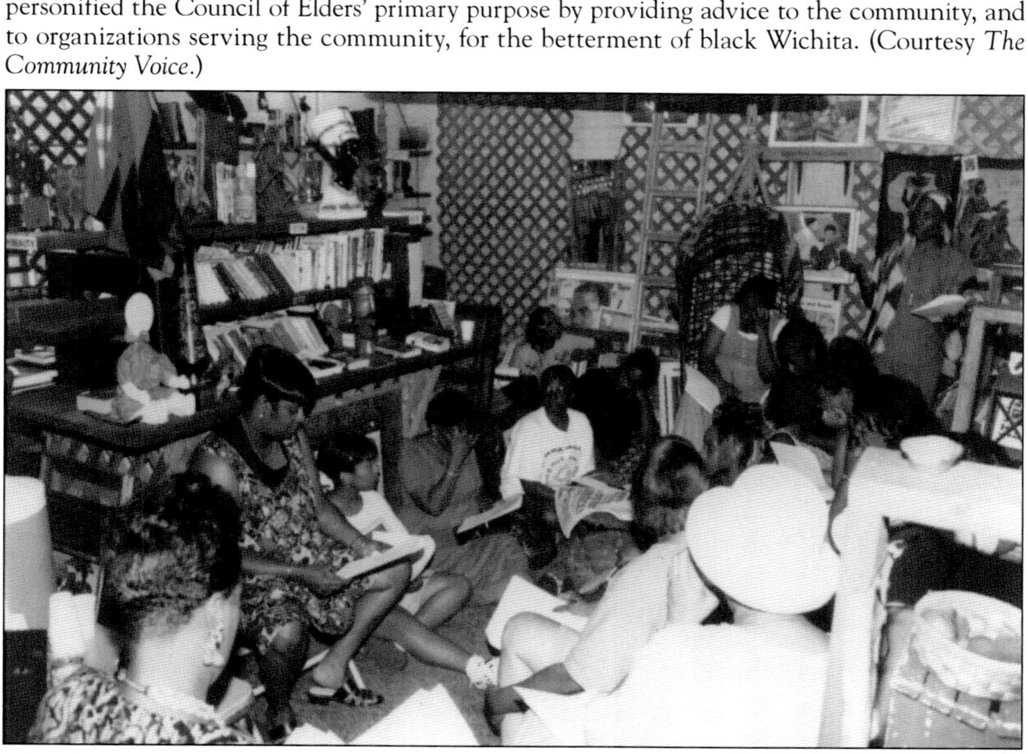

This photograph shows the inside the Iqraa Bookstore, located at 2219 East Thirteenth Street. Established during the 1990s, co-owners Maaskelah Thomas and her father, Jihad Muqtasid, sought to provide Wichita with a commercial enterprise that featured books, art, and other artifacts related to the African and African American experiences. (Courtesy *The Community Voice*.)

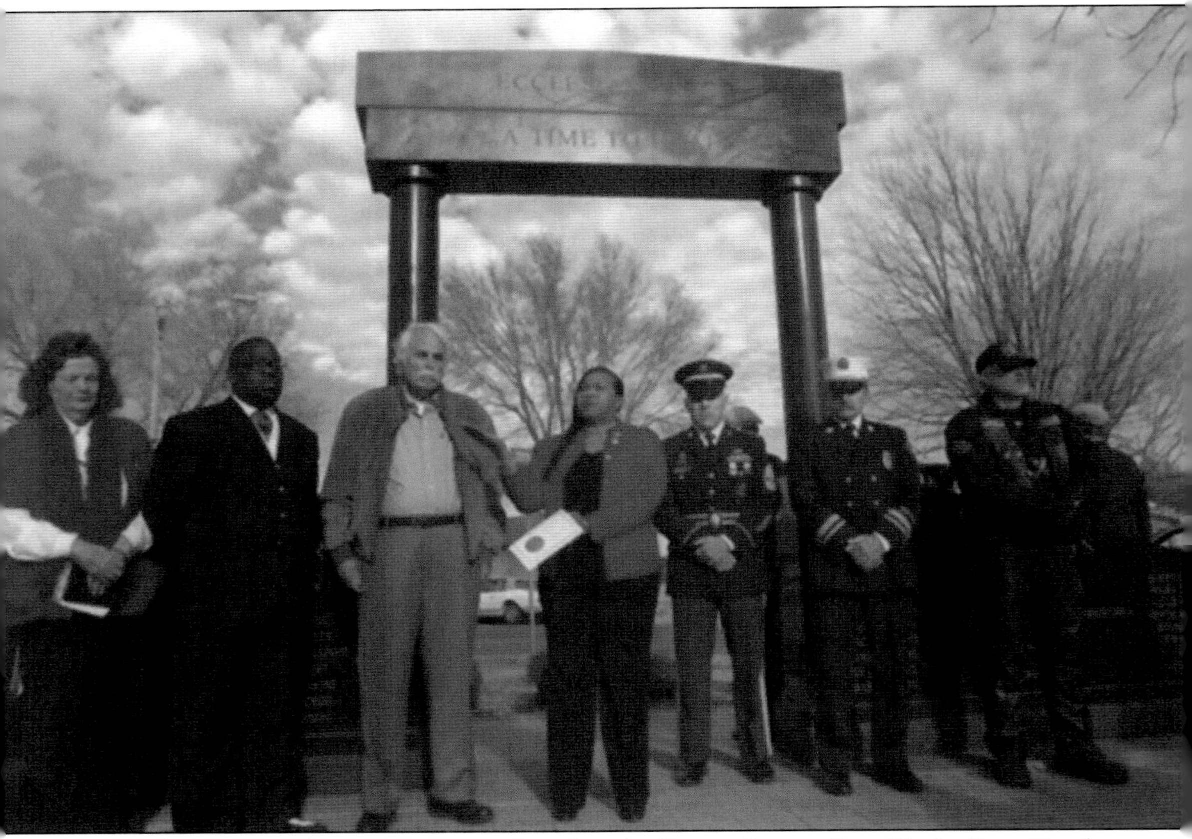

The first African American woman elected to the Kansas Senate, Sen. Oletha Faust-Goudeau (center), raised funds to establish this monument to those killed in the 1965 Piatt Street plane crash. (Courtesy Oletha Faust-Goudeau.)

Five

New Challenges, New Leadership

In 2007, Carl Brewer, who had a career in aviation before going into politics, became the city's first elected black mayor—serving two terms alongside the city's African American chief of police, Norm Williams, and fire chief, Ronald Blackwell. Black women were elected to the Sedgwick County Commission and the state legislature, with the first female black senator being Oletha Faust-Goudeau. In recent decades, residential segregation has decreased, and black families have dispersed to areas beyond the historic Northeast.

Newcomers from Africa have expanded black Wichita, while others have arrived through McConnell Air Force Base and the city's universities. Fraternities, sororities, social clubs, and churches have also continued, while performance groups like the Griots storytelling troupe promote African American traditions. Community leaders such as the Council of Elders have worked to preserve the legacy of culture. Despite this, the historic neighborhood has struggled, and while today's Wichita African Americans live in a community more residentially integrated, they still suffer from police harassment. "Driving while black" stops still take place, as do the shooting deaths of unarmed young black men by police officers who have never been held responsible. Wichita also continues to lack proportionate representation for its black citizens on the police force, which has led to new activism.

Meanwhile, a new generation of leaders is bringing energy and strategic savvy to their work addressing the continuing problems of the community. Among them are David Gilkey (gang prevention), Mary Dean (Black Women Empowered), Sandra Rankin, Lavonta Williams, and Kenya Cox (NAACP), Djuan Walsh (mass incarceration), Reuben Eckels (Sunflower Community Action), Brandon Johnson (Community Operations Recovery Empowerment), and Mark McCormick (The Kansas African American Museum). Others find success outside of Kansas: Sheinelle Jones, granddaughter of Dr. Val and Jo Brown, became the news anchor for the weekend version of NBC's *Today Show*. Cheryl and Charyl McAfee became, respectively, CEO and president/CFO of McAfee3 Architects in Atlanta. Kevin Merida became the managing editor of the *Washington Post*, and Deneen Brown an award-winning journalist at the *Post*. Others excel while away and then return, such as singer and actress Karla Burns—who won an Olivier Award in London and a Tony nomination for her Broadway performance in *Show Boat*—and singer Earnest Alexander, who has toured the world.

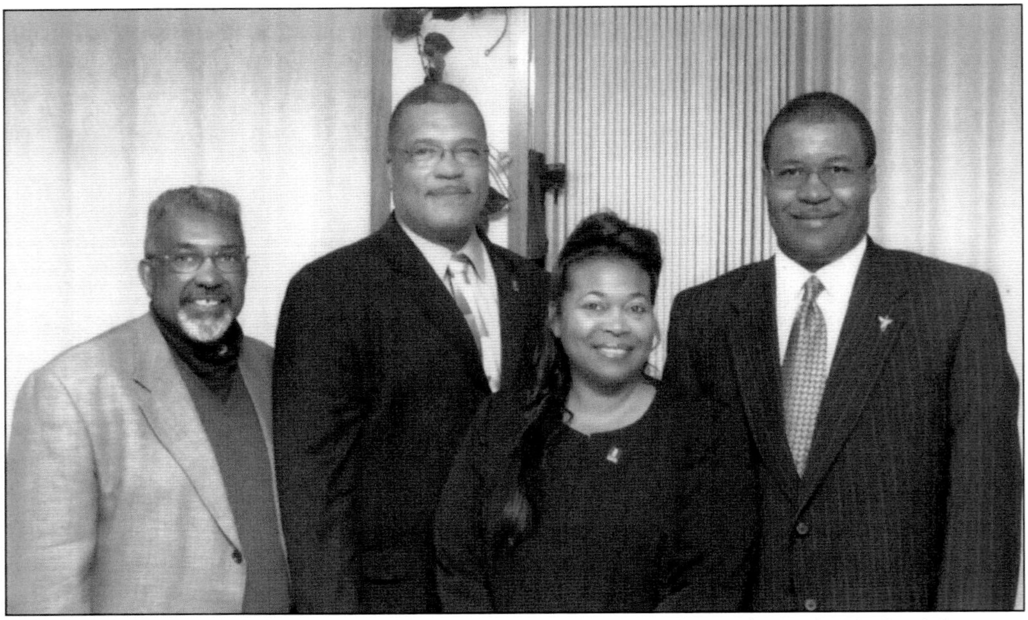

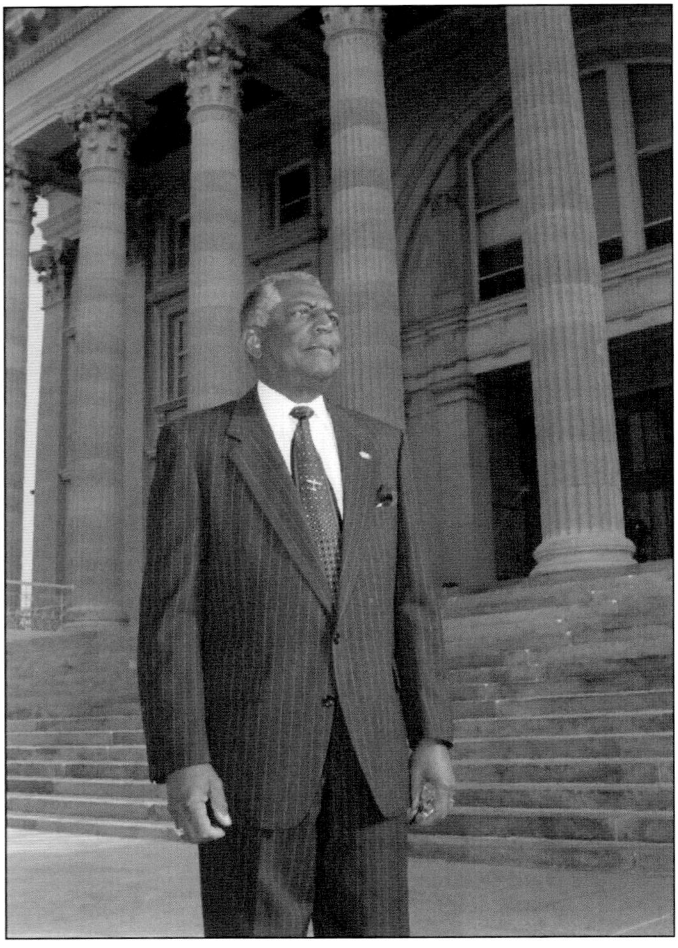

By the early 2000s, African Americans were elected to the top leadership positions in the city, including (from left to right) Ron Holt, assistant county manager; Carl Brewer, first elected black mayor; Oletha Faust-Goudeau, first African American woman elected to the Kansas Senate; and Norman Williams, first permanently appointed chief of police.

Ulysses Lee "Rip" Gooch, the child of Tennessee sharecroppers, became a pilot, ran an air charter service, trained pilots, and sold Mooney planes in Wichita until the company went under—owing him $100,000 that it never paid. Devastated financially, he paid off his creditors and was elected to the city council in Wichita before serving multiple terms in the Kansas Senate in the 1990s.

Judge Greg Waller has roots in Kansas that go back 100 years. This highly respected jurist of the Sedgwick County Court presided over the infamous BTK case and dispensed justice for 21 years, only to lose a reelection bid in 2014. *The Community Voice* editorialized about disproportionate incarceration of African Americans and Hispanics—referred to as "the new Jim Crow"—and called for the decriminalization and reform of sentencing guidelines of possessing small amounts of marijuana for personal use.

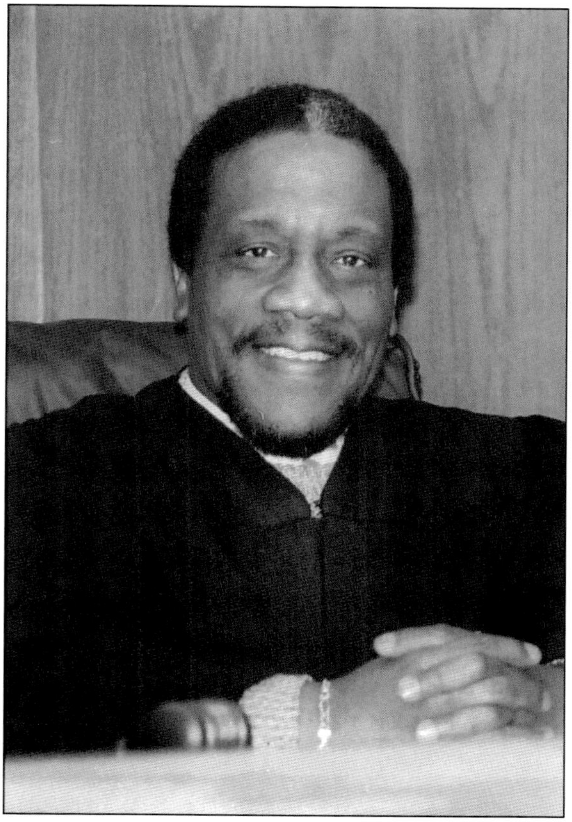

Three black women from Wichita joined Roderick Houston, Jonathan Wells, and Ruby Gilbert in the state legislature in the 1990s. They are, from left to right, Oletha Faust-Goudeau, Gail Finney, and Melody McCray Miller, with city councilwoman Lavonta Williams at far right. McCray Miller also was elected to the county commission. (Courtesy Melody McCray Miller.)

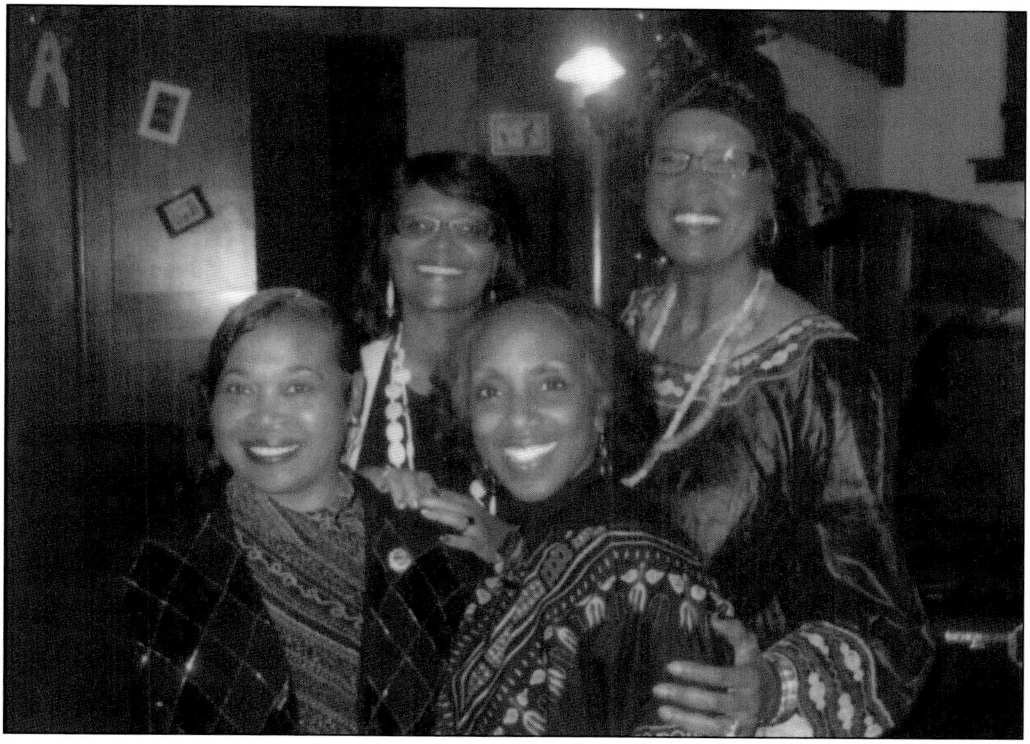

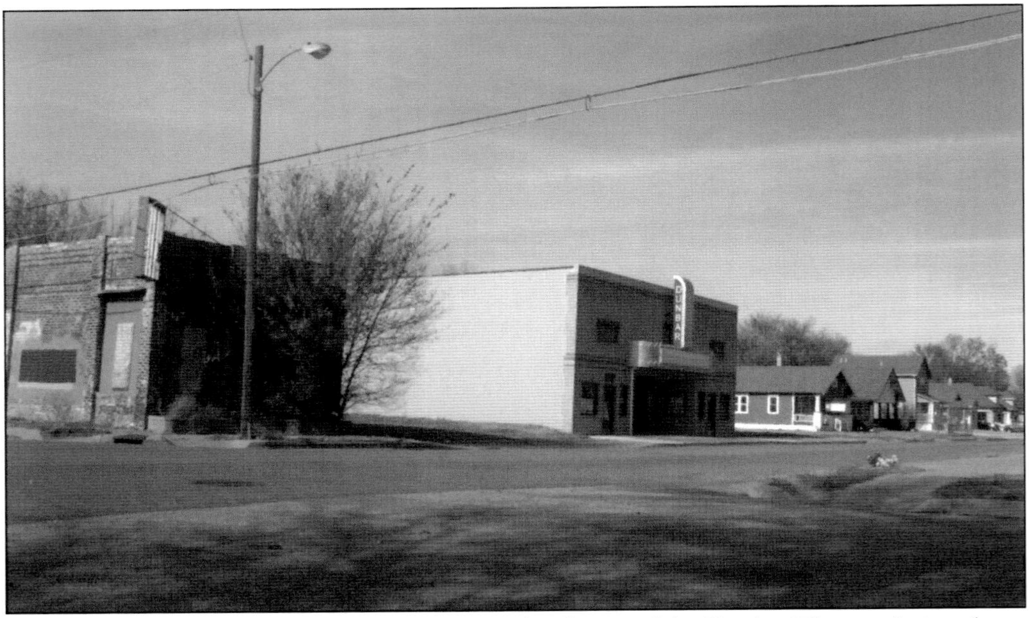

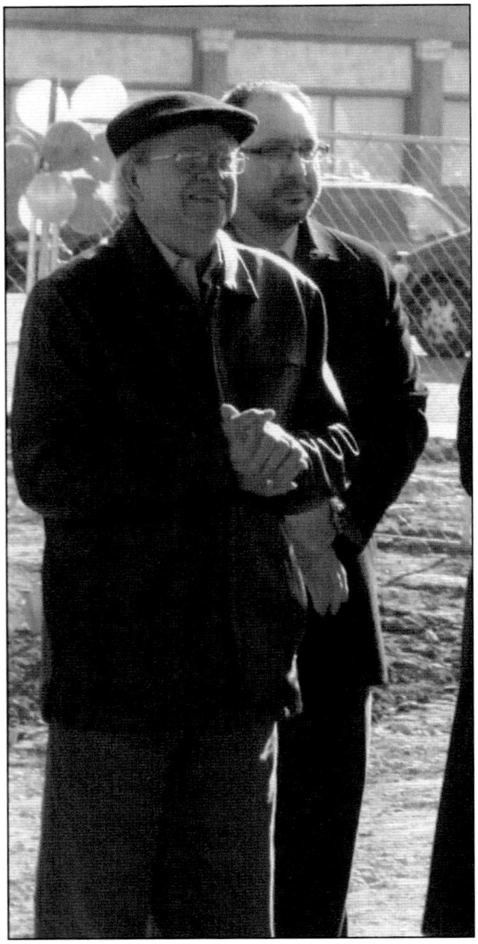

The closing of the Dunbar Theater during the 1970s marked the decline of the area around Ninth Street and Cleveland Avenue. By the 1980s, the larger McAdams neighborhood was plagued by closed businesses and high crime. Attempts to revitalize the area have included a 2008 effort to list the Dunbar Theater in the National Register of Historic Places. McClinton's Store was listed in the Register in 2011 but was torn down in early 2015.

When Robert Alford came to Wichita from Oklahoma, he went into the lighting business. Alford Electric Company sold, and even made, light fixtures for residential and commercial customers, including Pizza Hut franchises. By the 1980s, Alford also became active in the efforts of the First National Black Historical Society of Kansas, preparing the form that got Calvary Baptist nominated to the National Register of Historic Places.

In 1970, African Americans lived primarily in the north and east of downtown, save for small pockets like Oaklawn—in the far south of the city. In spite of two decades of activism, Wichita was still one of the most segregated cities in the country. (Courtesy Wichita City Planning.)

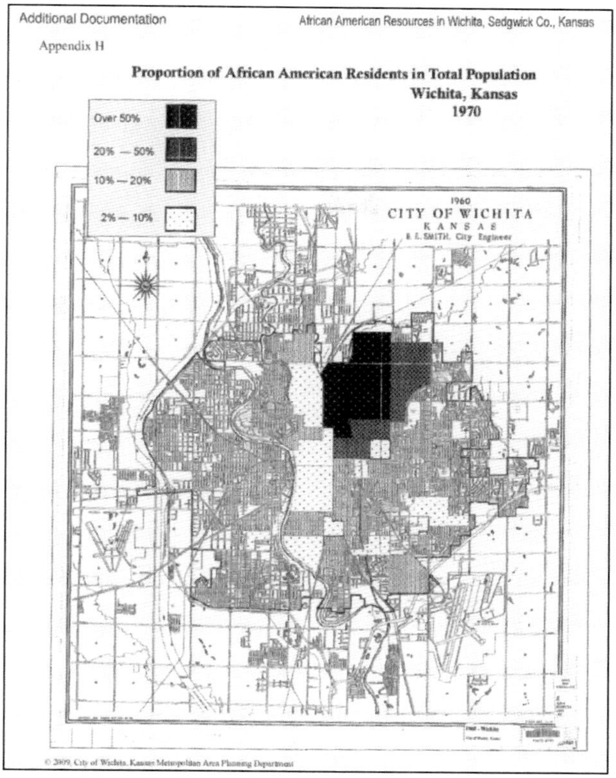

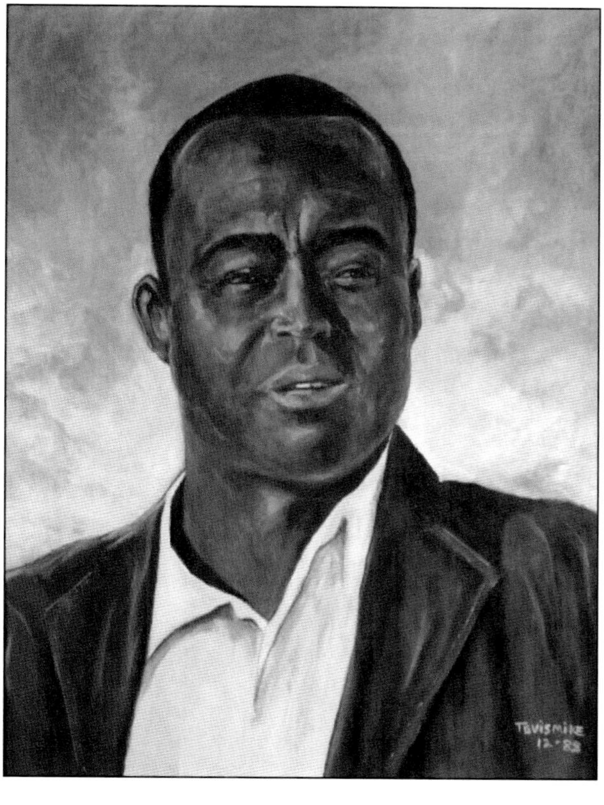

Originally serving on the Wichita police force, Emerson McAdams later became director of McKinley Park. In 1966, a few months after his death, the city renamed McKinley Park McAdams Park in his honor. In the decades that followed, the area around Ninth Street and Cleveland Avenue has come to be known as the McAdams neighborhood. (Painting by Tevis Mike, courtesy Jackson Mortuary and Pam Thompson.)

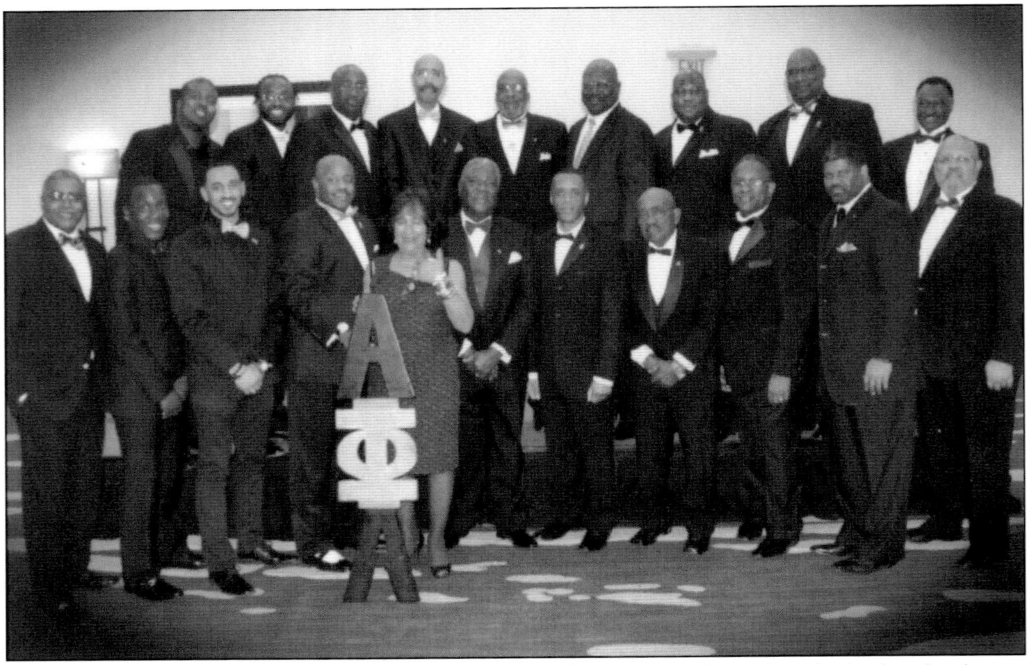

For the past several years, Wichita's Alpha Phi Alpha chapters have hosted a scholarship fundraiser to increase public awareness and appreciation of the important role of historically black colleges and universities. In this photograph from the 2013 event, fraternity members are shown with Dr. Carolyn Meyers, president of Jackson State University. (Courtesy Charlie Jenkins.)

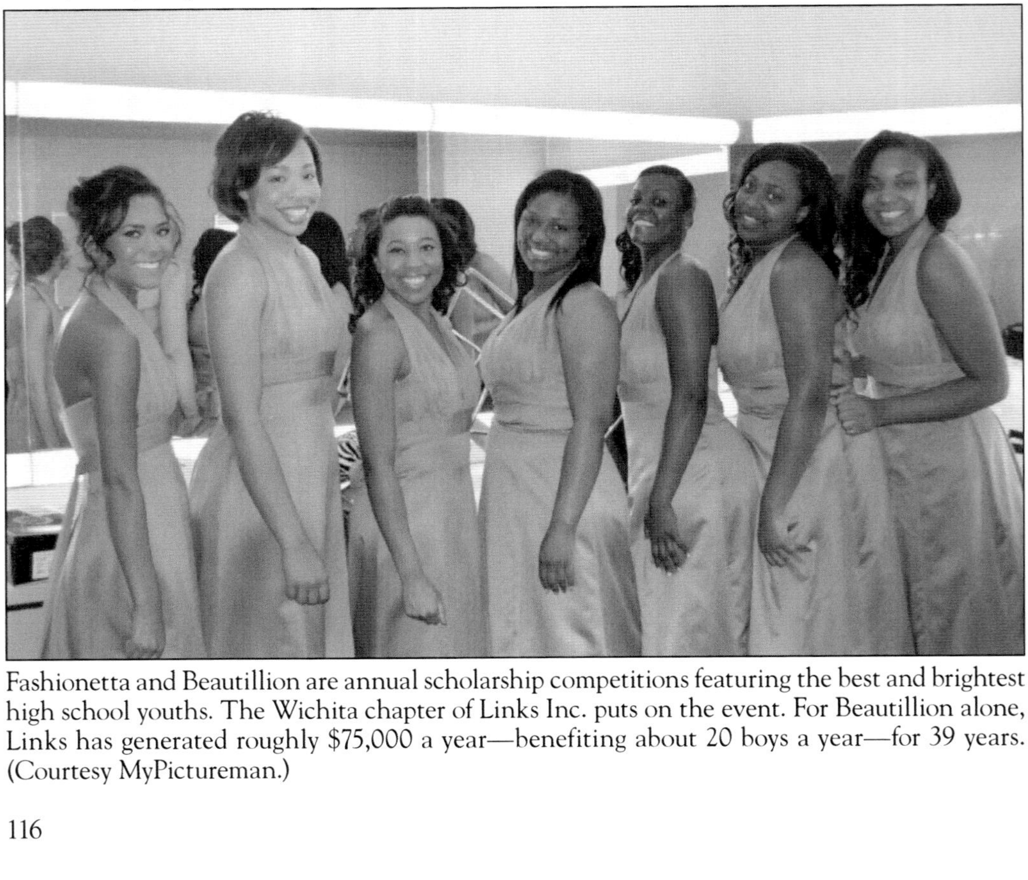

Fashionetta and Beautillion are annual scholarship competitions featuring the best and brightest high school youths. The Wichita chapter of Links Inc. puts on the event. For Beautillion alone, Links has generated roughly $75,000 a year—benefiting about 20 boys a year—for 39 years. (Courtesy MyPictureman.)

Since the early 20th century, the Greater Wichita Ministerial League has brought community religious leaders together to work on issues and projects that benefit the African American community. One of their most prominent events is the annual Martin Luther King Jr. celebration. One current project is a voting initiative called Souls to the Polls.

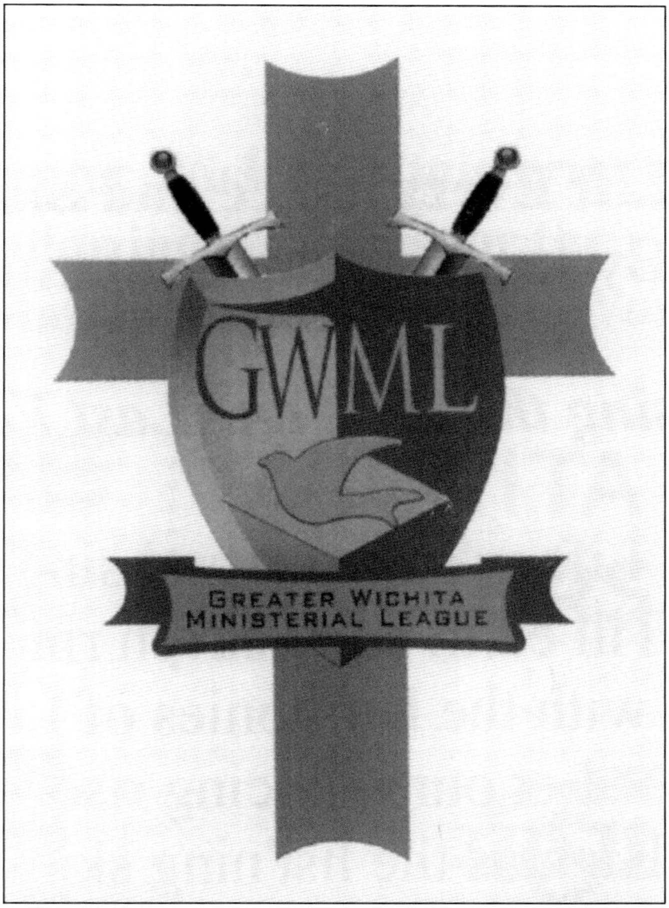

In 2002, at age 24, Donald Betts Jr. was elected to the Kansas House for two terms—becoming the youngest person to serve there. When Sen. Rip Gooch stepped down in 2006, Betts ran for his seat and won. In 2008, Betts ran unsuccessfully for the US Congress. (Courtesy Gretchen Eick)

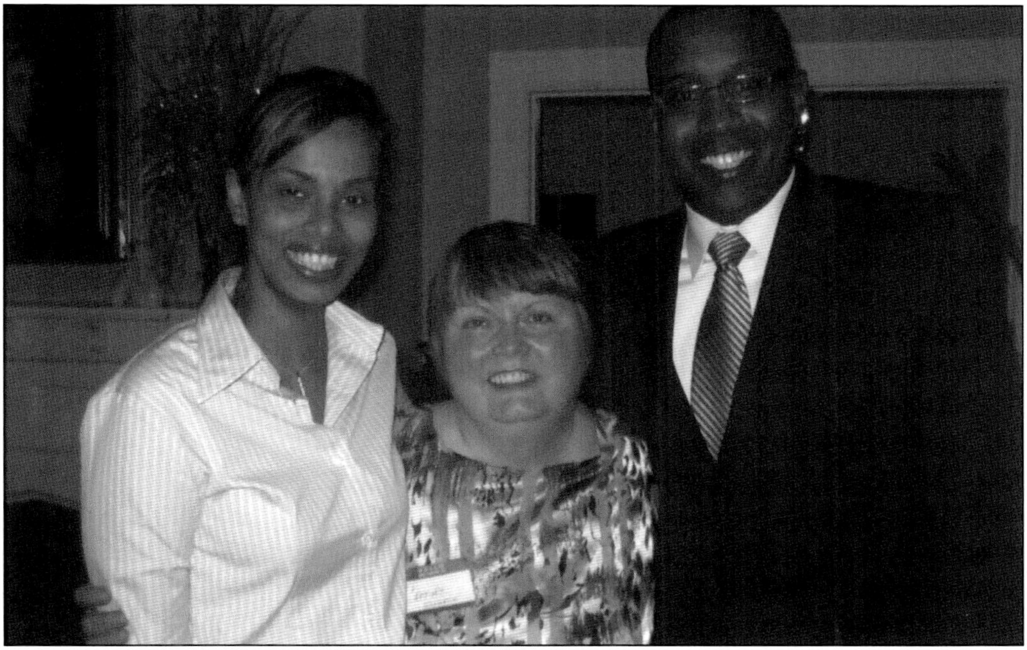

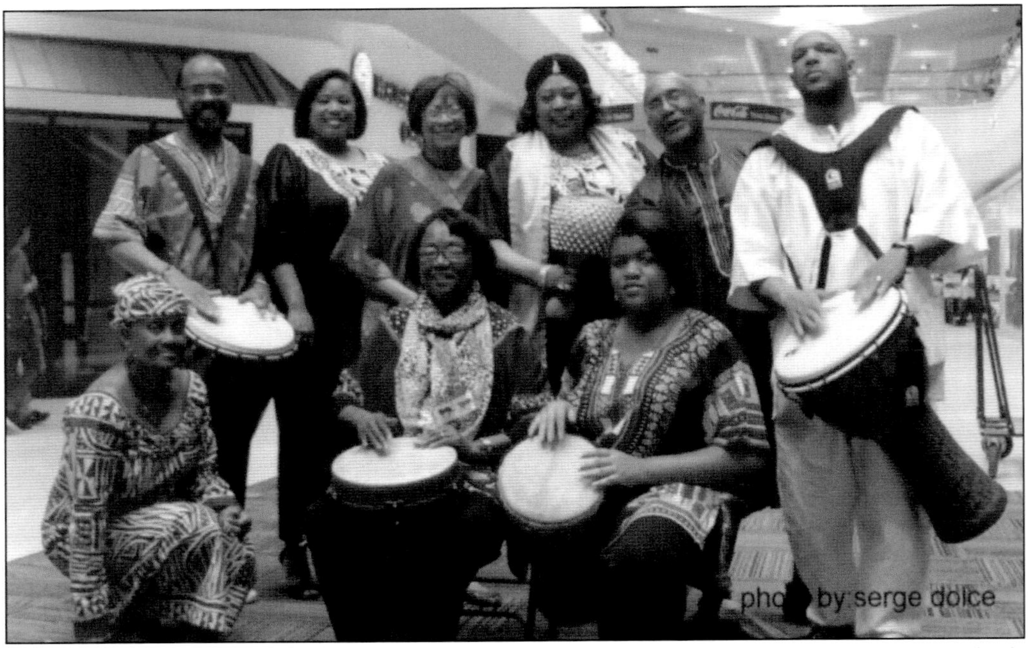

In 1998, retired librarian Jean Pouncil-Burton and a consortium of like-minded individuals established The Wichita Griots: Keepers of the Stories. In 2003, the group became the Griots Cultural Arts Storytelling Institute. This nonprofit organization, which partners with other arts and cultural organizations, uses storytelling as a means to further expose youths and others to positive principles like respect, responsibility, and integrity. (Courtesy Jean Pouncil-Burton.)

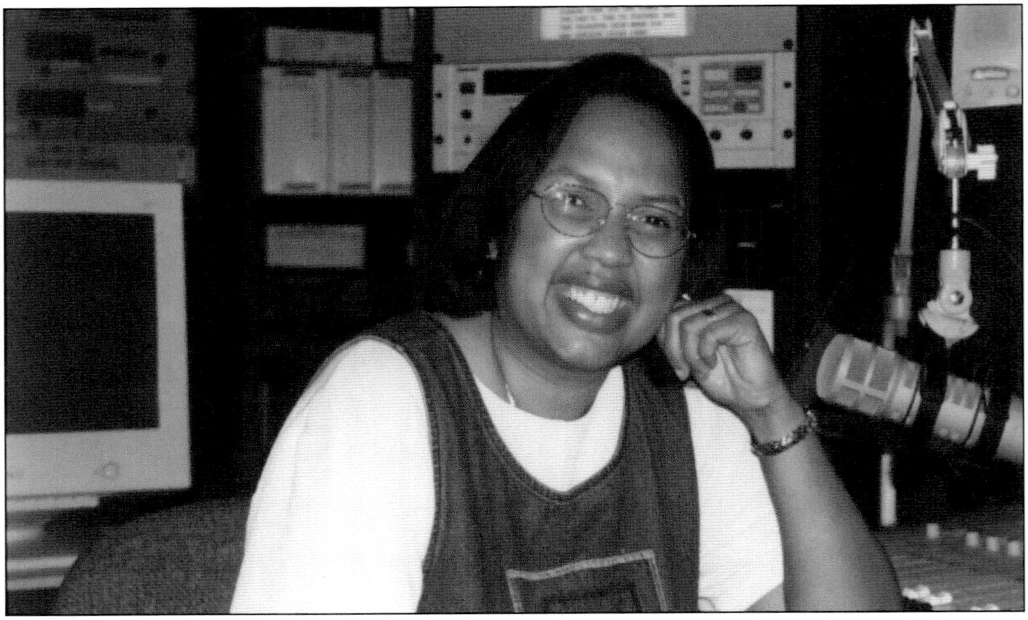

Carla Eckels, a Wichita native, has had a distinguished career as a radio professional. She is an award-winning journalist at KMUW—the public radio station on the campus of Wichita State University. Eckels has also distinguished herself as the host of gospel music programming in a variety of venues, including KSJM 107.9 JAMZ—Wichita's first black-owned radio station—and Soul Sensations on KMUW. (Courtesy *The Community Voice*.)

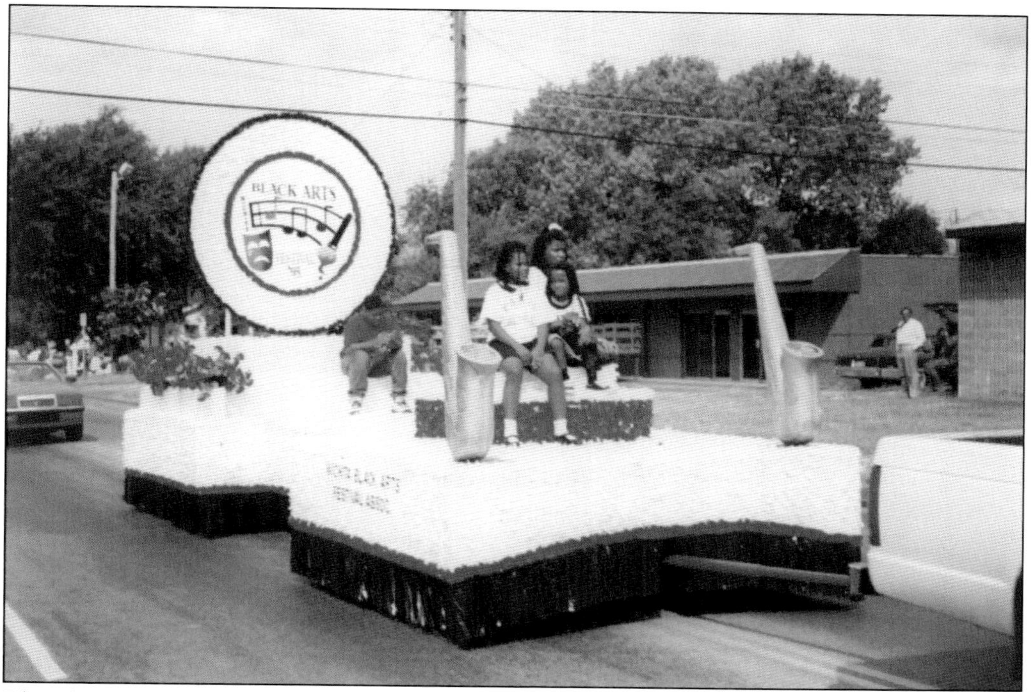

The Black Arts Festival was established in 1968 and remains an annual celebration of black life in Wichita. It is usually held over Labor Day Weekend and features a parade through Northeast Wichita. (Courtesy *The Community Voice*.)

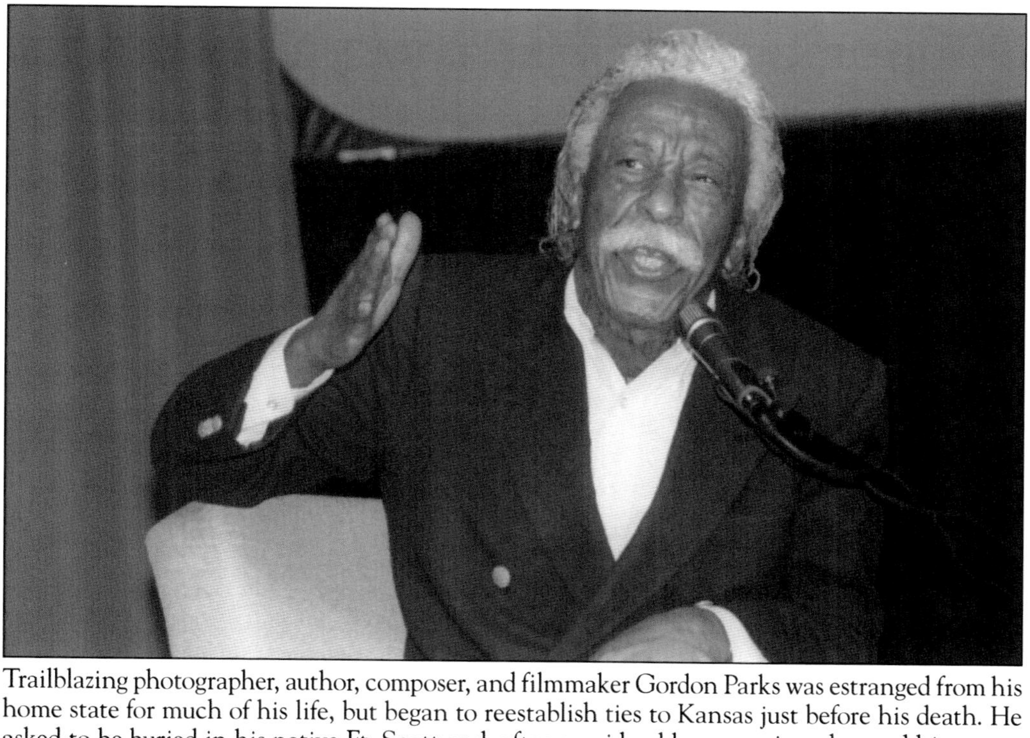

Trailblazing photographer, author, composer, and filmmaker Gordon Parks was estranged from his home state for much of his life, but began to reestablish ties to Kansas just before his death. He asked to be buried in his native Ft. Scott and, after considerable persuasion, donated his papers to Wichita State University. (Courtesy Chester Thomas and *The Community Voice*.)

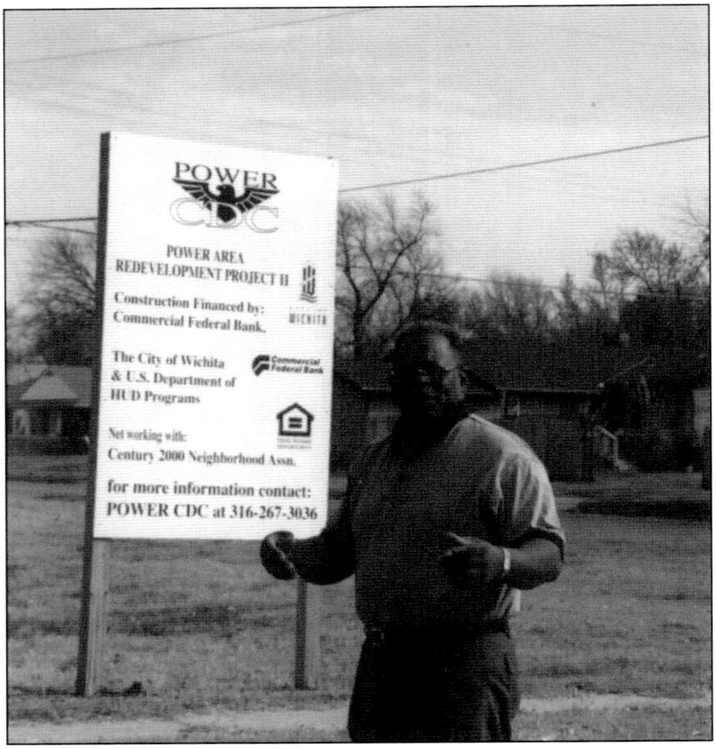

The Power Community Development Corporation, headed by James Arbertha, has engaged in a variety of initiatives in black Wichita. Power CDC's specific activities include the building of affordable single-family homes, bringing the Save-A-Lot Supermarket to Thirteenth and Grove Streets, and restoring the historic Dunbar Theater to promote the cultural arts among young people.

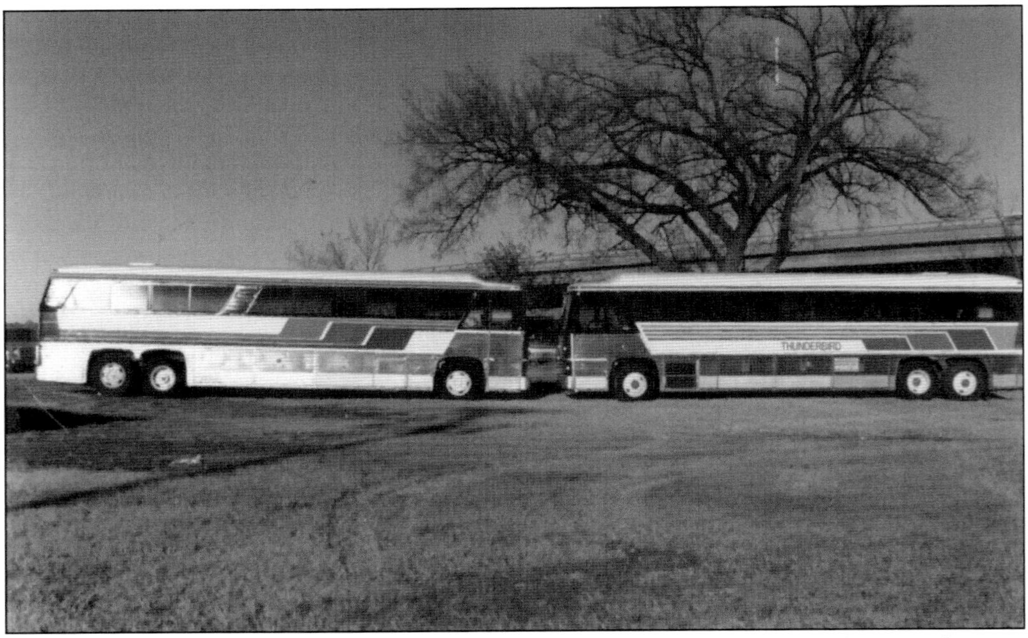

When it received its common carrier certificate in 1979, Wichita's Thunderbird Express became the first black-owned bus company in the state of Kansas. A consortium of black Wichitans including Jim Porter founded the company, which within two years had grown from three to six buses and had purchased a new garage and headquarters at 1212 East Seventeenth Street. Until its sale in the early 1990s, Thunderbird Express controlled an important niche in the marketplace. (Courtesy Karen Porter.)

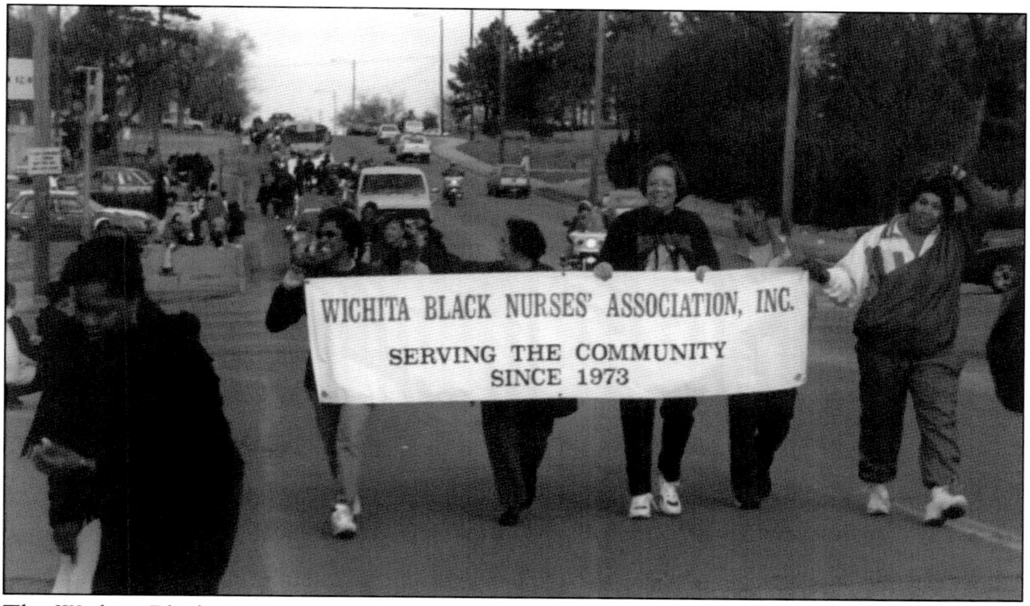

The Wichita Black Nurses Association, established in 1973, is linked with the National Black Nurses Association. Over the years, the Wichita Black Nurses Association has educated the public on ways to prevent illness. To do this, they have urged local churches to host health fairs and screenings. The Wichita Black Nurses Association has also prioritized assisting nursing students by providing both mentoring and scholarships. (Courtesy *The Community Voice*.)

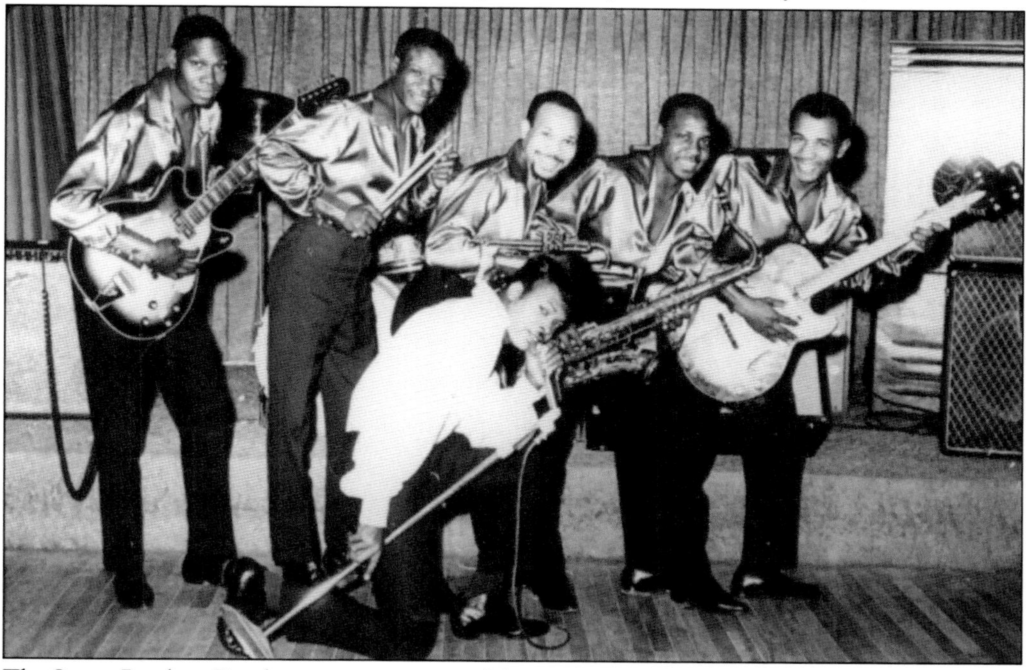

The Smart Brothers Band was a pioneering and dynamic musical act. In 1962, the band's passion for music and entrepreneurial spirit led them to open Smart's Palace at 1007 East Ninth Street, which served as both a restaurant and a music venue. The band played Kansas-wide and was a staple of clubs, fraternities, and sororities. They were one of the first African American bands to play the Cotillion Ballroom and on the local dance show *Hi-Five Hop*. (Courtesy Smart Brothers.)

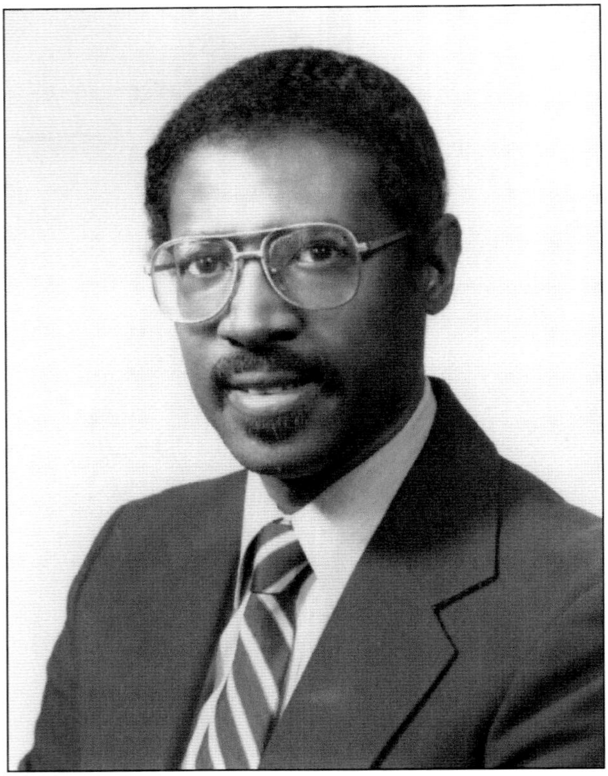

Dr. Ronald Walters, president of the NAACP youth chapter that conducted the Dockum sit-in, moved to Washington, DC, to advise the Congressional Black Caucus and Jesse Jackson's presidential campaign. He became nationally known through his books and appearances on TV news programs. Walters died in 2010 and is celebrated in a book by his colleagues. Other Dockum veterans, including Dr. Galyn Vesey and Dr. Robert Newby, also left Wichita to succeed.

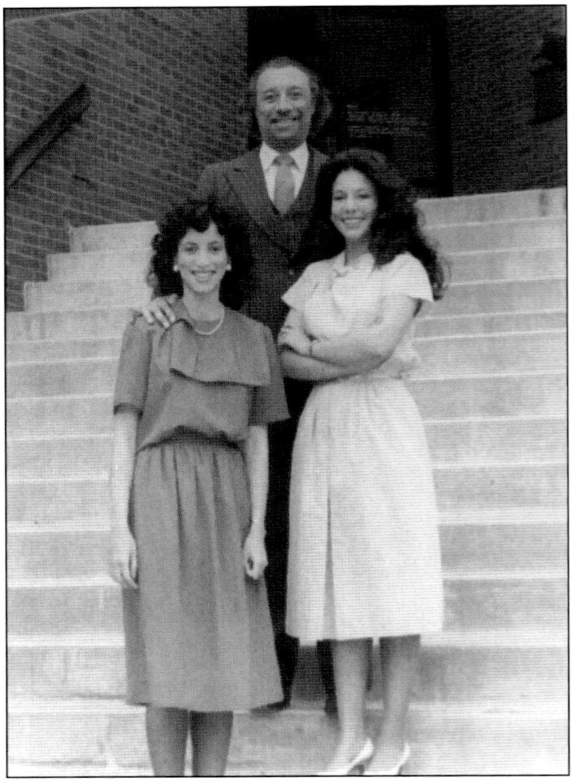

Charles McAfee's daughters, Charyl and Cheryl, followed their father into architecture—Charyl, after pursuing a masters' degree in architecture from the University of Texas, and Cheryl after earning a masters' from Harvard in architecture, urban design, and planning. Kim, not pictured here, received her master's in public administration from the University of Texas and is a hospital administrator in Fresno, California. (Courtesy Charles McAfee.)

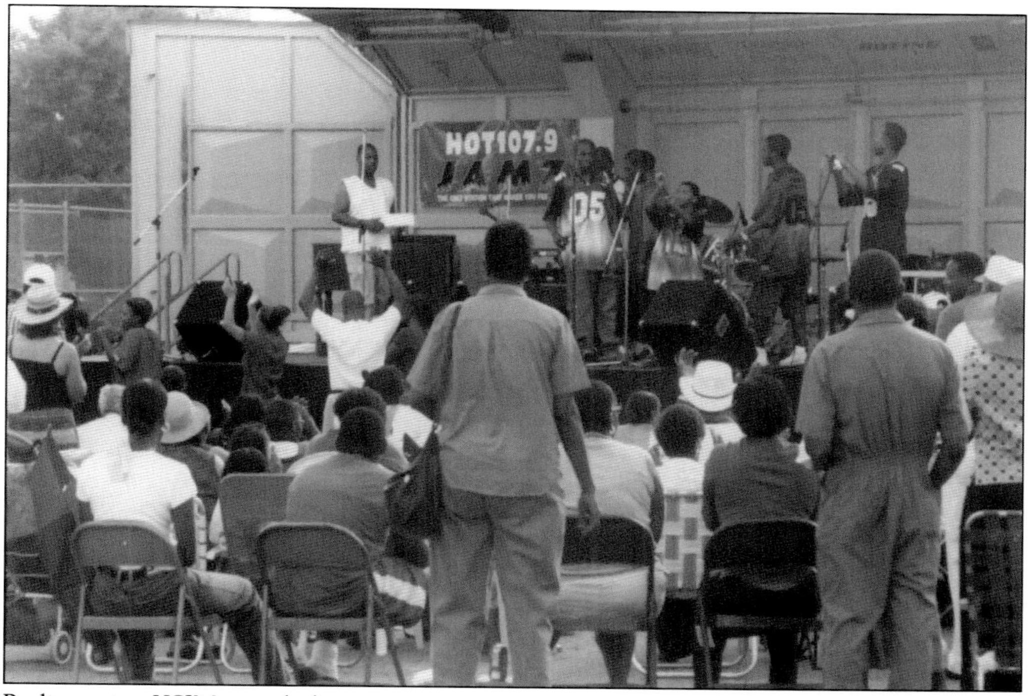

Radio station KSJM, popularly known as 107.9 JAMZ, debuted in 2000 and had the distinction of being Wichita's first black-owned station. Owned and operated by Don Sherman's Sherman Broadcasting Company, it brought urban-formatted programming to the Wichita airwaves. Later, Sherman Broadcasting entered into a partnership with the Carter Broadcast Group of Kansas City. In 2007, they sold the station. (Courtesy *The Community Voice*.)

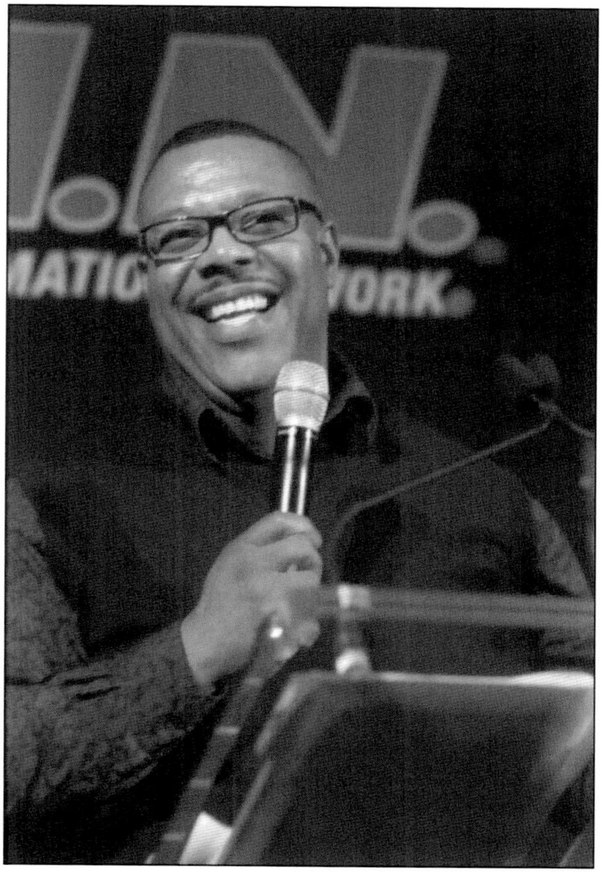

Greg Williams, affectionately known as "Hitman," is a Wichita radio legend. After ending several years at station KKRD, he went to KDGS (Power 93.9) as its program director in 2000. Since then, KDGS has consistently been Wichita's number one station in the 18 to 34 age bracket. Williams is pictured on stage at the National Radio Awards, receiving the award for America's Best Program Director for 2013. (Courtesy Greg Williams.)

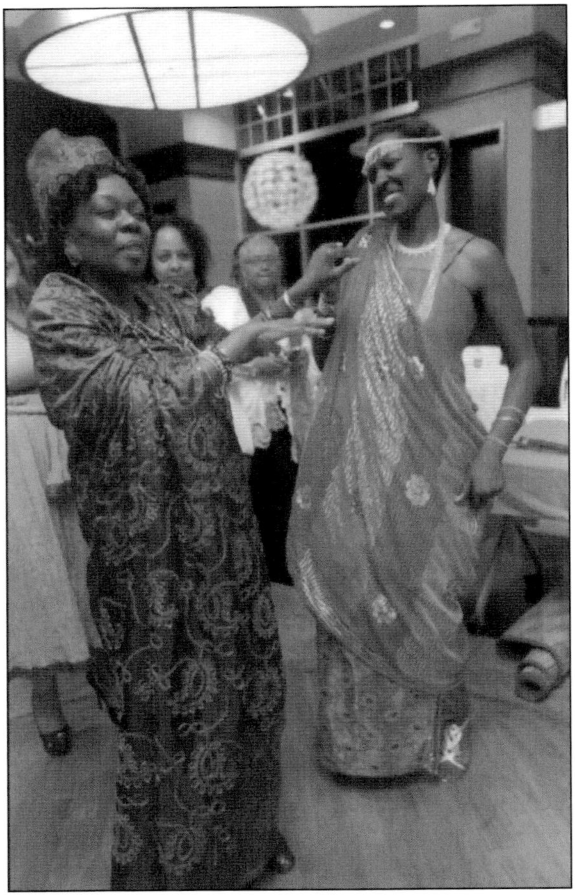

Bride Deborah Muhwezi Gladney dances with her mother at the African part of her wedding celebration in 2014. Her wedding was sponsored by her parents, Dr. Dan Muhwezi and Dr. Akiiki "Daisy" Kabagarama, professors who came from Uganda three decades ago. (Courtesy Akiiki Kabagarama.)

Wichita State University faculty member, poet, and author Chinyere Okafor is seen at right in this picture with friends. The Nigerian-born Okafor is an example of the many Africans, such as Kenyans and Nigerians, who are migrating to Kansas for their education. West African culture, especially as it relates to women's issues, is an important part of her work. (Courtesy Chinyere Okafor.)

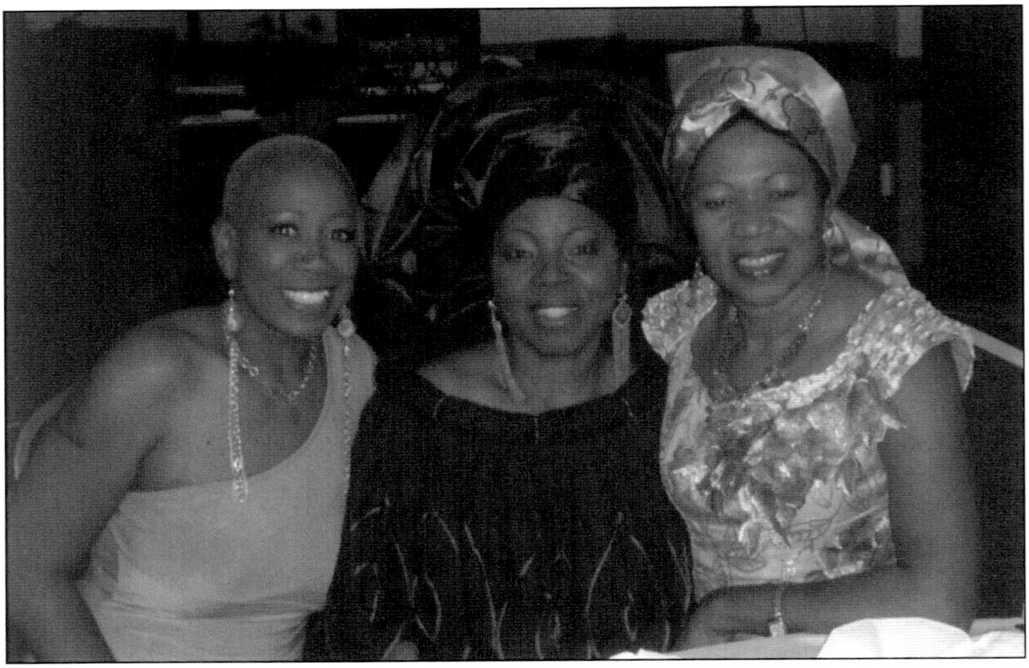

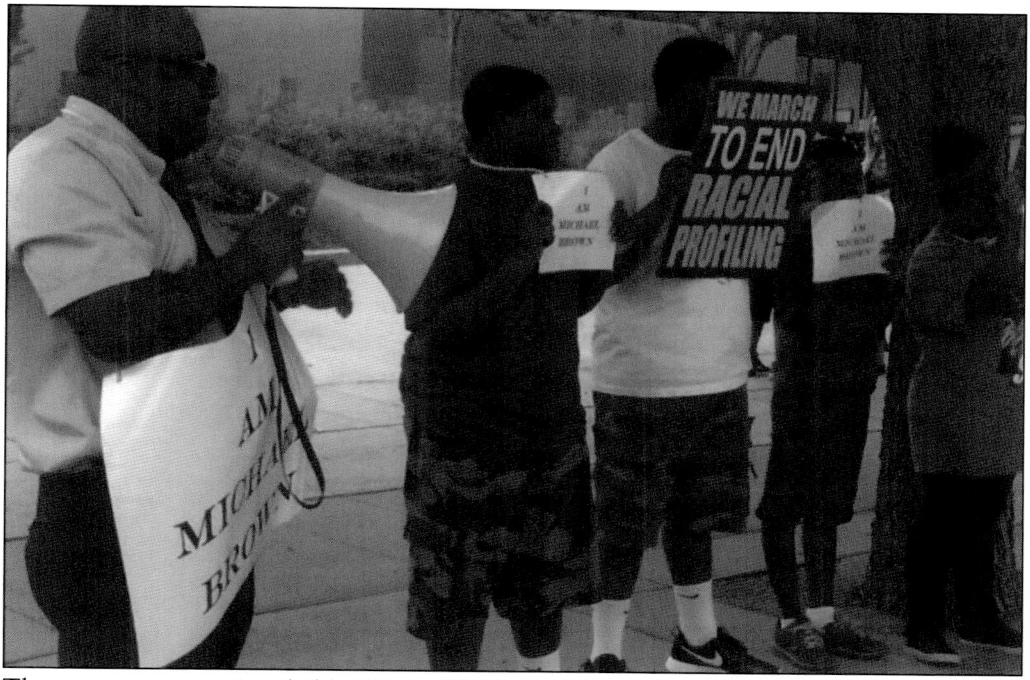

The younger generation, led by Djuan Walsh, Brandon Johnson, and Mary Dean, organize protests against racial profiling, "driving while black" stops, and local police shootings of young people of color. Their protests raised awareness of the disproportionate number of young black men incarcerated for the possession of small amounts of marijuana.

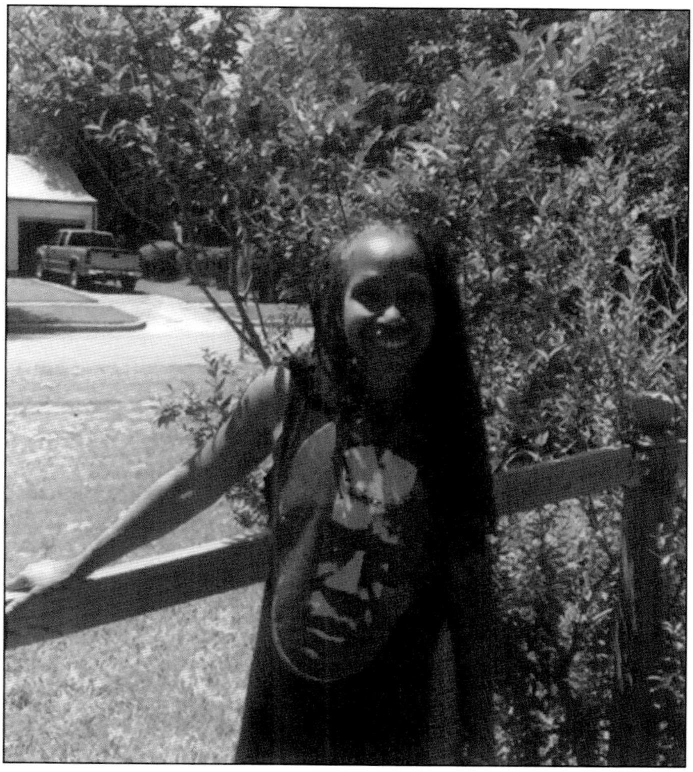

Shukura Jamila was a registered nurse but made her mark as an activist by highlighting the horrific black infant mortality rate in the 67214 zip code—one of the highest in the nation for more than a decade. She sounded the alarm about police brutality and the need for political organization, and sold books and videos to foster black consciousness. (Courtesy Michael Poage.)

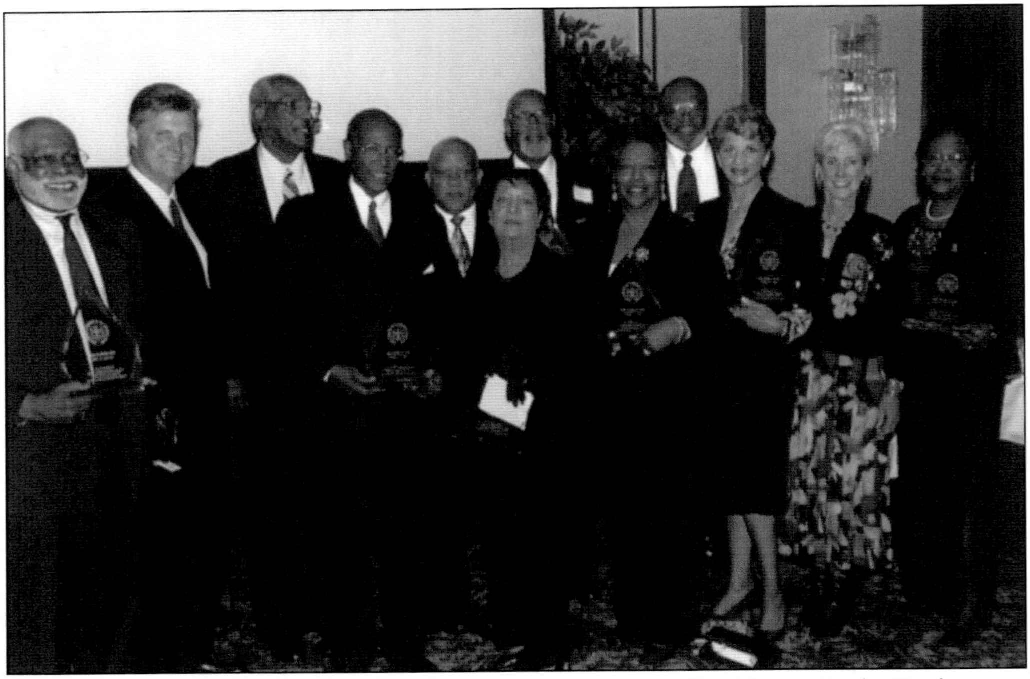

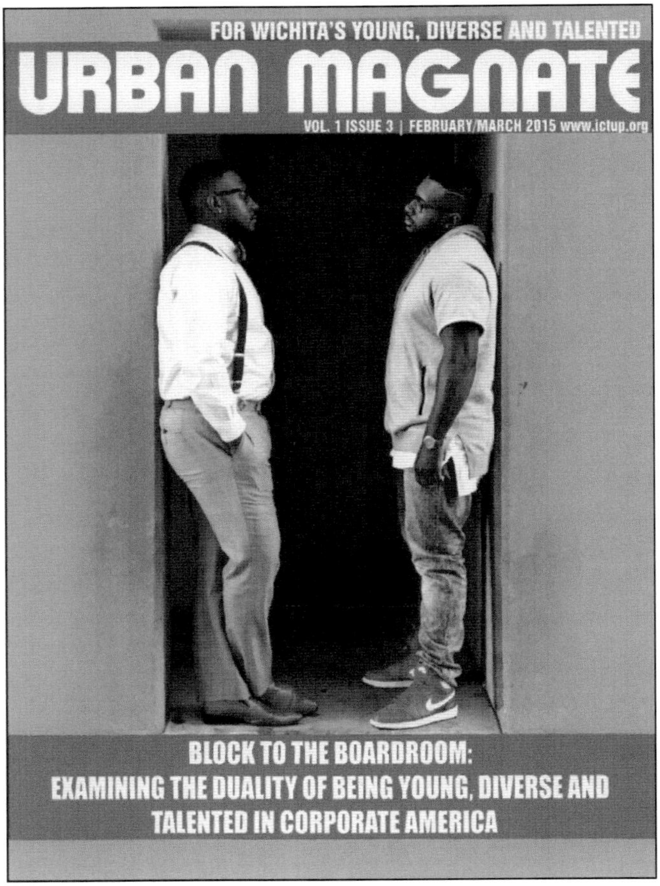

Participants in the Dockum sit-in were honored by the city and Gov. Kathleen Sebelius. Kevin Myles, then president of the Wichita branch of the NAACP, received retroactive recognition from the national office for Wichita as the site of the first successful student-led sit-ins, and under his leadership, the branch won three Thalheimer Awards.

Urban Magnate, the brainchild of Jonathan and Christina Long, is a publication linked with Wichita Urban Professionals. This organization, which targets African Americans under the age of 40, seeks to develop a network of future community leaders. *Urban Magnate*, according to its mission statement, covers "events and issues of interest to the city's young, diverse, and talented." (Courtesy Jonathan Long.)

Bibliography

Carter, D.W. *Mayday over Wichita: The Worst Military Aviation Disaster in Kansas History*. Charleston, SC: The History Press, 2013.

Eick, Gretchen. *Dissent in Wichita: the Civil Rights Movement in the Midwest, 1954–72*. Urbana, IL: University of Illinois Press, 2001/2007.

Gooch, Rip. *Black Horizons: One Aviator's Experience in the Post-Tuskegee Era*. Wichita, KS: Aviation Business Consultants, 2006.

Johnson, Judith R., and Craig Torbenson. "Stories From The Heartland: African American Experiences in Wichita, Kansas." *Kansas History*, Vol. 21 (1998/1999).

Long, Richard M. *Wichita Century: A Pictorial History of Wichita, Kansas 1870–1970*. Wichita, KS: Wichita Historical Museum Association, 1969.

Miner, Craig. *Wichita: The Magic City*. Wichita, KS: Wichita–Sedgwick County Historical Museum Association, 1988.

McCray, Billy. *Between These Walls: Working for the People*. Wichita, KS: McCray Publications Inc., 2000.

Rutledge, Carol. *The Brothers of the Ark Valley*. Self-published, 1985.

Sanders, Barry, and Mark E. McCormick. *Barry Sanders, Now You See Him: His Story in His Own Words*. Clerisy Press, Emmis Books, 2003.

Van Meter, Sondra. *Our Common School Heritage: A History of the Wichita Public Schools*. Wichita, KS: Board of Education of Unified School District No. 259, 1977.

Wolfenbarger, Deon. "African American Resources in Wichita, Sedgwick County, Kansas." National Register of Historic Places Multiple Property Documentation Form, 2011. www.kshs.org.

Yearout, Joshua L. *Wichita Jazz and Vice Between the World Wars*. Wichita, KS: Rowfant Press, 2010.